CHURCHILL'S COLD WAR

The IRON CURTAIN Speech that Shaped the Postwar World

PHILIP WHITE

DUCKWORTH OVERLOOK

First paperback edition 2013
First published in the UK in 2012 by
Duckworth Overlook
30 Calvin Street, London E1 6NW
T: 020 7490 7300
E: info@duckworth-publishers.co.uk
www.ducknet.co.uk
For bulk and special sales, please contact
sales@duckworth-publishers.co.uk
or write to us at the address above.

A catalogue record for this book is available
from the British Library

ISBN 978-0-7156-4577-2

Book design by Linda Mark
Printed and bound in Great Britain by
Ashford Colour Press, Gosport, Hants

For Nicole, Nan, Johnny & Harry

Contents

INTRODUCTION

PICTURE WINSTON CHURCHILL on May 8, 1945. He stands on a London balcony on a warm spring afternoon, holding aloft his celebratory "V" sign to thousands of people cheering his name in the streets below. Against all odds, he had kept Britain in the fight against Hitler until the United States entered World War II, and now, five arduous years after becoming prime minister, he had finally vanquished his foe. Yet, just weeks later, his victory would be soured by a tumultuous General Election, a fearsome battle of wills with Russian premier Joseph Stalin, and the continued spread of Communism across Eastern Europe and beyond.

Though the celebratory scenes of early May stick in the memory, it was Churchill's collision with Communism in the early postwar years that set the course for the remainder of his career, defined the divisions of the Cold War, and, ultimately, inspired Thatcher, Gorbachev, and Reagan to settle their nations' differences through diplomacy instead of armed conflict.

Churchill's strong reaction against Communism dated back to the Russian Revolution in 1917, when he scornfully labeled Bolshevism "a pestilence." In *The Aftermath*, the final book of his

World War I series, he attacked Lenin, who "repudiated God, King, Country, morals, treaties, debts, rents, interest, the laws and customs of centuries, all contracts written or implied, the whole structure . . . of human society."[1]

Churchill deplored everything about Communism. He had devoted his life to the preservation of democracy, and so was revolted by a totalitarianism under which individual liberty was subjugated and freedom constrained. In addition, having been born in Blenheim Palace into a noble lineage going back to the first Duke of Marlborough, he was an ardent monarchist who his wife would later call "Monarchial No. 1."[2] Thus, the Bolsheviks horrified Churchill when they wiped out the Russian ruling family in the course of their revolution.

Moreover, Churchill firmly believed in the virtues of capitalism, because he felt it provided the individual the best chance to prosper while affording industry the opportunity to advance his beloved Britain in international trade. In Leninist and then Stalinist Russia, the economic system was throttled and replaced by collectivization, which sought to eliminate the entrepreneurship, competition, and potential for growth that Churchill supported.[3]

In his capacity as Minister of Munitions during World War I, Churchill had pressed British Prime Minister David Lloyd George to bolster the small Allied force that supported anti-Bolsheviks. The premier and Churchill went back and forth on the issue for several months, until President Woodrow Wilson finally vetoed the plan.[4]

During the twenty-year interwar period, Churchill turned his attention first to domestic affairs and then, while out of office in the middle to late 1930s, to the imminent danger posed by Hitler. In no way did he ignore the ills of Communism, however, and he criticized Russia's collectivization and suppression of individual liberties in numerous opinion pieces. Still, Churchill did not claim to have all the answers. "It is a riddle, wrapped in a mystery, inside an enigma" he famously said of Stalin's homeland in a radio address in October 1939, "but perhaps there is a key. That key is Russian national interest."[5]

The Molotov-Ribbentrop nonaggression pact of August 1940, which bound the fates of Germany and Russia, had infuriated Churchill. Yet soon enough, Hitler's fateful decision to break his alliance with Stalin and declare war on Russia on June 22, 1941 (a decision that Churchill had predicted and tried to warn Stalin about the previous year), changed everything.

Of course, dissolution of the Russo-German accord had put Churchill in an awkward position. Staunchly opposed to Communism, he nonetheless accepted Stalin as an ally. The Red Army's engagement of Hitler's troops on the Eastern Front, after all, diverted manpower away from the German advance in Western Europe. And so, though Russia was far from his partner of choice, Churchill acknowledged that supporting Stalin was necessary to win the peace.[6]

For all the conflicting ideological interests of the three Allied powers, there had seemed to be a breakthrough at Yalta in February 1945, when Churchill, Stalin, and Roosevelt signed a declaration of postwar aims, including a guarantee of free elections in Poland and other Eastern European countries. Shortly after the conference, Churchill told Canadian Prime Minister Mackenzie King that he thought Stalin would honor their gentlemen's agreement: "Personally, in spite of my anti-Communist convictions, I have good hopes that Russia, or at any rate Stalin, desires to work in harmony with the Western democracies."[7]

As 1945 progressed, however, it became clear to Churchill and Roosevelt (and, later, Truman) that Stalin had no intention of honoring the Yalta Declaration, and that puppet Communist governments would soon roll over Eastern Europe. Even as Churchill declared faith in Stalin to Mackenzie King, Stalin's ruthless Deputy Commissar for Foreign Affairs (and the former Grand Prosecutor who oversaw countless deaths in Stalin's purges), Andrey Vishinsky, was leading Soviet forces in the takeover of Bucharest.

The Soviet monopolization of Eastern Europe was now virtually complete, and Churchill would soon discover the full extent of Stalin's treachery. Just days after the Red Army marched across Romania, Churchill found out that Russia's alternative to "free elections" was the nomination of solely its own chosen apparatchiks for government positions. Stalin later agreed to broaden the government to include the prewar Polish leaders then sheltering in London, only to renege soon after. Meanwhile, Churchill learned that Polish intellectuals and priests had been sent to Soviet labor camps and six thousand Polish soldiers were arrested and sentenced, though there was no court hearing or potential for appeal.[8]

On March 8, 1945, Churchill sent a memo to Roosevelt saying that Stalin had deceived Britain and America. Just as he had done when facing down Hitler, Churchill courted the support of his American counterpart.[9] And just as in the early phases of the war, Roosevelt proved reluctant to put his full weight behind the forceful Briton's proposals, which included delaying the withdrawal of American troops once Hitler met his fate. This inertia is partly attributable to the idealistically favorable impression of Russia in the United States at that time—an impression that failed to take into account the privations enforced by Communism.

Whatever hope Churchill had in Roosevelt as a foil to Stalin was dashed by the president's death on April 12. Churchill knew only a little about the man who replaced FDR, Vice President Harry S. Truman. Still, the prime minister realized the necessity—both for successfully concluding the war and for securing Britain's prominent place in peacetime—of cultivating a friendship with this brusque, untested Missouri native.

Twelve days into May, Churchill sent a telegram to Truman stating boldly that "[a]n iron curtain is drawn down upon their [Russia's] front, and I do not know what is going on behind." He called attention to Stalin's flagrant violations of the Yalta Declaration, and warned that after "the Muscovite advance into the centre of Europe . . . the curtain will descend again to a very large extent, if not entirely. Thus a broad band of hundreds of miles of Russian-occupied territory will isolate us from Poland."[10] To further explain his views on Russia and to advance the personal diplomacy in which he placed so much stock, Churchill needed to meet Truman. He would get his chance at the final wartime summit at Potsdam, Germany, in July.

Over the next several months, Churchill's ideological position on Russia and the relationship between Britain and America would crystallize, perhaps more clearly than in any other period of his public life. It is my intent in these pages to chronicle very clearly how this powerful perspective formed in Churchill's post-war understanding—an understanding that had its expression at one of the most unlikely venues imaginable: Westminster College in Fulton, Missouri, in March 1946. Indeed, this is a story of the conviction and bravery both of a public figure at a cross-roads in his illustrious career and of the small town that gave itself as his stage.

CHAPTER 1

THE BLACK DOG:
CHURCHILL AT THE FINAL WARTIME
CONFERENCE IN POTSDAM

Cecilienhof palace at Potsdam, with a red geranium "Stalin's Star" on the front lawn. CREDIT: KAYNI'S CORNER CAFÉ BLOG

Democracy is now on trial as it never was before, and in these Islands we must uphold it, with all our hearts, with all our vigilance, with all our enduring and inexhaustible strength.

—Winston Churchill to the House of Commons
(August 16, 1945)

H E SAT WITH BOTH ARMS on the great circular mahogany table, poised to leap from his chair at any moment if the need arose, which it had so often in these past few days. His wrinkled, rotund face, familiar now around the world, ought to have looked drained from five years of fighting Hitler and nine nights of toast after toast with his fellow leaders. Yet the ever-alert eyes and the defiantly jutting jaw, set firm as he forcefully made his case, made it clear to all assembled that he was anything but fatigued.

For Winston Churchill, this final wartime conference at Potsdam in July 1945 was the chance to punctuate his legacy as the finest British statesman of his age, a worthy successor to exemplary prime ministers of years past, and a resolute defender of democracy in defiance of totalitarianism.

Built for a German prince, the Cecilienhof palace is a steeply sloping tile-roofed structure with tall red-brick chimneys and black crisscrossed stonework, giving it the appearance of a Tudor-style English manor house—clearly a building befitting the magnitude of Churchill's task at Potsdam at this first plenary session on the morning of July 17. Across the table sat a man with whom Churchill was just getting acquainted: the short, blunt, bespectacled Missouri native Harry Truman, who had taken office only a few weeks before. Truman was determined to see Roosevelt's dream of the United Nations come to fruition and to solidify America's preeminence in the West, while overriding Churchill's imperial aims if necessary.[1]

And then there was the final member of the "Big Three." Clad as ever in his olive Russian military uniform adorned with an overflow of medals was the squat and elaborately mustached Joseph Stalin. His nickname "Uncle Joe" (bestowed by the American wartime propaganda machine and frequently used in correspondence between Roosevelt and Churchill), jovial story-telling, and congeniality with Churchill and Truman in the high-spirited atmosphere of the conference banquet hall belied a ferocity and ruthlessness that had claimed millions of his own people's lives.

Churchill was used to outfoxing opponents with his biting wit and a superior command of the English language. But Stalin was an altogether different kind of adversary. Churchill's pugnacious demeanor could not intimidate him, nor was he a helpless victim of the Englishman's sarcasm. And while he did not have the benefit of five decades of parliamentary jousting, he was battle-tested in ways that Churchill could not fathom.

Since becoming general secretary of the Communist Party in 1922, Stalin had forced everyone around him to follow orders, or face fatal consequences. The man who had overseen vast purges rivaling the Holocaust in scope and malevolence, who had brutally forced collectivization upon his citizens, and who had sent political and ideological opponents to either Siberian labor camps or their graves had come to Potsdam under the unlikely banner of friendship.[2] Stalin's staunch defense of his homeland in the face of the advancing Wehrmacht troops was one of the primary reasons for the demise of the Axis, and yet in many ways the Grand Alliance between Russia, the United States, and Britain was a sham.

For all parties it had been a marriage of convenience. Britain could not overcome Hitler and his wartime partners without the Americans' military might, while Washington could not act decisively against Japanese and German aggression without British intelligence, military bases, and new technologies. As Russia repulsed Hitler's troops during the biting Russian winter of 1941–1942, Stalin had sought and obtained tanks, planes, and armaments from the United States, all the while pushing for the Western Allies to make the final decisive invasion on the beaches of Normandy. Stalin's real prize for his participation in the tripartite arrangement, justifying in his mind the unequaled loss of life his country endured at a military and civilian level, was of immeasurable value—dominion of Eastern and, if he could get away with it, Central Europe.

Churchill himself was partly culpable for this. His "Percentages Agreement" of October 1944, drawn up in the interest of saving Greece from the likely ravages of Communism, served only to acknowledge Stalin's grip on Bulgaria, Romania, Yugoslavia, and Hungary.[3] As Churchill took his seat at Potsdam, it is conceivable that he was seeking atonement for this fateful decision by fighting for whatever semblance of sovereignty remained in these countries and those facing a similar fate.

He was also on the offensive over Stalin's claims at the Yalta Conference in February 1945 that there would be "free and democratic" elections in those nations and in Poland—an assurance subsequently exposed as the blatant falsehood that it had always been. It became clear that, in signing the Yalta Agreement, Stalin was paying mere lip service to Churchill and Roosevelt, buying himself time until the force of his Red Army, abetted by the guile of his political underlings, turned Eastern Europe's governments into Communist puppets.[4]

Churchill never evaded a fight, no matter how long the odds were. Even as Hitler's armies cut a fearsome swath across Europe, toppling the Low Countries and France with ease and pushing all the way to the English Channel in just weeks, Churchill had refused to yield. And when the British Expeditionary Force (BEF) was routed in its initial advance, forced to flee from the beaches of Dunkirk in May and June 1940, Churchill was again undaunted. Instead of conceding what at the time seemed a hopelessly one-sided conflict, he rallied his countrymen and resisted those elements of his Cabinet that pushed him to parley with the Führer.

His next great success was securing vital armaments from Franklin D. Roosevelt through the Lend-Lease Act of March 1941, long before the Japanese onslaught at Pearl Harbor and Germany's fateful declaration of war on December 11. Now that military triumph in Europe was accomplished, Churchill again wanted U.S. leaders to stand side by side with him. This time, however, the common enemy was not the evil force of Nazism—his sworn foe since he began warning his countrymen about it in the mid-1930s—but Communism itself.

The wartime decision to embrace Stalin as an ally had not been an easy one for Churchill, who during the 1917 Bolshevik Revolution had declared Marxist theory to be "a disease" and vowed to "strangle Bolshevism at its birth."[5] He had finally accepted partnership with Russia after Hitler had turned on Stalin, realizing that supporting Russian resistance would further divert Hitler's attention and resources away from the West and buy him valuable time not only to redouble the BEF's strength but also to take advantage of America's ever-growing military and industrial might. As he told his private secretary Jock Colville on June 21, 1941, "If Hitler invaded Hell I would at least make a favorable reference to the Devil in the House of Commons."[6] Certainly, Churchill loathed Communism and its obliteration of the personal and societal freedoms he held sacred, but this was, at least temporarily, secondary to the survival of his own nation and, as he saw it, those same liberties.

In public, Churchill praised Stalin for the remainder of the war, yet privately, he was ever wary of the man's mendacity and ruthlessness. Churchill realized that Potsdam presented his final chance to regain the ground lost at Yalta, and to hold Stalin to his promise of allowing democracy in Eastern Europe.

The Big Three convened at the expansive Potsdam estate on the afternoon of July 15, 1945. British, American, and Russian officials could not have picked a more visually appealing setting. The ivy-covered stone walls, lush gardens lined with marble statues, and hundreds of newly planted trees and shrubs of every hue held a treat for the eyes around every corner. Churchill would stay in a low stone villa two blocks from Truman's three-story yellow stucco residence, both of which offered magnificent views of the wooded valley and the shimmering surface of the Jungfernsee—"The Lake of the Virgins."

The only unpleasant surprise was a gigantic star in the middle of the central lawn at the Cecilienhof palace. The unmistakable sweet aroma of the red scented geraniums that formed the Communist emblem was a strange juxtaposition to the ominous nature of this Russian power symbol, which Soviet conference organizers had ensured would be seen by Churchill and Truman each time they walked to join Stalin at the negotiating table. The British and Americans soon dubbed it "Stalin's Star."[7]

Before the conference began, Churchill and Truman met for the first time. Truman was impressed with their first encounter, noting in his diary, on July 16, that "I had an instant liking for this man who had done so much for his own country and for the Allied cause. There was something very open and genuine about the way he greeted me."[8] The Briton was equally complimentary, declaring Truman to be "a man of exceptional character."[9] The two leaders might have differed in their views of how Communism would

Winston Churchill and Harry Truman meet for the first time at the Potsdam Conference, July 1945. CREDIT: HARRY S. TRUMAN LIBRARY

grow in influence abroad, but they agreed that it was the single greatest threat to a post-Nazi world.

The next day, Churchill took a car into Berlin with his kindly physician Lord Charles Moran, his suave foreign secretary Anthony Eden (whom Churchill had also made Leader of the House of Commons), and the permanent undersecretary for foreign affairs Alexander Cadogan, whose ever-serious countenance mirrored his taciturn, no-nonsense personality. The Reichstag—once resplendent with its stunning Italian Renaissance, Gothic, and Baroque architectural details and signature glass copula—was now demolished. A crowd of Berliners had set up an impromptu market in the square outside. Eager for any cash they could get to help them survive the ravages of the decimated city, they loudly hawked fountain pens, watches, and clothing to enthusiastic Russian soldiers and bartered items they couldn't sell for binoculars, boots, and other military-issue keepsakes. This scenario was somewhat strange, as the Red Army had arrived to finish off the resistance of the Third Reich, but now that the occupiers' guns were silent and their objective of Nazi surrender achieved, they posed no threat to the German citizens who milled around.

To reduce the chance of an unpleasant interaction with the crowd, Churchill's bodyguards had intended to take their charge all the way to the Chancellery. However, this was not Churchill's way. He motioned for the driver to halt the car, and got out among the people, cigar clenched between his teeth. Unsurprisingly, some turned their backs on the man who had led their wartime enemy; but others, glad to be rid of the yoke of more than a decade of Nazi rule and the ruin it had wreaked about them, hailed him enthusiastically. Though he could not speak German, Churchill developed an easy rapport with the crowd, and one young blonde woman in a vividly patterned dress got a little too close for the bodyguards' liking and they gently ushered her away. Outpourings of emotion were common at Churchill's post-war appearances in the U.K. and abroad, but here, in a city so recently vanquished and with some animosity toward Britain understandably lingering, it is astonishing that an unknown person could have breached the security cordon so easily.

After a few minutes, Churchill returned to the car and went into the Chancellery. Once a picture of Nazi order as envisioned by Hitler's architect Albert Speer—strictly clean lines, seemingly endless rows of unadorned windows and intimidating large, rectangular columns—Hitler's seat of power was now in shambles. Rubble lay strewn about, gaping holes dotted what was left of the roof, and slivers of broken glass threatened to pierce the shoes of visitors who failed to watch their step. The few walls that were still standing were now pockmarked with jagged gashes from artillery shells, and disfigured steel rods poked haphazardly out of the stonework. Churchill, clad in a lightweight army uniform appropriate for the hot Berlin afternoon, acknowledged a group of Royal Marines and British sailors who saluted him and cheered as he passed by; then, with Cadogan, Eden, Moran, his security detail, and a gaggle of reporters in tow, the prime minister walked somberly into the wreckage.[10] He carefully stepped over and around the piles of debris blighting the hallways, which formerly had been lined with German paintings and sculptures like the exhibit rooms of a museum, and made his way to Hitler's office.

At one time, visitors of the Führer were escorted by armed sentries through imposing, solid oak doors and across Hitler's vast office to his gigantic marble-topped desk. There they stood until instructed to sit by the man himself, who held court from a high-backed red leather chair. On the dark wood-paneled walls had hung paintings of former German leaders Hitler had admired, including a Lenbach portrait of a brooding Otto von Bismarck above the fireplace that faced the Führer's desk. High above the floor were several large gold Nazi eagles, which perched menacingly atop swastikas.

Now, the office designed to convey Hitler's power and to intimidate guests (including Neville Chamberlain, who had signed there the paperwork that handed the Czech Sudetenland to Germany in 1938) was in ruins—the marble desktop smashed, the desk itself upended, the dust-covered red carpet littered with Iron Crosses, chandelier fragments, and official papers. Churchill slowly inspected the carnage and then strode into the adjacent dining room. He looked up at what was once the ceiling, blinking in the bright daylight that streamed through the hole where an elaborate glass dome had been.[11] Then, following Eden and Moran, he traipsed across the courtyard to the entrance of Hitler's underground bunker. The rank, damp air irritated the men's nostrils as they carefully picked their way down the concrete steps. There they found more chaos—gas masks and trash haphazardly flung on the floor, pictures with ripped canvases hanging at grotesque angles, water seeping from an unseen plumbing breach. A vase containing a forlorn branch stood eerily intact. Churchill had seen enough; walking back to the main level, he sat wearily on the first unbroken chair he found. "Hitler must have come up here to get some air," he told his attendants, "and heard the guns getting nearer and nearer."[12]

After a day of recouping from the apocalyptic scene in Berlin, Churchill was ready to begin deliberations at the round table that accommodated five delegates from each of the three Grand Alliance nations. In the middle of the oak circle, which rested on a wide hardwood post set on thick-pile burgundy carpet, were the flags of Russia, Britain, and the United States. These signified, at least visually, continued unity among the Big Three. The three leaders sat in gilt-edged chairs more suitable for a royal parlor than for a political negotiation room: Truman facing the window, Churchill with his back to it, and Stalin three seats to Churchill's left. There was to be no serious work that day—just a shot across the bow from the Briton. Churchill looked Stalin straight in the eyes as he told him and Truman in the opening session that he considered "early holding of free elections in Poland which would truly reflect the wishes of the Polish people" to be a top priority. The marshal, staring back stony-faced, declined to comment.[13] Light streamed through the giant, white-latticed window that dominated the back wall, contrasting the gloomy portent of this first exchange.

The statesmen's mood brightened somewhat that evening as Churchill, Truman, and Stalin indulged their palates at one of the sprawling silver-service feasts that had become standard practice at the wartime conferences. As a multitude of servers bustled about the immense table with trays of caviar, goose liver, and duck, Churchill made small talk with the Russian leader. He thanked him for hosting his wife, Clementine, on her recent Moscow visit and stated that his nation "welcomed Russia as a Great Power."[14]

"Stalin was very amiable," Churchill told Lord Moran before bed that night. And what of Truman, Moran inquired. "He is a man of immense determination," Churchill observed. "He takes no notice of firm ground, he just plants his foot down firmly on it." To emphasize his point, Churchill lifted his great form several inches into the air and crashed back down onto the bathroom floor with two feet.[15]

It did not take long for Churchill to realize that Truman's steely determination would prove invaluable, or that "frustration was the fate of this final Conference of 'the Three,'" as he recalled in his war memoirs. In the second plenary session, Poland was the flashpoint. Stalin demanded that all assets belonging to the leaders of the exiled Polish government, whom Churchill had sheltered when they fled in the wake of Nazi occupation, be turned over to the puppet Communist administration. Churchill had reluctantly joined Roosevelt in recognizing the new Polish leadership, known as the Lublin Poles, several months earlier— mainly because the Soviets' rulers of choice were already in full control of the country—but he didn't hesitate now in barking his refusal to this proposal.

Churchill then insisted that exiled Polish soldiers who had fought against Hitler's forces should be welcomed back to their homeland without fear of reprisal for declaring allegiance to their London-based leaders. When Truman leaned forward to deflect the bullets from the opposing Russian and British sides and suggested that the three foreign ministers discuss the Polish situation at a later session, Churchill saw a window of opportunity and leapt through it. "Including elections," he growled at Stalin. "The Provisional Government have never refused to hold free elections," came the nonchalant reply. This infuriated Churchill because it was a blatant lie, and Stalin knew it. Though the Yalta Declaration had supposedly guaranteed the Poles the right of determination, Stalin's agents had ensured that the new Polish government was an autocracy that served the will of Moscow.[16]

With that, the session adjourned, after just an hour and forty-five minutes. Churchill had failed to gain a concession from his Russian counterpart, but that evening did manage to strike a blow that foreshadowed the fierce debate to come.

Tuning out the clinking of glasses, the frenetic conversations between Russian, British, and American diplomats and their interpreters, and the ceaseless parade of German delicacies ferried into and out of the room, Churchill and Stalin argued about Eastern Europe.[17] When Churchill brought up Romania and Bulgaria, Stalin denied that his agents were pressing Communist aims in those countries and went on to claim that Greek operatives were threatening Russian interests. It was Greece, after all, that Churchill had saved from Communist takeover by writing in the Percentages Agreement that Russia was to have zero influence there.[18]

Churchill also voiced his concern over the fate of Hungary. The Soviet leader, quaffing vodka from a tiny glass that he refilled frequently, insisted that "Russian policy was to see a strong, independent sovereign state" in all of the Eastern European nations freed from Nazi oppression and that he desired open elections.[19] Churchill knew this to be a falsehood: the Kremlin's interpretation of "free elections" entailed intimidation of the supporters and candidates of non-Communist parties, and eventual elimination of them if it saw the need.[20]

The discussion was proving futile. Churchill downed what was left of the whiskey, now a little warm from his tightening grip around the glass. Hoping to get at least a fragment of truth from Stalin about his intentions in postwar Europe, Churchill looked past his encroaching tiredness and mounting frustration, and tried again. This time he produced a map and a silver pen from his jacket pocket, scraped a line through the middle of Europe, and reeled off the growing list of capitals to its east that the Red Army controlled. Then came his gruff query: How many more countries would Russia overrun as it marched its troops westward? Again, Stalin parried, claiming that the advance was over and that more than 2 million Russian troops would be heading home within the following four months. Churchill stood up slowly, feeling every one of his seventy years. He excused himself from the table and, with grim musings percolating, retired for a fitful night, unsure of how to bend or break his former ally—as formidable an adversary as Hitler had ever been.

Churchill had most of the next day to recharge, but the third session showed no more promise for a satisfactory conclusion. After he declined to meet Stalin's demands to break off diplomatic relations with Franco's right-wing government in Spain and for Russia to acquire a third of the captured German Navy vessels, the Russian dug in his heels over Yugoslavia. The British Foreign Office wanted Churchill to pressure the Communist Yugoslav leader—stern, broad-faced, autocratic Josip Tito—to conform to the June 1944 Tito-Šubašic Agreement. This had bound Tito to share power with the nation's non-Communist partisans, which he did in name only, and to hold democratic elections, which he had no intention of doing. While Stalin and Tito's relationship was strained by the latter's refusal to do the Kremlin's bidding to the letter, Tito's actions were consistent with the pattern of Sovietization of Eastern Europe—forced takeover, crushing of democratic institutions, and suppression of resistance.[21]

Stalin refused to take action without bringing Tito to Potsdam, an idea Truman dismissed. As impasse followed stalemate, it became increasingly clear to all present that the Grand Alliance now existed in name only. Indeed, Truman was so exasperated that he recalled wanting to "pack up and go home" and later "felt like blowing the roof off the palace."

Several days passed, with frustrations deepening all the while. Evenings spent indulging in lavish soirées satisfied the participants' palates but did little to advance their diplomatic aims. On the third night of the conference, Churchill and the quick-minded Clement Attlee joined Truman for a state dinner at his residence. Formerly the home of a film producer, it was nicknamed "The Little White House," despite its yellow exterior and the fact that it was anything but small. The home was surrounded on three sides by evergreen trees and bushes, with a private rear lawn extending to the shore of the Jungfernsee. Once inside, Churchill and Attlee found a U.S. Army sergeant sitting at the piano, leading a violinist from the Metropolitan Orchestra and two Russian violinists in the melodic tones of Chopin's *Nocturne* and *Waltz in A Minor*, which were favorites of Stalin. Truman, a competent pianist, then took over at the keys, playing Paderewski's *Minuet in G*. Less than enthusiastic about the Chopin recital (having never cared for the composer) and exhausted from the fruitless sparring at the conference table, Churchill retired early.[22]

On Saturday, July 21, Churchill was temporarily invigorated by an Allied victory parade through the Tiergarten in central Berlin. Clad in a khaki uniform, he stood beside General George Marshall and Admiral Ernest King as the tanks of the British Seventh Armored Division (known as the "Desert Rats" after their fierce battles with Germany's Field Marshal Erwin Rommel in North Africa) rolled by the raised viewing platform. Late that afternoon, Churchill strode enthusiastically down the winding, red-carpeted corridors that linked the 178 rooms of the Potsdam palace, his walking stick tapping a hopeful path into the fifth conference session, which opened with good news: Stalin reiterated his commitment to Anglo-American possession of the Austrian zone.[23]

But with the contentious topic of Poland's borders moved to the top of the agenda, the sense of progress vanished. As the leaders sat together once more around the great table, Stalin insisted that the western Poland border be moved further yet into German territory. Even as Churchill stiffened, preparing to make his objection, Truman jumped in, telling Stalin: "We ought to keep to the zones we agreed at Yalta."[24] Seizing the momentum, Churchill stated that the change Stalin proposed would take away a quarter of Germany's food-producing farmland and displace yet more citizens, making a total of 8.5 million Germans who were forced to uproot.[25] Britain and the United States would be compelled to make up the shortfall in food, he argued, not to mention a sizable fuel deficit.

Bristling at what he saw as a combined attack, Stalin rejected Churchill's food and population estimates as exaggerations. Truman and Attlee, sensing a looming deadlock, spoke up to bolster Churchill's position. Still, Stalin stood his ground, and then asked gruffly, "Are we through?"

The next morning, Churchill got some much-needed good news. U.S. Secretary of War Henry Stimson, who had presided over the retooling of the U.S. Army in 1940, handed Churchill a piece of paper with the coded message: "Babies satisfactorily born." Churchill understood its significance: the atomic bomb was ready.[26]

The Allies had lobbied Stalin to join the war in the Pacific so that they could send Japan to its final defeat, but had feared giving Stalin further leverage in his demands for more territory. The completion of this terrible new weapon removed the need for Russian involvement, Churchill realized. "Stimson, what is gunpowder?" he asked. "What is electricity? Meaningless. This atomic bomb is the Second Coming in Wrath."[27] The need for Russian involvement against the dogged Japanese, it was immediately clear to the prime minister, had ended with the mushroom cloud in the New Mexico desert.

A proving ground for this sentiment came within hours, at the sixth session. From the get-go, Churchill was on the attack, with Stalin his target. Echoing his finest parliamentary performances, Churchill sharply restated his previous reasons for opposing moving the Polish frontier further west: namely, a lack of food, fuel, and land for German citizens, economic disunity in Germany, and the massive displacement of German citizens.

Never one to back down, Stalin lowered his head and rhetorically charged like an enraged bull: the Englishman's claims were unfounded, he blustered, and Poland (which, given the Communist government, was essentially now his) must be compensated for German atrocities.

Looking to avoid an insurmountable rift, Truman intervened, rereading the Yalta Declaration passage that promised Poland more land to the west, but then telling Stalin that the Poles would not be allowed an occupation zone within German borders.[28]

The conference had come to a head, with Churchill and Stalin standing on opposite sides. Where Truman himself stood remained to be seen. Ideologically and during some of the Churchill-Stalin exchanges he was, of course, much closer to Churchill, but like Roosevelt before him, he was leery of British imperialism. Now, with the summit on a knife-edge, the Big Three agreed to summon Polish leaders to Potsdam to make their case.

The day's defining battle was over, but there were still skirmishes. Stalin was adamant that Russia be granted a Turkish base in the Dardanelles, a progression of his demand in previous weeks that the Turkish provinces of Ardahan and Kars be annexed to Russia. And while Churchill had affirmed the rights of the Soviet Navy several times during the preceding days, he couldn't allow the Soviets unfettered access to the Mediterranean or, worse, the Suez Canal, its waters the very lifeblood of British trade in the region. Now Vyacheslav Molotov, the Russian foreign minister, joined in to bolster Stalin's arguments. The British, he pointed out, had just called for international control of the Black Sea Straits, so why not apply the same principle to the Suez Canal? British rights in Egypt's waters extended back seventy years, Churchill retorted, so why shake things up now? Anthony Eden, Churchill's deputy and the man Churchill had anointed as the next leader of the Conservative Party, chimed in, explaining

Churchill, Truman, Stalin, and twelve diplomats from Britain, the United States, and Russia sit around the Potsdam Conference table, with their interpreters alongside. CREDIT: U.S. ARMY, COURTESY HARRY S. TRUMAN LIBRARY

that control of the Suez Canal had been settled long ago by Britain and Egypt. With yet another line of conversation at a standstill, Stalin and Churchill reluctantly agreed with Truman to discuss the matter further at subsequent sessions.[29]

As the evening sky darkened portentously, the plenary ended, prompting the diplomats who were seated in a ring behind the Big Three to shuffle papers back into manila folders, speaking quietly in twos and threes as they left the table. Churchill's labored walk up the many steps of the switchback staircase that led out of the conference room proved less of a challenge to his old legs than Stalin's seemingly insurmountable obstacles.

The meetings resumed on Monday, July 23, after a round of unrelenting thunderstorms—chaos in the human realm mirrored by chaos in nature. Nor did this disorder show any sign of abating at the seventh plenary. Churchill and Stalin sparred over the question of a Russian base in Turkey, neither man giving ground. Churchill eventually proposed that the Russian Navy instead be allowed to move through the channel between the Black and Aegean seas—a proposition far less threatening to British trade interests—but Stalin refused to consider this alternative.[30]

Several hours later, Churchill put his burdens aside as he hosted the Russian and American delegations for dinner, with Stalin seated on his left and Truman on his right. Stalin spoke enthusiastically about Russia joining the war in the Pacific, ignorant still of the atomic weapons that had rendered such a commitment a moot point should Truman decide to authorize their use against Japan. He almost certainly would, given the United States' commitment of more than $2 billion to the Manhattan Project, Truman's reluctance to bring Russia into the Pacific theater, and the grim alternative of American forces invading Japan.[31]

As Churchill bade farewell to his guests and walked slowly back to his private quarters, his mind drifted from international to domestic matters. On July 5, British voters had gone to the polls for a General Election that would decide whether Churchill and his Conservative Party returned to power. The old man had made several missteps in the campaign—not least outrageously accusing his fellow Potsdam attendee Attlee of wanting to install "some form of Gestapo" government. Churchill's extreme condemnation of Labour's socialist program had hardly endeared him to voters or his opponents.[32]

In contrast, Attlee promised full employment, better social services, and the revitalization of an economy decimated by the costs of war—issues that were paramount in the minds of British citizens after victory in Europe. Attlee's position as the face of a caring, compassionate, and progressive Labour Party struck a chord with voters in all social classes, while the Tories feebly criticized Labour's plans for an expanded welfare state without establishing their own key policies. In the words of Churchill's former colleague William Beveridge (upon whose landmark 1942 report on Britain's social woes Labour had based its manifesto): "The Conservatives are fighting this election not on their own program at all, but on the popularity of Mr. Churchill."[33]

Still, in the wake of victory in Europe, Churchill was confident of success in the election, which had been pushed back three weeks to count the votes of the 3 million British troops still stationed abroad. Cautious of undue optimism, Churchill called his friend and confidant Max Beaverbrook, the newspaper tycoon. In his diary, Churchill's physician, Lord Moran, recalled Beaverbrook's contention: that Churchill might not attain the decisive 100-seat majority his campaign managers had predicted only a few weeks before but would certainly win enough seats for a working majority.[34] And so, placing the black receiver back into its cradle on the small circular nightstand, Churchill clambered into bed and slept soundly.

The following morning, Churchill attended the final meeting of the Anglo-American Joint Chiefs of Staff. Needing to salvage something from the conference, Churchill then petitioned Truman for a significant extension of the Lend-Lease Act that Roosevelt had conceived four years earlier. Truman's openness boosted Churchill's mood considerably as he left the president to meet with the recently arrived eight-man Polish delegation.

To the latter, Churchill reiterated that having entered the war to defend Polish liberty, Britain now wanted to see "free and unfettered" elections and to include "moderate elements" in the new government.[35] Finally, he advocated unrestricted access to such democratic processes for Western diplomats and journalists alike.

Ignoring Churchill's talk of elections, Polish leader Boleslaw Bierut, his dark eyes fixed on Churchill, pressed the joint Stalin-Polish claim for territorial compensation from Germany as a just measure. Frustrated by the insolence of these men, whom he had told King George were "the greatest villains imaginable," Churchill reiterated that he could not support this land grab.[36] With neither man giving an inch, Bierut and Churchill set a follow-up meeting for the next day.

By now in a thoroughly foul mood, Churchill followed Attlee and Anthony Eden into the wood-paneled meeting chamber to confer with Stalin and Truman for the eighth time. Allowing the Russian leader no chance to make the opening remarks, Churchill complained about the restrictions placed on British diplomats in Bulgaria and Romania. "They are not free to go abroad," he insisted, pausing for effect. "An iron curtain," he continued, letting the phrase linger in the smoky air, "has been rung down."

Stalin mulled this for a moment, before smiling once again as he contradicted his supposed ally. "Fairy tales," he laughed dismissively. No, Churchill insisted, these were facts, confirmed by top-ranking officials who were tired of being followed and denied access to many parts of Bucharest. Stalin then tried to pawn him off by agreeing that the Big Three must work out, on their own, how best to deal diplomatically with Romania, Bulgaria, Hungary, and Finland. To reroute the conversation, Stalin asked Truman to declare his position on recognizing the governments of Romania and Bulgaria, both of which, by this time, were dominated by Communists in key ministries. When Truman demurred, Stalin once more changed the arc of the discussion, this time pressuring Churchill on proposals for a Russian naval base in Turkey. After a brief period of sparring during which each man restated his previous positions, Truman requested that the three foreign ministers draw up a paper stating the conclusions reached thus far.[37]

Hoping to move the threesome to a topic they could agree on, Truman then turned to plans for Japan. He proposed the peace terms—Japan's full disarmament, return of conquered islands, and protection of Roosevelt's Four Freedoms for Japanese citizens. On this, at least, Churchill and Stalin concurred. Then, as the session ended, Churchill looked on as the Man from Missouri strode over to Stalin, his interpreter in tow. "I knew what the President was going to do," Churchill later recalled. Only now would Stalin learn the secret of the atom bomb.

Churchill had little time to appreciate Stalin's reaction before keeping his second appointment with the Polish leader Bierut, whom he was rapidly coming to loathe for his lack of propriety and sheer bloody-mindedness. Done playing games with these people, whom he regarded as usurpers and traitors to their nation, Churchill asked Bierut flat out whether he planned to push Poland into the Communist model. Never, Bierut insisted; on the contrary, his government would be founded on the tenets of British democracy. It was as if Bierut were not only a pawn of Stalin's but an outright imitator.

"There must be free speech," Churchill insisted, "so that everyone can argue matters out and everyone can vote." This was, of course, a sharp contrast to what had already happened in much of Eastern Europe: the establishment of "police government." In response, Bierut claimed that the Russians were leaving Poland to its own devices, and that religious and political freedom was the order of the day. Elections would be "even more democratic than those in England."

Summoning all of his diplomatic tact in suppressing his contempt for this outlandish declaration, Churchill told Bierut that he would entertain the idea of the Polish moving their western border to certain points along the Oder River but first needed assurances over the questions of supplies and reparations. He then said his good-byes, feigning geniality as he shook hands with Bierut and his aides and left for the ninth plenary—his last at the summit before he would return to London for the election results.

Stalin, predictably, was just as uncooperative as his Polish minions. The marshal still sought millions of tons of coal from Germany's Ruhr district for the Russian occupation zone and the

Poles. Impossible, Churchill insisted, but he would allocate some British coal if the Russians would reciprocate with food for Germans living in the British zone. Stalin would not budge, so this matter was added to the ever-growing list of items for the three foreign ministers to discuss at their meetings later that year.[38]

After the plenary ended, the Big Three made a passable attempt at joviality as they posed for photographers outside the Palace—Churchill in green army fatigues, Truman wearing a black suit, and Stalin in a white-jacketed, gold-buttoned military dress uniform. With this formality now concluded, Churchill, Moran, and Churchill's valet, Frank Sawyers, left for a nearby airfield along with Churchill's twenty-three-year-old daughter Mary, whom he affectionately called "Mouse" when not in such official circles.

Winston Churchill, Harry Truman, and Joseph Stalin pose for photographers at Potsdam. CREDIT: U.S. ARMY, COURTESY HARRY S. TRUMAN LIBRARY

As their black Rolls Royce made its way tentatively along the winding, tree-canopied road, Churchill mulled over the previous week's events: the frustrating encounters with Bierut, the ebb and flow of Truman's support, and the stubbornness of Stalin. At least, Churchill reassured himself, he would be able to put Stalin in his place later that week. In just a few short hours, the polls would hand the people's champion, good old Winnie, another five years at 10 Downing Street.

Churchill's silver Skymaster plane landed in the glow of a gloriously sunny afternoon on July 25 at west London's Northolt Royal Air Force base. From here, RAF and Polish Air Force fighter planes had just weeks before staged assaults against the Luftwaffe. Upon alighting, Churchill was delighted to see his younger brother, Jack, waiting for him on the tarmac, along with Clementine, his personal assistant Jock Colville, and his dear friend Lady Mountbatten. Colville relayed the Conservative Central Office (CCO) prediction that Churchill would claim a decisive majority when the next day's results came in, which only improved his employer's mood.[39]

The Tory leadership chose to ignore the fact that Labour had enjoyed a lead of up to eighteen points over the previous six months. By 1946 Gallup had been in operation for ten years, but the methods of this poll and its imitators were considered crude and unsophisticated by the Conservative Party campaign managers, who trusted their own instincts above the findings of some newfangled data-gathering company. The idealistically sunny forecast CCO staffers relayed to Churchill that day was predicated on anecdote, on laudatory conservative press coverage, and on the natural desire of party managers to please their demanding boss, if only through exaggeration and flattery.[40]

Despite their unempirical nature, the CCO's assertions hit the mark with Churchill, whose passion for the office of prime minister was as ardent in July 1945 as when he had won it in May 1940. The wartime leadership was his destiny, he believed, and having achieved victory in Europe, he wanted to lead Britain into peacetime recovery. Britain's significant postwar economic and social challenges would certainly be a trial for any politician: supporting the families of the 200,000 lost in wartime service, repairing or replacing more than 400,000 homes damaged or destroyed in the Blitz, and resuscitating a near-bankrupt economy.[41]

Churchill proceeded to Buckingham Palace to brief King George VI on the events of the Potsdam Conference. The Royal Family eyed Churchill with suspicion when he supported George's brother, Edward, before he abdicated the throne in 1936, and again when Churchill became prime minister ahead of their favorite, Lord Edward Halifax, following Neville Chamberlain's resignation in 1940. But during the war Churchill ate lunch with the king almost every Tuesday, and the two developed a rapport that extended well beyond obligatory loyalty.[42] Churchill's standing at Buckingham Palace improved all the more with the defeat of Hitler, and on the afternoon of July 25 he was a most welcome guest.

Following his royal appointment, Churchill returned to his Number 10 Annex residence—a modest, handsome white stone building constructed opposite the resplendent St. James Park in 1916. There he met briefly with his friend Max Beaverbrook. Years of experience in the newspaper industry had given Beaverbrook an uncanny understanding of the public's preferences. And when it came to choosing between the reserved Clement Attlee or the forthright Churchill to get Britain back on its feet, Beaverbrook had no doubt that the electorate would go for the latter. After sharing this sentiment with Churchill, the Canadian tycoon, whose wrinkled forehead conveyed the impression of permanent consternation, took his leave.

As dawn broke on July 26, Churchill recalled waking "suddenly with a sharp stab of almost physical pain. A hitherto subconscious conviction that we were beaten broke forth and dominated my mind. . . . The power to shape the future world would be denied me. The knowledge and experience I had gathered, the authority and goodwill I had gained in so many countries would vanish."[43]

Quickly dismissing this feeling of impending doom as a mere nightmare, he went back to sleep until 9:00 A.M. Typically, upon waking, Churchill spent several hours eating a large, cooked English breakfast (including bottled orange juice, black cherry jam, and steak or chicken from the previous evening's dinner), splashing around in the first of two daily baths, and reading the morning papers and government documents.[44] In anticipation of this day's unusual events, however, he abbreviated his breakfast and jettisoned the newspapers, remaining propped up in his bed just long enough to compose a note to Truman.

Just before 10:00 A.M., he heard a knock at the bathroom door. At Churchill's bidding, in came Richard Pim, the tall, sharp-featured Irish naval captain Churchill had hand-picked to establish and run the Map Room—the nerve center of the British war effort. Pim was used to delivering ill tidings of Allied shipping losses, but his face looked particularly grim as he shared the first election results—10 Labour wins. Churchill demanded a towel, which Pim handed him, and then strode unashamedly into the bedroom, where he donned his blue velvet "siren" suit.[45] Now dressed, he led Pim out of the room and down a short flight of concrete steps to the subterranean Map Room.

As a stark reminder that the war against Japan was yet ongoing, hundreds of pins with flags representing Japanese, American, and British ships dotted a huge, wall-mounted map of the Pacific Ocean. Color-coded telephones that enabled staff officers to relay orders to regional commanders fought for space on the writing desks littered with naval charts, import/export graphs, and the operational briefings that Churchill had spent so many hours poring over during the past five years.

The initial voting returns were unfavorable, but the Conservative camp was hopeful that the ballots from traditional Tory strongholds such as Southeast England and the Midlands would tell a different story. However, as the morning went on, these gains failed to materialize. Negative result followed negative result, and Churchill's dark premonition soon became reality. "By noon," he later wrote, "it was clear that the Socialists would have a majority."[46]

When the votes were tallied, the results amounted to a massive defeat for the Conservative Party: Labour had won an unthinkable 393 seats, while Churchill's Tories languished with a meager 210. It was the first true Labour majority government in the party's history as well as the Conservatives' worst election loss since the debacle of 1906, when it was left with just 156 seats.

Like a deflated balloon, Churchill slumped into an armchair in the Map Room, the worn cushions offering little hope of rest for his weary frame.[47] How could this be? How could the electorate have cast him out? Was it not he who had galvanized the nation, and arguably the entire democratic West, against the wretched Nazis?

Now, in July of 1945, even as he was leading his country to the successful conclusion of its long and exhausting fight against tyranny, even as he was making a lasting peace with Truman and a reluctant one with Stalin, he had been ousted from the role of prime minister. No longer feeling like the bold vanquisher of Hitler, he was, just then, an exhausted seventy-one-year-old losing his grip on his career. Trying to console her suffering husband, Clementine told him that leaving 10 Downing Street might just prove "a blessing in disguise." Ever the quick wit, Churchill glumly retorted, "At the moment it seems quite effectively disguised."[48]

Churchill's beloved daughter and confidant Mary painted a grim verbal picture of her father's mood in late July: "The next few days were, if anything, worse than that dreadful Thursday. After years of intense activity, for Winston now there was a yawning hiatus. The whole focus of power, action, and news was transferred to the new Prime Minister. Letters and messages from friends and from countless members of the public started pouring in, sweet and consoling, expressing love, indignation, and loyalty. But nothing and nobody could really soften the bitter blow."[49]

Churchill's family and friends had experienced his bouts of self-pity before—a downcast mindset he dubbed "the Black Dog"—but this uncharacteristic surrender to apathy shocked them. They were familiar with his tendency to sequester himself in his study to toil long into the night, when he was not striding purposefully through the corridors of Whitehall or working on yet another building project in the grounds of his Chartwell estate. Now, however, at least for a time, his ever-spinning wheels had ground altogether to a halt. His despondency was encapsulated in the message he left in the guest book at Chequers, at the end of what was likely to be his final stay at the prime minister's country retreat: "Finis."[50]

His previously exhausting routine had meant that Churchill usually slept soundly during his four to seven hours of daily repose. Even this brief nightly rest, however, was disrupted in the weeks following the election, as he wrestled with the defeat and churned Stalin's dismissive claims about Soviet atrocities—"fairy tales"—over and over in his troubled mind. For it was not just the return to 10 Downing Street that had eluded him but also his chance to prevent the march of expansionist Communism. Moran reported that "futile speculations filled his mind."[51]

Churchill seemingly could not shake the fear that he was finished as a politician, unwanted by the electorate, and helpless to shape the postwar peace. As he stated in his war memoirs: "Naturally I hoped that power would be accorded to me to try and make the settlement in Europe, to end the Japanese war, to bring the soldiers home. . . . I had the world position as a whole in my mind. I could not believe this would be denied me."[52]

Now that the country had put Attlee in 10 Downing Street, Churchill had little choice but to compose himself and move on. Throughout his life he had craved something to combat, from his

infantry service to opponents in the House of Commons, and
then to the military fight against Nazi Germany. With the fall of
Hitler and Mussolini, Europe was safe from the ravages of fas-
cism, but not from an equally extreme and, in Churchill's mind,
dangerous ideology: Communism. Devastated that he could not
return to Potsdam to fight Stalin over the fate of Eastern Europe,
he became resolved to find another way to protect freedom and
democracy from the Politburo's aggressive posturing.

In some ways, Churchill's enforced exodus from the Potsdam
Conference and the corridors of power was indeed the veiled opportunity that his wife had predicted immediately following news
of his defeat. Free of the burdens of high office, his mind could
devise a strategy for preventing war between the estranged members of the Grand Alliance. Without the affairs of state to occupy
his business, he began to look at the Soviet conundrum from new
angles, which would ultimately impact the postwar world as
much as any accord he may have reached if he had rejoined the
Potsdam deliberations.

For it was when forced from a position of power that
Churchill was at his most vigorous, his most eloquent, and his
most determined. This he had proven to dramatic effect in his
1930s "wilderness" campaign, when, despite being on the outside
of the Conservative Party's inner circle, he had almost single-
handedly awakened a dormant Britain to the harsh reality of
Nazism's threat.

Experience, then, told Churchill that he didn't need the bully
pulpit of 10 Downing Street in order to make an impact on the
world stage. And so, his pen—or more specifically, the pens of
his patient and frequently exasperated secretaries—went into
immediate action during the summer of 1945. And having overcome his initial defeatist reaction to the election, Churchill now
set about making sure that his voice would be heard regarding
Russia.

One August evening, as he paced back and forth in his study, an idea dawned. Churchill might have lost the opportunity to confront Stalin face-to-face at Potsdam, but he still had open to him a platform that would garner political and media attention at home and abroad: the House of Commons. Inspired to deliver a speech, Churchill began unfurling an impassioned treatise against the menace of Communism.

After days spent refining his message, Churchill made his first major speech in the new parliamentary session. The date he quite deliberately chose was August 16, the very day that Stalin and his minions in the Polish government were to ratify their new Russian frontier, and just twenty-four hours after Japan's surrender to the Allies. Eager not to let victory in the Pacific obscure the stranglehold of Communism in Eastern Europe, Churchill rose to address Parliament. Peering through his circular black-rimmed reading glasses, he consulted his notes for the last time. And then he spoke: "It would be wrong to conceal the divergences of view which exist inevitably between the victors about the state of affairs in Eastern and Middle Europe," he told them. This was met by a shuffling of order papers and mumbles of disagreement from both sides of the House.

Then, noticing that Ernest Bevin, minister of labour in Churchill's wartime coalition government, had arrived twelve minutes late, Churchill briefly digressed. Smiling at Bevin, he said: "I am very glad to see the new Foreign Secretary sitting on the front bench opposite. I would like to say with what gratification I learned that the right honorable gentleman had taken on this high office." Bevin "scowled" at Churchill, prompting *Time* to report: "Few can pay compliments so gracefully as Churchill; few can receive them as gracelessly as Bevin."[53]

Churchill then got back to the task at hand. "Spare and unguarded accounts of what has happened and is happening have filtered through," he told the House, "but it is not impossible that tragedy on a prodigious scale is unfolding itself behind the iron curtain which at the moment divides Europe in twain." He had used the term *iron curtain* three months earlier in a memo to Truman, and now, with the bombing of Hiroshima and Nagasaki having concluded war in the Pacific, it was time to introduce it to his countrymen.[54]

"Almost everywhere," Churchill told the House, "Communist forces have obtained or are in the process of obtaining dictatorial powers."[55] Churchill then offered a vivid description of what citizens living under Communist "police governments" in Eastern Europe could expect if they questioned their totalitarian leaders. He set the scene of a family "gathered around the fireside to enjoy the scanty fruits of their toil" and then described how a "father or son, or a friend sitting in the cottage is taken out into the dark, and no one knows whether he will come back again, or what his fate has been."

To press his point, Churchill moved on to the central theme of his speech: the tension between the "four freedoms" enjoyed by the Western democracies and "fears of the common man" living "in servitude" under puppet Soviet governments east of the Curzon Line. As he had done when cautioning against inaction in the face of Nazism, Churchill now issued a stark warning that echoed his "Blood, Toil, Tears and Sweat" address of May 13, 1940, saying: "Democracy is now on trial as it never was before, and in these Islands we must uphold it, with all our hearts, with all our vigilance, with all our enduring and inexhaustible strength." He paused for effect, and several shouts of "here, here" rang out on both sides of the chamber. Churchill barely looked at the small stack of notes in his left palm as he rolled along like a steam engine that had reached its head of speed.

During his election campaign, Churchill had slammed the Labour Party for embracing socialism. Now he attempted to heal the rift by stating that Attlee's administration and his Opposition ranks were "agreed in the main essentials of foreign policy and in our moral outlook on world affairs." He looked straight at Attlee and Bevin as he said this, and the two nodded back in appreciation.[56] This posture of bipartisanship demonstrated to the assembled MPs Churchill's belief that tackling the rising menace of Communism was not merely a Labour issue nor a Conservative one—it was the duty of any and all elected officials in Britain to take a stand.

Eager to continue airing his warnings about Russia, Churchill recognized the urgency of recovering from the exhaustion of the war effort, election campaign, and Potsdam Conference. And so, at the insistence of Lord Moran, he set out on September 2 for a four-week trip to the temperate climate of the Mediterranean. Sarah Churchill, who had served as her father's aide at the Teheran and Yalta summits, accompanied his party on the journey to a waterside villa with breathtaking views of the expansive, mountain-lined Lake Como. The international news corps had followed Churchill to the idyllic village of Moltrasio, but the red-tiled private villa on the western edge of the lake, offered to him by Field Marshall Harold Alexander, was heavily guarded and offered complete seclusion.[57] Other than traveling forty miles south through Italian vineyards and olive groves to see Mussolini's grave in Milan, Churchill and his fellow guests kept to themselves.

It was in the quietness of the villa, with its panoramic views, that Churchill turned again to a familiar source of solace—his easel and brushes. He had discovered the joys of painting in the aftermath of a previous traumatic event—resignation as First Lord of the Admiralty after being blamed (not unfairly) for the ill-fated Dardanelles offensive in 1915.[58]

Thirty years and several political calamities later, Churchill purged his creeping self-doubt by recording resplendent waterside vistas on canvas. With each bold sweep of the brush, the troubles that had weighed so heavily on his mind drifted across the late summer horizon like fleeting clouds. As Sarah put it, "Painting was often to save my father's temper and mind."[59]

Now at last Churchill had the benefit of several weeks of uninterrupted rest. In a letter to Clementine on September 5, he indicated that her steadfast support and patience during his malaise had yielded dividends:

> It has done me no end of good to come out here and resume my painting. I am much better in myself, and am not worrying about anything. We have had no newspapers since I left England, and I no longer feel a keen desire to turn their pages. This is the first time for many years that I have been completely out of the world. The Japanese war being finished and complete peace and victory achieved, I feel a great sense of relief which grows steadily, others having to face the hideous problems of the aftermath. On their shoulders and consciences weighs the responsibility for what is happening in Germany and Central Europe.[60]

Knowing Winston's tendency to write overly positive letters to allay her concerns, Clementine had asked Sarah for frequent updates on his progress. On September 8, Sarah wrote to her mother: "He is looking tremendously well and is much happier with every lovely picture. Care slips away. Last night he said, 'Every day I stay here without news, without worry, I realize more and more that it [the election defeat] may very well be what your mother said, a blessing in disguise. The war is over, it is won and they have lifted the hideous aftermath from my shoulders. I am what I thought I never would be until I reached my grave, sans soucis [*sic*] et sans regrets.' The only thing he misses is you."[61]

The same day, Moran confirmed in his diary that making time for artistic indulgence had given his patient much-needed perspective on the previous months' upheaval. "With my painting I have recovered my balance," Churchill told him. "I'm damned glad now to be out of it. I shall paint the rest of my days."[62]

Indeed, while at the Lake Como villa he finished nine oil paintings, which he sent back to England with Lord Moran and Sarah before he moved on to Genoa and then to the luxurious millionaire's seaside playground of Monte Carlo. He spent the warm morning of September 22 on the golden sand and then set up his easel after lunch to record the crystalline waters of the Mediterranean.[63]

Churchill had put the deterioration of the Grand Alliance out of his mind for the first few days of his Mediterranean trip, but he could not keep a lid on his growing concerns for long. Press reports about the stalemate between Bevin, Molotov, and Byrnes at the London Conference that he read at Monte Carlo's palatial, white-stone Hotel de Paris spurred him to write to Clementine on September 25:

> The Bolshevization of the Balkans proceeds apace and all the Cabinets of Central, Eastern, and Southern Europe are in Soviet control, excepting only Athens. This brand I snatched from the burning on Christmas Day. The Russians have no need of agreement and time is on their side, because they simply consolidate themselves in all these countries they now have in their grasp.
>
> I regard the future as full of darkness and menace. Horrible things must be happening to millions of Germans hunted out of Poland and Czecho-Slovakia into the British and American occupied zones. Very little is known as to what is happening behind the Russian iron curtain, but evidently the Poles and Czecho-Slovakians are being as badly treated as one could have expected.[64]

Increasingly resolute about Russia's misdeeds, Churchill was now convinced that in Eastern and Central Europe only Greece, by virtue of his Percentages Agreement, would remain outside the Politburo's expanding sphere of influence. His concern for the fate of displaced Germans is also notable. He had expressed similar sentiments at Yalta and Potsdam, demonstrating magnanimity toward his former enemies, even as he aired grave suspicions about his former allies. He also wished to avoid a repeat of the overly punitive Treaty of Versailles, which Churchill had called "malignant" and believed had stirred German support of Hitler's nationalism during the interwar years.[65]

Few maintain the energy or desire for top-level politics in their seventies, but at the age of seventy-one, Churchill was determined to lead his Conservative Party back to power. From the pinnacle of his leadership of free Europe to electoral defeat and from the bustle of 10 Downing Street to enforced rest in the Mediterranean, 1945 had been a tumultuous year for him. He had lost the chance to gain the upper hand with Stalin at the peacemakers' table, yet was resolute that he would, by whatever means necessary, prevent tyranny from again consuming the Continent.

With the year drawing to a close and "the Black Dog" muzzled, Churchill's spirits were sufficiently refreshed that he could turn his attention to his last great crusade: alerting the world to the divisions between Communist Russia and the democratic West, and urging strong diplomacy to avoid an armed struggle.

The only question that remained was how and where to share his insights with a global audience. Little could he have known that his opportunity would come from the most unlikely of sources, more than 4,000 miles away.

CHAPTER 2

DETERMINATION OF ANOTHER KIND: BULLET MCCLUER AND THE MISSION OF WESTMINSTER COLLEGE

Franc and Ida Belle McCluer. CREDIT: MCCLUER FAMILY ARCHIVES, PROVIDED BY RICHMOND MCCLUER, JR.

IN THE SMALL, UNASSUMING TOWN of Fulton, Missouri, another orator was hard at work. It was 1946, the guns of war were silent, and President Franc Lewis McCluer was busy establishing Westminster College as one of the leading men's colleges in the Midwest.

Seated in his small study, McCluer was reviewing a tall stack of administrative paperwork on his full but neatly organized mahogany desk. He periodically got up from his chair to refill his pipe with tobacco, or to pluck a hardback from the expansive oak bookshelves. When writing an important letter or preparing a speech, McCluer paced meditatively across the well-worn carpet in front of the shelves, eyes scanning the beloved volumes—several of which were components of larger books that he had commissioned the school's publisher to rebind in more manageable sections—looking for the perfect poetry, prose, or quote to inspire his own words.[1]

He was born into a humble home, a small, white board house in the hamlet of O'Fallon, Missouri, on March 27, 1896. His father, Clarence (known to everyone as C.E.), was a hard-working lumber merchant who had stoked Franc's interest in politics. As a young man, Franc was also profoundly influenced by the strong Presbyterian faith of his maternal grandfather, the charismatic Reverend Savage. When Franc was eight, his father sold the family business and moved his wife, Martha, and their three young sons to Fulton, a modest-sized yet thriving agricultural center whose residents were predominantly churchgoing folk and seemingly always elected Democrats. They relocated primarily so that the boys could attend the well-regarded Fulton High School and, later, Westminster College. A few weeks after arriving in town, the ambitious C.E. went halves on a new business venture with Fulton entrepreneur Willie Hereford and the twosome soon opened the Hereford McCluer Grocery Store at the intersection of St. Louis and Bluff streets, in the heart of Fulton's cobbled business district.[2]

Like Churchill, McCluer grew to an inconsequential height, standing barely five feet three inches. But he quickly dissolved whatever negative deductions people based on his stature with an eager mind, an indefatigable work ethic, and fast-paced persuasive rhetoric that, as a local reporter wrote, "captures his audience and holds them until he leaves the platform followed by enthusiastic applause."[3] He had become Westminster's president when he was only thirty-seven, with the Board of Trustees picking him unanimously despite his lack of administrative experience and competition from more seasoned professors.

Franc McCluer met many people in his new role and quickly endeared himself to them. Though very proper in manner and appearance, his oval-shaped face frequently creased with laughter as he sat and talked with students over lunch, hosted friends, faculty, and trustees for dinner at his yellow-brick campus home, or mixed with acquaintances at local political functions.[4] The only thing overflowing more than his ever-full appointment book was an overactive imagination, which constantly churned out new ways to improve Westminster's educational offerings to its students and to boost the college's national standing.

On McCluer's mind in late summer 1945 were fiscal planning for the college, research for the many state committees he sat on, and an especially pressing question: Who could he bring to his rural Missouri town to continue the rich tradition of the John Findley Green Lecture Series?

He had started this program in 1936, when the widow of prominent Canadian lawyer John F. Green, a Westminster College graduate in 1884 and a member of its Board of Trustees between 1906 and 1932, established a lecture program in memory of her husband. The resulting $20,000 endowment empowered McCluer to reach out to major figures in the Republican and Democratic parties and to foreign dignitaries between 1937 and 1942.

McCluer's involvement in revamping the Missouri constitution and in guiding Westminster through the economic perils of the late war years meant that he was unable to schedule Green lectures between 1943 and 1945. With the ratification of the new state constitution and the privations caused by the draft behind him in the summer of 1945, McCluer turned his attention back to the speaking schedule, regretting that he had let it languish for so long.

McCluer's interest in oration had begun in 1908, when he tried out for the high school debate team and earned a place on it. Described by one professor as "enthusiastic, energetic, popular, intellectually brilliant," he had enrolled in the freshman class at Westminster College in September 1912. With its elevated position affording panoramic views, a rocky creek running behind the campus, and six administrative, teaching, and residential buildings lining a horseshoe-shaped driveway, Westminster had a picturesque appearance and a reputation for sending many students on to medical and postgraduate programs. It was also a strict Presbyterian institution, which, though possibly deterring applicants from more socially permissive backgrounds, was an attraction for the devout and disciplined grandson of a minister.

Despite McCluer's rhetorical prowess, he faced stiff competition for the six places on the varsity debate team that year. Belying its small size, Westminster already had a nationwide reputation for excellence in debate, particularly in McCluer's favorite type—forensic debating. This method appealed to him because of his inquisitive nature (which led him to spend entire days in dusty libraries surrounded by piles of dog-eared volumes) and his uncanny ability to recall even the most obscure details at the podium.

During McCluer's junior year his persuasive rhetoric earned him a nickname, "Bullet," that would stick with him for the rest of his life. One of the debaters from the University of Texas team, which the Westminster boys defeated, said in awe of his vanquisher: "He shoots words like bullets."

Bullet's senior year was his most successful yet as a debater. Under his captaincy, the squad won the state championship for a sixth consecutive year.[5] He was mentored by professor John J. Rice, who had left a lucrative legal practice to teach a heavy load of English, political science, and history courses at Westminster and served as interim president three times. Rice's decision to forsake a high-salary career for education left an indelible mark on his protégé, who was named valedictorian at his 1916 graduation. To get the teaching experience required to lecture at Westminster, McCluer returned to Fulton High School, where he quickly became popular with students and fellow teachers. He maintained his connection with Westminster by studying for his Master of Arts degree there and devoted what little spare time he had to youth ministry at the First Presbyterian Church, which was just a short walk away from the campus on Court Street, Fulton's main drag.[6]

At the same time, McCluer got involved in the war effort. When the United States entered World War I on April 6, 1917, he

volunteered for foreign service, with a local bank manager rec-
ommending him to the chief signal officer in Washington as being "held in high regard in our community." Fulton lawyer J. R.
Baker supported this claim by writing that Bullet was "not only
bright and industrious, but thoroughly reliable." Despite his
willingness to serve in Europe, the Callaway County Draft
Board, which he later represented during World War II, decided that McCluer should continue teaching while serving in
the Missouri Fourth Minute Men division for home training
and defense.[7]

When the Board of Trustees at Westminster approached Mc-
Cluer about the vacant position of assistant professor of English
in the summer of 1918, he jumped at the chance to return to his
beloved alma mater. He quickly put his domestic military service
and in-depth knowledge of world events to use, teaching a "War
Issues" class.

Two years later, in 1920, McCluer took a major step in his personal life, marrying twenty-one-year-old Ida Belle Richmond on
September 2. The daughter of a Presbyterian minister who had attended Westminster College and now preached in tiny, rural Paris,
Missouri, the soft-spoken Ida Belle was the perfect foil to the
gregarious Bullet. Their marriage endured for sixty-nine years.[8]

This was also the year McCluer received his Master of Arts in
philosophy from Westminster. The cerebral topic of his thesis,
titled "Bergson and His Critics"—an evaluation of French
philosopher Henri Bergson's work—shows the range of his academic curiosity and acumen. His own studies temporarily behind him, McCluer wanted to make his mark on the student
body in his new role as professor of history and economics (with
a colleague now taking over his duties in the English department). Starting a tradition that they would continue throughout
their time at Westminster, Bullet and Ida Belle took many of
their meals in the expansive student dining hall, eating with a
different group each time. As his close friend Russell L. Dear-

mont (a longtime Westminster College trustee and future president of the Missouri Pacific Railroad) later put it, "The students
and alumni affectionately refer to him as 'Bullet' and many of
them have told me that their years at the College would have
been well spent if they had gained nothing but close association
with McCluer."[9]

His pupils elected McCluer as their faculty representative on
the 1921 student council, and he oversaw the *Blue Jay* yearbook
and *Fortnightly* newspaper. He also renewed his involvement
with the increasingly successful debate team, taking over as
coach in 1921, just weeks before Ida Belle gave birth to their first
and only son, Richmond, on November 26. The squad won
thirty-four of forty contests and defeated Cambridge and Oxford
in a 1928 tour of the U.K.—a tour that one observer described as
"[t]he most effective and pleasing speakers . . . so far welcomed
from any American college."[10]

Though Bullet enjoyed guiding his students to success, he was
also eager to advance his own education. To this end, he enrolled
in the University of Chicago's prestigious School of Sociology, the
first independent school in this discipline in the United States
and a pioneer of urban sociology. His decision to complete the
course while remaining in Fulton prolonged his studies from the
usual three years to six, including a semester of academic leave
from Westminster to make use of Chicago School of Sociology
resources in person. The bustle of America's second city, the sight
of ivy-covered, white stone Gothic buildings standing alongside
gleaming modern towers at the university, and the tutelage of
some of the world's leading sociologists provided quite the experience for the small-town McCluer. Following a dissertation on
the plight of Chicago's urban poor, he received his PhD in sociology and anthropology on August 31, 1928.[11]

The Chicagoans surveyed in McCluer's thesis were still dealing with the crippling consequences of the 1921–1923 economic
slump. Little did they or he know that worse times were to come.

The Wall Street Crash of 1929 hit Westminster College hard. Enrollment dropped 9 percent—to fewer than three hundred students—for the first time in a decade, alumni contributions fell off, and the rotten fruits of ill-conceived investments in local farms consumed in the Dust Bowl drained the school's coffers even further. In 1930 and 1931, beleaguered President M. E. Melvin let the business manager go, reduced faculty and staff salaries, and froze hiring.[12] McCluer, like his colleagues, accepted a pay cut, despite his promotion to professor of economics and sociology in 1931.

Always looking for new ways to stretch himself, McCluer volunteered his services to the Calloway County office of the Democratic Party in 1932, which put him to work as a campaigner for Franklin D. Roosevelt's presidential bid. That suited McCluer's outgoing and affable demeanor perfectly, and he wasted no time adding local senators and congressmen to his contacts book.

McCluer soon put his interest in local politics aside to focus on addressing Westminster's mounting financial woes. On May 6, 1932, he and his colleagues accepted President Melvin's austerity budget, which cut the money-draining football program and slashed faculty and staff salaries by 20 percent. Showing their dedication to the school, McCluer and his fellow faculty members, along with the trustees and residents of Fulton, contributed $20,000 to the general fund by January 1, 1933, despite economic hardship.[13]

This effort was not enough to prevent President Melvin's resignation on March 29, a self-sacrificing action he undertook to prevent further faculty cuts. Since his appointment in 1926, Melvin had built a new gym, boosted the endowment fund, and secured accreditation from the prestigious Association of American Universities, but he lacked the mettle to steer Westminster College through the Great Depression.[14]

McCluer took up that intimidating task when he accepted the Board of Trustees' offer of the presidency on May 29, following a unanimous vote in his favor. Professor Peoples made the burden of expectation clear when he told his still-young colleague, "McCluer, I congratulate you on your courage but not on your judgment!"[15]

On October 26, McCluer was sworn into his new role in front of 920 people, who crammed into tiny Swope Chapel to see the ceremony. Benjamin H. Charles, president of the Board of Trustees, explained why the school selected McCluer: "He is steeped in Westminster traditions. He knows the romance and the tragedy of her history. . . . [H]e knows that he will be faced with a mountain of difficulty. . . . [H]e . . . will be undaunted."[16]

McCluer soon showed courage with an unsparing budget. He proved that he was indeed undaunted, telling the Presbyterian Synod of Missouri, "The financial problems of the college are serious, though the Board feels that with cooperation and continued effort they will be solved." He delivered on this promise, keeping finances in the black. McCluer's bold leadership—and the fact that it came from a rookie president—inspired the fourteen faculty members, who, despite the privations placed on them by the hard times, showed their loyalty to McCluer by remaining in all of their posts. Russell Dearmont, who towered over the diminutive Bullet, rhapsodized, "The members of the Board are devoted to him, the members of the faculty are most cooperative with him and believe in the strength of his leadership."[17]

Certainly the Saturday morning student-professor hikes through the nearby Dark Hollow woods and the Faculty Club gatherings every two weeks in professors' homes contributed to camaraderie and unity in the face of pay cuts and heavy course loads. While schools were closing at an alarming rate in the Great Depression vortex, unable to withstand a 70 percent nationwide average drop in alumni giving and a 40 percent reduction in government funding, McCluer helped safeguard the future of his school by fostering a unique togetherness between students, faculty, and alumni.[18]

McCluer was just getting started in his new role, and yet his reputation as a capable administrator was already spreading. In 1933, the director of the American Association of Colleges named him president.

In 1934, Westminster's enrollment was back up. Astonishingly, given the fiscal plight of many Dust Bowl schools, it reached 356, an all-time record. McCluer again balanced the budget, and repeated this feat the following year. McCluer did not conduct Westminster's financial affairs in isolation but, rather, worked diligently with the state government to take advantage of President Franklin D. Roosevelt's New Deal. In 1935, a quarter of the students who worked on campus did so as part of the National Youth Administration program.[19]

The next year, McCluer's endeavors to promote public speaking and political debate on the Westminster campus received an unexpected boost with the Green family endowment. For the inaugural Green Lecture in 1937, McCluer secured Oscar D. Skelton, undersecretary for foreign affairs for Dominion of Canada, who, like McCluer, had completed his postgraduate studies at the University of Chicago. The soft-spoken Skelton lectured to a crowd of several hundred Fultonians on "Our Generation: Gains and Losses."[20] This was published by the prestigious University of Chicago Press, bringing the Green Lectures to a wider audience and helping the school to attract other prominent orators.

Later that year, McCluer showed his commitment to civil rights by bringing noted African American scientist, prominent civil rights figure, and fellow Missourian George Washington Carver to town to dedicate a middle school that bore Carver's name. This was a bold move, considering the lynchings that still plagued Missouri in the 1930s and the influence of white supremacists with local government officials and police officers. Still, the seventy-three-year-old Carver heard only cheers as he cut the new school's ceremonial ribbon.

Bullet also began what was to become a tradition for the Green Lectures and other Westminster speaking engagements—inviting scholars, journalists, and politicians to address the student body—with the arrival of Spanish Civil War reporter John Langdon Davies. Believing that the public speaking series should raise his students' global awareness, McCluer then brought to Fulton returning U.S. Ambassador to Germany William E. Dodd (1938) and Francis B. Sayre, former High Commissioner to the Philippines (1940). McCluer encapsulated the ethos of the Green Lectures thus: "One must be devoted to something bigger than himself, and so eager to accomplish a worthy purpose that he can push himself toward with the vigorous and enthusiastic abandon and the joy of self-forgetfulness."[21]

When the 1940 presidential election campaign got under way, McCluer was again in the thick of it. In early May, he hosted what *Time* called "the biggest college rump convention ever staged," at Westminster College, which, seven years into Bullet's tenure as president, was "politically-conscious beyond all proportion to its size."[22] The next month, McCluer landed for the Green Lecture arguably his biggest political catch so far—New York Mayor Fiorello LaGuardia, the cigar-smoking dynamo who had revitalized the Big Apple and whom McCluer had met at the World's Fair.

At each of these lectures, according to the school's marshal and historian Charles F. "Dog" Lamkin, "[c]rowds filled the gymnasium where the visitors spoke as their speeches were broadcast, delegations from distant points coming to Fulton to greet the distinguished visitors."[23]

How was McCluer attracting such dignified speakers to his humble college of three hundred young men, with its six small buildings, when they were in demand to speak at institutions of far greater enrollment and prestige? The answer is twofold. First, McCluer had social grace and charisma in abundance. As Russell Dearmont put it, "He has a charming personality, which draws people of all ages to him."[24]

Second, there was the sheer boldness of his invitations: Mc-Cluer believed he could petition anyone, from the president of the United States down, and succeed in getting that person to speak in Fulton. Professor Edgar Dewitt Jones, who knew Mc-Cluer from his son's PR job at Fulton's nearby William Woods College, remarked, "President McCluer is one of those go get 'em gentlemen who usually hook what they fish for."[25] McCluer's chief success, in addition to landing Mayor LaGuardia, was drawing FBI director J. Edgar Hoover to campus.

Juggling engagements with the military, which brought a civilian pilot training program to Westminster in the fall of 1940, and preparing a budget that ensured an eighth year of surplus funds, McCluer continued Westminster's burgeoning speaking program in the 1940–1941 school year. A new theme, "The Unity of the Western Hemisphere and the Means to Its Defense," attracted an eclectic array of guest speakers, from arch-isolationist Kirby Page and the hawkish Admiral William Standley to pragmatic architect M. Todd, whose firm designed the iconic Radio City Music Hall and the Cunard Building in New York. Delivering the commencement address on May 1941, Governor Forrest Donnell urged the Westminster student body to put service to their country above all else, even if the United States formally entered the war and they were dispatched to Europe.[26]

The Lend-Lease program escalated and America joined the struggle after Germany and Italy declared war on December 11, 1941. The topic of McCluer's ambitious lecture series seemed more prescient and fitting than ever. Still, it took a back seat to the escalation in American materiel supply to Britain. McCluer invited Vice President Henry A. Wallace, but he declined on April 30, 1943, "because of the exigencies of the war and the great demands on my time."[27]

In recognition of his jump-starting Missouri's constitutional review, including hosting the kick-off meeting, McCluer was elected president of the finance committee for the Missouri Constitutional Convention in September 1943. At the same time that McCluer was beginning work for the Convention, his son, Richmond, was sent to Europe as a paratrooper in the 101st Airborne Division, or "Screaming Eagles" as they were commonly known. For a parting gift, McCluer bought his son a small brown ceramic pipe and several tins of Dunhill's Medium tobacco from Jost's Pipe Shop in St. Louis.[28] In retrospect these items appeared to be a good-luck talisman, as Richmond survived the war without serious injury and was recognized for distinguished service.

Though worried about his son's fortunes in Europe, McCluer was engaged in his own battle to again pull Westminster College out of a deep financial rut. During World War II the college had, like most other higher-education institutions on both sides of the Atlantic, seen traditional enrollment drop precipitously due to the draft, presenting the school's most formidable fiscal challenge since its struggles in the wake of the Great Depression.

On November 25, 1943, McCluer summarized the root of the enrollment problems in a letter to Dearmont: "Students who have reached their eighteenth birthday cannot enter college under present service regulations. . . . It is unlikely we will have more than 25 freshmen."[29] To keep the school afloat, McCluer shrewdly negotiated with the U.S. Navy and secured funding for officer cadets in the V-12 program. This move was unpopular with the civilian student body because the cadets took over the dormitories, but it staved off likely bankruptcy.

With Westminster's financial situation stabilized, McCluer switched his focus to auditing the sixty-eight-year-old Missouri Constitution (now woefully outdated by the cultural, social, and economic circumstances of the 1940s). In a memo written on May 19, 1944, McCluer described his proposed solution to what he called the "wasteful awkwardness" of multiple offices dividing financial control: "It became apparent as we studied the fiscal problems of the state that it was desirable for all agencies of government dealing with financial administration to be grouped into one department, the Department of Revenue."

McCluer also proposed a radical improvement in public schooling. Up to this point, education in Missouri was dramatically underfunded and no minimum was set for the percentage of state revenue that would be appropriated for schools. Rural schoolhouses were consequently falling apart, with the only money for books and supplies coming from residents still recovering from the aftermath of the Depression. McCluer sought to remedy these issues, declaring: "In no case shall there be set aside less than twenty-five percent of the state revenue to be applied annually to the support of free public schools." He was also determined to offer state support for learning through reading, stating that "the policy of the state shall be to promote the establishment of free public libraries."

In keeping with the focus of his postgraduate work and his correspondence with executives of the National Association for the Advancement of Colored People (NAACP), McCluer tried to desegregate Missouri schools and colleges, which were strictly separated under the old constitution. Racially motivated violence was not as endemic as in Mississippi or Alabama, but the Ku Klux Klan was active in Missouri and there were numerous cases of violence and harassment each year. McCluer realized that the conservative Missouri populace was unlikely to approve wholesale integration, so he attempted to get a measure through the back door by way of compromise. This is explained in a letter from his friend J. A. Thompson dated April 27, 1944: "Your section made it possible for colleges and universities to admit negro students on their own terms. At any rate, your proposition was sensible and yet recognized the prejudices of a former slave state. It is time the former slave states were recognizing their obligations to their negro citizenship. Missouri, being a border state, is in a position to set a good example to the states of the 'Deep South.' We are glad that men such as yourself are members of the convention."[30]

This brave amendment was ultimately stricken by McCluer's colleagues. Yet that should not diminish how forward-thinking the proposition was. The *Brown v. State Board of Education* case, in which the U.S. Supreme Court ruled that school segregation violated the Equal Protection Clause of the Fourteenth Amendment, would not be heard for another decade. Despite numerous defeats of his ambitious proposals, McCluer was determined to bring about social change. As he later wrote: "We must become one people, united by the way we feel toward one another and not merely by laws that seek to establish equality of opportunity."[31]

When he was not busying himself with state, local, and national politics at his desk, McCluer loved being outdoors. He cultivated roses and a rainbow of dahlias in the garden outside his office window, regularly played tennis with students and faculty members, and was a keen golfer.[32]

Beneath his often reserved demeanor lay a rebellious streak, typified by his love of driving far in excess of Callaway County's draconian speed limits. Years later, his son, Richmond, wrote his wife: "I've driven the Buick since I've been here. Ribbed Bullet about how sluggish it is compared to our own Chevy. Told him I didn't think it'd do over 60. He admitted having had it well above 90."[33]

After commencement in June each year, McCluer combined his passions for fishing and family time, packing luggage and fishing gear into his black Buick coupe and driving to Cape Hatterass, a sand-dune-lined island with a distinctive black and white swirl-painted lighthouse in North Carolina's Outer Banks. His other favored destination was the lake house he purchased in the late 1930s in Ludington, Michigan's picturesque Epworth Heights neighborhood, which boasts a golden sand beach, a renowned golf course, and Cape Cod–style cottages in every color and hue imaginable. He renamed the two-story wooden home "Dunvagen" after the Scottish castle owned by his ancestors and made several trips there each year when he had breaks in his frenetic schedule. The McCluers spent evenings reading in the spacious living room, with Bullet occasionally breaking the silence by sharing passages from C. S. Lewis, James Michener, and the Bible.[34]

McCluer took any opportunity to express his profound faith in the formative powers of the humanities and their ability to influence political thought. In his 1945 report to the Board of Trustees, he included a brief essay titled "The Responsibility of Education for the Future." In it, he wrote: "For the practical task of defending civilization we have need of liberal education. The training of youth in the mastery of ideas provides the understanding and the appreciation of values vital to our democratic way of life. Technicians with expert hand, keen eye, and sharpened faculties may win the battles, fill the barns and launch the ships, but with these skills must go the human and enlightened heart."

He then moved on to the important contribution that college students would make when the war was over: "People, not dictators, must make great decisions in the post war days. Appreciation of great values and of eternal principles must be accomplished in some measure in countless minds if our decisions are to be just and wise."[35]

With these thoughts in mind, McCluer turned his attention to finding a speaker for the first postwar Green Lecture. While on a bass fishing trip at North Star Lake in Minnesota "one beautiful afternoon," on July 11, 1945, he discussed possible orators with Ida Belle. While "sitting lazily relaxing in our fishing boat . . . in a daydreaming mood," he suddenly exclaimed, "How about Winston Churchill?"

"I thought he was saying it with tongue in cheek," Ida Belle later recalled. "But I replied that we could dream, and after all, what did we have to lose?" "Harry Vaughan could help arrange it," she insisted.[36] Vaughan was a Westminster alumnus, a longtime friend of the McCluers, and, most significantly, a naval aide in the Truman White House.

On returning to Fulton, McCluer developed the proposal. On September 10, he wrote to Estill I. Green, son of John Findley Green and Bullet's old teammate on the Westminster College debate squad, to see what he thought of the idea. In addition to requesting feedback, McCluer wanted to know if Green, who had been an aide at the League of Nations, could help "get some of our government officials to urge him to accept our invitation." Green was skeptical, replying three days later that "it would be fine to have Winston Churchill if that is feasible. However, I would anticipate possible delays and difficulties."[37]

Undeterred, Bullet also shared his idea with several other close friends, who encouraged him to move ahead, including Westminster College trustees Neal S. Wood and Estill Green's brother, John Raeburn. So McCluer went to the red-brick Callaway County Bank with its distinctive two-story arched window and concrete American Eagle perched atop the roof, to talk to longtime confidant Tom Van Sant, an executive at the bank. Van Sant was an old friend of President Harry Truman and frequently shared his opinions as "Mr. Average Voter," who claimed to be in touch with the needs and views of small town America. Truman must have respected Van Sant's judgment as he offered him the role of secretary of agriculture, but the Fultonian turned it down.[38]

After graduating from Westminster College, Van Sant enlisted in the U.S. Army in World War I and fought in France and Belgium. When hostilities ceased in late 1918, he traveled to London and took a one-year, postgraduate course at the prestigious London School of Economics. Upon his return to Fulton, news of this qualification prompted Van Sant's cousin, William C. Harris, to appoint him cashier—the equivalent of Chief Financial Officer—at the Callaway County Bank, of which Harris was a part-owner and executive.

When he heard Bullet's idea, Van Sant immediately agreed with Ida Belle McCluer: yes, inviting Churchill to Fulton was audacious, but Bullet had landed big fish in the past, so why not just try. He also seconded her recommendation to get Harry Vaughan involved, and offered to contact him.

Van Sant was a persuasive fellow, although his method differed from McCluer's typical approach of logical argument. Favoring volume over rationale, Van Sant made good use of his six-foot-plus frame to lean in close to his listeners, disarming them by invading their personal space. He then boomed his opinion in no uncertain terms, and few argued. Bullet valued his friend's judgment and, combined with the encouragement of the Green brothers and Ida Belle, it was enough to spur him to act on his plan.[39]

Back at his office, McCluer concluded that asking Churchill to come would cost him little, whatever the outcome. "If he will not come it means nothing more than he said, 'No,' and if he does accept, Westminster will have one of the greatest men it could ever hope to attain for the lectureship," he later remembered thinking.[40] At age forty-nine, McCluer convinced himself that he could pull off the biggest coup of his educational and political career: bringing Winston Churchill to Fulton to deliver five lectures in the spring of 1946.

As fate would have it, the former prime minister was considering taking a long trip to the United States, with the dual purpose of enjoying the coastal waters of Florida and helping Britain secure a postwar loan of several billion dollars by meeting with Truman and influential friends such as New York financier Bernard Baruch. The trip was also recommended by Churchill's personal physician, who was troubled by the former prime minister's mounting health concerns. Even Churchill himself admitted to his potential host in Miami, Canadian Colonel Frank Clarke, that "I stand in need of some rest and sunshine and . . . hope it would be possible for us to live very quietly indeed with you for some few weeks."[41]

This planned journey came at just the right time to accommodate McCluer's plan, but his invitation was still a long shot at best. After all, Churchill was arguably the most recognized figure in world affairs and received dozens of invitations each month, most of which were dismissed by his secretaries before even reaching his desk. And in any case, at the moment McCluer dispatched his letter, Churchill had not committed to coming to the United States. Bullet had used his political contacts to bring Hoover and LaGuardia to Fulton, but bringing *the* iconic figure of his age to campus was an altogether different proposition.

In the face of long odds, McCluer resolved to give it a shot, as he always did when asking a prominent figure to speak at Westminster. Just as Ida Belle and Van Sant had suggested, McCluer asked the latter to reach out to his old classmate Harry Vaughan, the star center on Westminster's football team and a member of the Phi Delta Theta fraternity.[42]

A year after graduating from Westminster with McCluer in 1916, the jovial Vaughan became friends with Harry Truman while the two were in military training in Oklahoma. In World War I, Vaughan won the Silver Star as an artillery field captain and was promoted to Major in 1928 and to Lieutenant Colonel in 1935.

Vaughan, whose large facial features later made him an easy target for political cartoonists, was treasurer for Truman's senatorial campaign in 1940 and his secretary the following year. He was appointed Liaison Officer for the Truman-Mead Commission in 1944, and later that year was promoted to Military Aide to the President. The major general's critics claimed that he carried "little weight or responsibility" in the White House. A *Time* reporter dismissed him as "The Amateur General" (one of the many negative things this publication printed about him), but there is no question that Vaughan was in Truman's inner circle.[43] The president personally appointed him and frequently called on his old friend to share his views on national defense.

After McCluer and Vaughan exchanged several phone calls and letters about the proposed visit by Churchill, the major general invited Bullet, who knew Truman from the Missouri political circuit, to the White House in early October. McCluer dictated version after version for his secretary Dorothy Canada to type and, after filling the wastebasket with crumpled rewrites, finally settled on the final iteration just before his visit to Washington.[44]

Vaughan later recounted the details of hosting Bullet:

He came into my office one day and said, "Mr. Churchill is going to be in the United States in the spring. It sure would be great if we could get him to come out to the college and make a talk." I said, "Well, why don't you write to him?" He said, "I got a letter right here."

He handed it to me and I read it. I said, "Let's go in and see what the Boss [President Truman] thinks about that." So, I called Matt Connelly and I said, "Is the Boss busy?" He said, "No, his last appointment left and he hasn't got another appointment for ten minutes—fifteen minutes, something like that."

I said, "Bullet McCluer is here and we'd like to see him." [He responded:] "Well, if you come right over now. I'll have to throw you out in about five minutes but you can get in right now." So, we went over in a hurry and went right through [presidential secretary] Rose Conway's office. I stuck my head in and I said, "Boss, I've found you've got five minutes free and I've got a guy here from Missouri who wants to see you—Bullet."

He said, "Well, come in, Bullet. How are you?" They chatted for a minute and I said, "He's got a letter he wants you to look at."

Bullet gave it to him and the president said, "I think that's a good letter. That might work. Wait a minute." So he took up his pen (it was a short letter so there was plenty of room on the bottom) and wrote on the bottom in longhand. He said, "Now, you send him that."[45]

On returning to Fulton, McCluer took the president's advice, dispatching his audacious letter on October 3. Despite Truman's endorsement, Bullet had no inkling of what Churchill would decide.

CHAPTER 3

A Date Is Set:
Harry Truman and
Winston Churchill Accept

*This is a wonderful school in my home state. Hope you
can do it. I'll introduce you.*

—Harry Truman's addendum on Franc McCluer's
letter to Winston Churchill (October 3, 1945)

EARLY ON A COLD MORNING in early October, 1945, Winston Churchill rifled through a stack of mail, looking for something meaningful enough to command a few minutes of his precious time. An envelope with a U.S. State Department postmark caught his eye. He opened it, pulled out two pages, and read the first:

My dear Mr. Churchill:

In 1936, an English-born woman, Mrs. John Findley Green, established at Westminster College a memorial lectureship to be known as the John Findley Green Foundation. The lectureship was established to bring to the college campus each year a man of international reputation who would discuss economic, social, or political problems of international concern in a series of three or four lectures. After the lectures are delivered, the lecturer leaves the manuscript with the college in order that they may be published in book form.

This letter is to invite you to deliver the Green Lectures in the winter of 1945–1946, or in the spring of 1946. We should be glad to arrange the date or dates to suit your convenience.

The arrangement for the scheduling of the lectures may be made to suit your convenience. It had been our thought to have one lecture at the college one evening and to have another lecture delivered in St. Louis, Missouri (U.S.A.) on the evening of the following day. The college is located one hundred miles from this metropolitan center and we should like to arrange for your appearance under the auspices of the Green Foundation before the great audience which would assemble in St. Louis to hear you. We know that any discussions coming from you and delivered from this forum here in the heart of the United States will be of immense and enduring significance, and will promote the international understanding requisite to the maintenance of peace. We earnestly hope that you will do us the honor of accepting this invitation.

A suitable honorarium will be provided. In this instance, we shall also be glad to allow you to arrange for the publication of the lectures, or we shall make the arrangement and allow you to share in the royalties.

Enclosed you will find [an] excerpt from the Instrument of Gift, establishing the John Findley Green Foundation Lectureship at Westminster College.

Yours respectfully,

F. L. McCluer

President

An intriguing proposal, certainly, but Churchill received so many like it. Then he scanned the postscript:

> This is a wonderful school in my home state. Hope you can
> do it. I'll introduce you.
> Best Regards,
> Harry Truman[1]

This, Churchill suddenly realized, was not merely a letter from a president at some obscure college in America's heartland. With Truman's involvement and the full attention of the U.S. and British media, such an engagement could be the perfect opportunity to share his grave concerns about Communism and the potential solutions that had percolated since the election defeat four months earlier. He had certainly never heard of Fulton, Westminster College, or Franc McCluer, but this was of no concern: Truman would announce him, so the world would be watching and listening.

Churchill was an idealist who wanted to believe in his heart that Britain was still the strong Empire seat of yore, yet he was also a pragmatist. Indeed, with the U.S.S.R. now dominating Eastern and possibly soon Central Europe, the United States preeminent in the West, and Britain's powers waning, he knew that close association with America was vital to the preservation of the U.K.'s security and economic interests.[2] With blind faith in his personal diplomacy skills, Churchill believed that he could bring about such unity single-handedly if he had an audience with the president and a chance to speak to the American public.

With these factors in mind, he dictated his acceptance on November 8, sending it to Truman rather than McCluer to ensure maximum impact at the highest level. While eager to speak in Missouri, Churchill informed the former that he would "not be able to contemplate the effort involved in composing and delivering the four lectures of the Greene [*sic*] Foundation. Of course, however, if you, as you suggest in your postscript, would like me to visit your home State and would introduce me, I should feel it my duty—and it would be a great pleasure—to deliver an address to the Westminster University on the world situation, under your aegis. This might possibly be advantageous for several points of view."[3]

The decision to deliver a single lecture rather than a series is hardly surprising, given that Churchill gave his most potent orations as single salvos—most famously his "Blood, Toil, Tears and Sweat" speech delivered to a packed House of Commons on May 13, 1940.

Having communicated acceptance of the Fulton engagement, Churchill switched his focus, conveying his support of the U.S. president: "I dare say you will have seen from the speech I made yesterday how very much I admire your recent declarations and my great desire to carry forward the policy which you have announced by every means in the power of the Conservative Party."[4] In tone and content, such a comment was reminiscent of the early World War II years, when Churchill was courting the support of FDR. The new foe, or at least potential new foe, was no longer Germany, however, but Soviet Russia.

By soliciting the president's backing in person, Churchill knew he would have more leeway as a private citizen than when he had communicated with Roosevelt as prime minister. Now, he would not have to answer to a coalition Cabinet full of conflicting voices and opinions. In addition, as he implied in the memo to Truman, an introduction from the president of the United States would validate his message and provide an opportunity to talk to the Man from Missouri and his key advisers about other pressing matters, including a much-needed new American loan to Britain.

The combination of these factors and sheer audacity meant that Bullet McCluer had succeeded in making what once seemed

WESTMINSTER COLLEGE

CHARTERED IN 1853

FULTON, MISSOURI

October 3, 1945

The Honorable Winston Churchill, M. P. *(W. S. C.)*
London
England

My dear Mr. Churchill:

In 1936 an English-born woman, Mrs. John Findley Green, established at Westminster College a memorial lectureship to be known as the
John Findley Green Foundation. The lectureship was established to bring
to the college campus each year a man of international reputation who
would discuss economic, social, or political problems of international
concern in a series of three or four lectures. After the lectures are
delivered, the lecturer leaves the manuscript with the college in order
that they may be published in book form.

This letter is to invite you to deliver the Green Lectures in
the winter of 1945-1946, or in the spring of 1946. We should be glad to
arrange the date or dates to suit your convenience.

The arrangement for the scheduling of the lectures may be made
to suit your convenience. It had been our thought to have one lecture
at the college one evening and to have another lecture delivered in St.
Louis, Missouri (U.S.A.) on the evening of the following day. The college
is located one hundred miles from this metropolitan center and we should
like to arrange for your appearance under the auspices of the Green Foundation before the great audience which would assemble in St. Louis to hear
you. We know that any discussions coming from you and delivered from this
forum here in the heart of the United States will be of immense and enduring significance, and will promote the international understanding requisite
to the maintenance of peace. We earnestly hope that you will do us the
honor of accepting this invitation.

A suitable honorarium will be provided. In this instance, we shall
also be glad to allow you to arrange for the publication of the lectures, or
we shall make the arrangement and allow you to share in the royalties.

Enclosed you will find excerpt from the Instrument of Gift, establishing the John Findley Green Foundation Lectureship at Westminster College.

*This is a wonderful school
in my home state. Hope you
can do it. I'll introduce you*

Yours respectfully,

F. L. McCluer
F. L. McCluer
President

FLM:D
enclosure (1) *Best regards*

Harry Truman

Franc McCluer's letter to Winston Churchill with Harry Truman's
postscript, October 3, 1945. CREDIT: NATIONAL CHURCHILL MUSEUM
ARCHIVES, CHURCHILL, TRUMAN, McCLUER DAY COLLECTION,
FOLDER 07, IMAGE 267

a far-fetched idea become a reality: arguably the two most recognizable men in the world were coming to Westminster College.

Bullet McCluer was elated, Harry Vaughan remembered. "He called me up from Fulton and I think if he'd had the window open and his head out the window, he wouldn't have needed the phone. He said, 'Mr. Churchill said that he will come and make this talk and that it will be the only public appearance that he will make during this trip to the United States!'" McCluer dispatched an equally high-spirited note to his friend on November 30, 1945, telling Vaughan that Churchill's visit "will be one of the most outstanding days in the history of the college" and sharing his hope that Truman would consent to "nationwide broadcasting."[5]

At the same time, McCluer turned his attention back to budgetary challenges at Westminster College. At the end of the war, the Navy V-12 program that McCluer had brought to the campus and had saved the school financially was disbanded by the U.S. government, with more than a thousand officer cadets graduated. This left a huge gap between school spending and revenue—a gap that private donations would need to bridge if McCluer was to continue his remarkable twelve-year run of balancing the budget in the face of recession and war. There was also a decline in enrollment, with a mere third of the three hundred required students on campus after the Navy cadets departed. Fortunately for McCluer and the ever-fluctuating Westminster College finances, Churchill declined the offer of an honorarium, enabling this money to go into reserve for future Green Foundation lecturers.[6]

To help drum up new funds, Bullet packed a small wooden platform in the trunk of his black Buick town car and drove to a different Presbyterian church each Sunday, at the invitation of a minister he invariably knew from his long denominational involvement. At each countryside chapel he made a persuasive speech from his raised position, his surprisingly loud voice echoing around the sanctuary without amplification. Then the Westminster Glee Club struck up a hymn or two, and the resulting donations went into the college's coffers.[7]

However, no amount of churchgoers' generosity could contribute the required capital. On December 10, McCluer took up his persuasive pen once again, writing to Westminster's alumni requesting assistance to overcome the $50,000 deficit (equivalent to almost $600,000 today). He told them that "this will be the most difficult year during the war emergency period" and declared his hope that "this one year the friends of the college will make extraordinary gifts to operating funds to offset this loss." As was the case every time he made such an appeal, former Westminster students reached deep into their pockets, pulling out enough for Bullet to again put the balance sheet back in the black. The college, which sent a third of its graduates to medical school and 65 percent to postgraduate professional study, was out of danger once more.[8]

Demonstrating his ability to alternate easily between macro and micro decision-making, McCluer worked with Westminster trustee A. P. Green (no relation to the Green Foundation lecture donor or her sons) in mid-December to secure the large quantities of cured Callaway County ham that would be served at the honorary lunch for Churchill and Truman at his home.[9] The event was still three months in the future, but McCluer was eager that no detail would be missed.

A. P. Green, instantly recognizable by his ever-present circular-rimmed glasses and commanding frame, was happy to help. In addition to his service on the Board of Trustees, he had long been a financial backer of Westminster College, paying for an endowed English chair and coming to the school's aid during Westminster's intermittent fiscal travails. Given his past involvement with Westminster College, it was natural that the businessman and philanthropist would again step up to support McCluer in any way he could.[10]

The same day as he received Green's confirmation about the
ham order, December 13, McCluer again sent a letter to the
White House, telling Truman of his mounting excitement about
Churchill's impending visit. To honor the president's wish to announce the Fulton address in London and Washington simultaneously, McCluer held his exuberance in check and delayed until
December 19 his official proclamation about Churchill's decision
as well as the prospective speech date of February 5, 1946.[11]

It was hard to keep even small happenings secret in the intimate Fulton community, but the discreetness of the McCluers
and the loyalty of their friends prevented a media leak that would
have been inevitable at a larger school. First-term Missouri governor Phil M. Donnelly and his wife, Juanita, were among the
first people McCluer formally invited to the speech, even before
the formal announcement. For McCluer, this event was a chance
not only to draw attention to Westminster College and boost the
prestige of the Green Lectures but also to unite national and
international affairs with the Missouri political scene in which
he had been so involved for the preceding twenty years.[12]

Writing to Estill Green (one of John Findley Green's sons) two
weeks before the December 19 news release, McCluer diffi-
dently predicted that the event "will be carried rather generally
in the papers of the country."[13] He did not anticipate the media
frenzy that was in store once the announcement was made, with
the speech date now officially changed to March 5, 1946.

Newspaper boys struggled through snow and ice in Fulton on the
morning of December 19 to deliver warm tidings to *Fulton Sun-
Gazette* subscribers: "Winston Churchill to Speak in Fulton
March 5: Truman Coming." Tom Van Sant, the Fulton banker
whose encouragement had spurred McCluer to visit the White
House and seek Truman's endorsement of the Churchill invitation, described the hectic twenty-four hours that followed the
news release: "As you might guess, the announcement of this

man's appearance in Central Missouri has precipitated a flood of calls and demands on Dr. McCluer's time have him pretty well tied up. Up to noon today Dr. McCluer has received more than 100 long-distance telephone calls requesting seats."[14]

McCluer carved a few minutes out of the chaos to pen a note to Churchill, informing him: "It will be an honor to welcome you to this campus and to have the college offer the forum for the address, which we know will be of significance to the world."[15]

In his final communication of the day, McCluer typed a late-night note to Harry Vaughan. "I shall never cease to be grateful to the President and you for making this event possible at Westminster College," McCluer wrote.[16] He also confirmed that the two would meet in Kansas City two days after Christmas, their first face-to-face encounter since that fateful October day in Washington.

The news of Churchill's impending arrival demanded much from the already busy Bullet, and he was not the only member of the family affected. "It was like a bomb exploding in my living room," Ida Belle McCluer recalled. "Some students were already on their way home for the Christmas holidays that morning. . . . [T]hey began calling back, 'Is it really true?' and 'Why weren't we called?' I remember a London newspaper reporter calling about 3:00 A.M. the next morning. He wanted to know something about Westminster College and how all this came about. He had to meet a deadline, he said. He apologized for calling, as he put it, at this 'un-Christian hour.'"[17]

This was just the first of many interviews. In speaking with a reporter from the *St. Louis Globe-Democrat,* McCluer admitted, "I didn't have much confidence Churchill would accept, but I felt there wasn't any harm in asking." Certainly there was a greater degree of difficulty involved than if McCluer had invited one of his previous two prospects for the 1946 Green Lecture, accomplished though they were—Dr. John Mackay, president of Princeton Seminary, or Henning W. Prentis, Jr., head of the

Armstrong Cork Company. McCluer gave much of the credit for Churchill's unexpected acquiescence to Truman, saying, "We realize that his endorsement of it is partially responsible for the quick response."

Later in the *St. Louis Globe-Democrat* article, writer Margaret Maunder summarized the unique circumstances of McCluer's coup and the bafflement it caused among other higher-education administrators: "If there was ever a case of shooting for the moon and hitting it, the instance of Fulton and the British war leader is it. . . . The idea of such a small, remote school . . . getting Churchill to address it has caused larger universities to grow green with envy. The nerve of that little college!"[18]

The *Kansas City Times* shared similar sentiments with its readers: "The presidents of the great and powerful universities are scratching their heads and talking to themselves. . . . Small college presidents may shoot a sly grin at the big, famous universities with all their money and courses to solve every immediate problem of the world—except the problem of getting Winston Churchill as the main event."[19]

To reduce the administrative burden on himself, McCluer hired Joe B. Humphreys, a Westminster alumnus who had acted as press liaison for the U.S. Navy during World War II. Humphreys was almost as effervescent as Bullet, and the two sparked each other's efforts throughout Humphreys's stay on campus.[20] Bullet also appointed A. C. Huber to help manage public relations.

Bullet quickly realized that the efforts of these three men, with all the late nights in the world, would not be enough to manage the preparations for Churchill's visit. He reached out to the Fulton Chamber of Commerce, which formed a committee to oversee the considerable logistical challenges. The unanimous choice for chairman was the fifty-year-old superintendent of Fulton's Missouri State School for the Deaf, Truman L. Ingle, who was entering his thirteenth year at the institution's helm. This tall, energetic administrator wasted little time getting to work. He soon told McCluer about the subcommittees he had established: decorations, traffic control/parking, feeding, housing, airport, parade, information, and—ingloriously—restrooms.[21] The list soon grew to include a group dedicated to ferrying around the expected throng of reporters as well as a finance committee to keep spending under control. Through a city council allocation and the generosity of the Chamber's members, the latter soon had $5,000 at its disposal.

McCluer insisted that no committee member was to furnish individuals with more than two places in the gym unless given a personal exemption by him. The team-focused approach proved to be prudent, as no one person could have processed the thousands of ticket-related inquiries and media solicitations that flooded the campus in the ensuing weeks, much less the logistical minutiae such an event necessitated. As A. P. Green put it, the event would be "the biggest thing to happen here for years!"[22]

The only comparable event in Fulton history was the visit of Jefferson Davis in September 1875, when horse-drawn carriages blocked the roads into Fulton as Missourians flocked to see the former Confederate president. The town was in a unique position in the Civil War, having been part of the only county to sign a nonaggression treaty with the federal government. Callaway County leaders garnered a government vow to keep troops away if the Missouri district kept its promise not to carry arms.[23] Accordingly, the area became proudly known as "The Kingdom of Callaway County," ensuring that the thriving mule-breeding town of Fulton did not suffer the human and financial losses suffered by many other cities in the Midwest.

In more recent memory was the reception for Helen Stephens, the "Fulton Flash," who won the hundred-yard dash in a world-record time at the 1936 Berlin Olympics. Yet even this parade, which saw up to 20,000 people flooding the streets of Fulton to hail Stephens's triumphant return, was expected to pale next to the scope and scale of "Churchill-Truman Day" (or "C-T Day"), as locals had dubbed it.[24]

Though the mule trade had foundered by 1946, Fulton remained a thriving agricultural center, with one of the region's most popular livestock markets meeting each week just outside the city and more than 100,000 head of cattle, horses, pigs, and sheep on the surrounding arable land. There had been a turn to industry, though, with the largest employers being two shoe factories (including the International Shoe Factory, which had premises across the state), a terrace production facility, and the Harbison-Walker brickworks. The latter found plenty of local materials, as the central Missouri soil was predominantly composed of red fire clay. Indeed, many local children learned to swim in the water-filled clay pits on the outskirts of town.[25]

The town's retail and commercial interests were concentrated on the three-block, red-brick paved Court Street. On a typical day, black coupes were tightly packed into just-big-enough parallel parking spots, while their owners ran into Sault's or Dunavant's drugstores to pick up aspirin, Klobuchar Shoes for a new pair of heels or Oxfords, or Alexander's Hardware for the elusive screws needed to finish a home improvement project.[26]

Fulton's five churches—Methodist, Christian, Presbyterian, Catholic, and Baptist—provided many activities for their parishioners and were full every Sunday morning. For more secular amusement, Fultonians also frequented the bowling alley, where they could get a game for a dime, before heading over to Central Dairy for an ice cream sundae or milkshake. The Estes Café, which offered a sprawling lunchtime buffet, was popular with students for its low prices and the mountains of food they could pile on plastic plates. If still hungry, they went outside to the popcorn stand owned by elderly, white-haired Bob Mutson. A red wagon with large wooden spoke wheels, it looked more like an old prairie mail carriage than a makeshift store. Though confined to a wheelchair, Mutson was a cheerful soul who joked around with the kids before they headed into the Fulton Theater. Here they paid twenty-five cents each to watch a double-feature matinee, with Alfred Hitchcock's *Spellbound* (if the ticket counter clerk would let them see it), the Bing Crosby drama *The Bells of St. Mary's,* and Frank Sinatra as a singing sailor in *Anchors Aweigh* proving popular draws in 1945.[27]

Even before it received news of Churchill's visit, Fulton in late 1945 was, like most of the United States, in a buoyant mood. More than 11 million servicemen were home, or soon to arrive, and the country's newly honed industrial prowess promised to increase the proliferation and lower the cost of consumer goods when peacetime production started up again. With the advent of demobilization, employment and housing were in short supply in America's primary cities and union walkouts were growing in size and frequency—but in Fulton, jobs were plentiful and an optimistic atmosphere prevailed.[28] The mass return of Fulton's service personnel certainly gave the town's businesses a shot in the arm: Bo Jameson scribbled more than a hundred orders for new Ford, Mercury, and Lincoln models on his dealership blackboard. As historian Gary Donaldson wrote: "The Great Depression seemed little more than a bad dream. The war was over. The future was bright."[29]

With Churchill and Truman expected in a matter of months, Callaway County had even greater reason for optimism. Whether in the form of high-spirited teenage chatter outside the bright yellow lockers at Fulton High School or the more sedate discussions of regulars at the Old Spot Café, exuding its familiar aroma of eggs, bacon, and coffee, Fultonians ruminated on everything from the topic of Churchill's lecture to what they would say if they got the chance to meet him. Local tobacconists looked to cash in by rebranding their top-shelf stogies as "Churchill Cigars," though not every customer bought into the fad. In a letter to the *St. Joseph News-Press,* one Fulton resident expressed his hope that Churchill could be persuaded to switch

to a "Missouri meerschaum," a pipe made from a Black Sea min-
eral that changes color from yellow to orange, and finally to red,
as the smoker puffs away.[30]

On the Westminster College campus, aside from the busyness
of Bullet McCluer, Huber, and Humphreys, the myriad preparations of the facility services team, and the bags of ticket
requests flooding into the mail room each day, it was business
as usual.

The college experience at Westminster was far more intimate
than at larger private or state schools, owing to its small class
sizes, the close proximity of student and faculty housing to the
campus, and the wide range of activities that fostered campus camaraderie. McCluer frequently invited his colleagues to his campus home for dinner, the staff gathered frequently, and faculty
wives provided cookies and other treats for student-parent
events. The undergraduates reciprocated by hosting their professors at the fraternity houses, which, as at most colleges, were social hubs at Westminster—despite the school's prohibition of
alcohol on its grounds. In addition to the spring and Christmas
formals, both held simultaneously in the four fraternity houses
and open to anyone connected with the school, the frat brothers
regularly held "Vic" dances, where they played Frank Sinatra,
Nat King Cole, and Frankie Carle records for hours on Victor
Victrola turntable cabinets that reverberated the crooning off the
hardwood floors and plaster walls of the frat houses. If the boys
wanted female company, they did not have far to go, with the all-
girls William Woods College just a mile away.[31]

Westminster also had a reputation for excellence in instruc-
tion, with several professors who were well known in literary and
political circles. One such individual was longtime English professor Jeremiah Bascom Reeves. The congenial, forgetful fellow
known to students as "Jerry"—who had joined the faculty in 1913

and coached Bullet during his debating days—had published a well-received literary criticism volume in 1924 entitled *The Hymn as Literature.*

Beyond its academic reputation, Westminster was home to some extraordinary characters. The teaching prowess of one of Reeves's colleagues, Daniel Shaw Gage, was matched only by his renowned eccentricity. Gage was an academic stickler, giving students a daily quiz on Bible history and noting their grades carefully in his reporter's notebook.[32] A graduate of the Westminster class of 1889, he began his professorial duties there the following year, agreeing to teach Greek for just one year until administrators found a replacement for his predecessor, who had resigned due to ill health. Still in Fulton more than a half century later, student favorite "Danny" had enthusiastically added philosophy to his teaching repertoire of classical language and biblical studies.[33]

Gage's classroom manner typically matched his genteel Southern style, but he was fiercely passionate about his vocation and demanded that students apply themselves. After just a couple of class sessions, even naive freshmen quickly learned never to be late for Gage's lectures. He closed his classroom door at the exact start time, and if a latecomer knocked or asked to enter, Gage refused, drawling, "The train has already left the station."[34]

During World War II, the U.S. Navy had sent instructors as well as cadets to Westminster College for the V-12 training program. Chief Petty Officer Ben Vitale made the mistake of repeatedly running his class past the bell, preventing some students from making it to Gage's beloved philosophy class on time. Ignoring the fact that he was outmatched by Vitale's youth, height, and bulk, the small-statured veteran professor berated the military man in front of pupils and colleagues.[35] To Gage, nothing was more important than his students' education, and he would be darned if he was going to let a new guy on campus, even a military officer, impede his teaching.

With international press coverage focusing the world's attention on Fulton, McCluer could have moved Churchill's lecture to a large auditorium in St. Louis or Kansas City to draw a bigger crowd than could be hosted in the humble Westminster College gymnasium. But Bullet realized that this local event would be the culmination of his work to bolster the school's standing, a chance to thank Fultonians for years of strong support, and a way to ensure that the John Findley Green Lecture Series would take its place among the nation's premier speaking engagements.

And so he kept with the original plan, despite the logistical challenges it was presenting. Chief among these was managing the clamor for seats. Even if spectators could be jammed together with no regard for the luxuries of personal space, no more than 2,800 could be hosted safely in a facility designed to hold just 500. With this concern in mind, and with requests already far outnumbering tickets, McCluer informed A. P. Green on December 21 that he should favor those with a strong Westminster connection when allocating his ticket block: "My thought is that you may receive a great many applications from persons who have no special interest in the college and persons to whom we have no special obligation to reserve seats. . . . [W]e are eager to have people admitted who have a genuine interest in the college. We shall, therefore, issue notransferrable [sic] tickets for reserved seats."[36]

Green certainly had the best financial interests of the college in mind when he invited the likes of Mr. D. D. Davis, a wealthy brick company owner from Ohio and potential donor to Westminster College, to hear Churchill speak. Green told McCluer that Davis was "easily worth 10 million dollars. . . . I have talked to him about . . . Westminster."[37]

This is not to say that McCluer was calculating or mercenary in his ticket allotment—rich current and prospective donors comprised only a slight portion of the tickets issued. Before offering a place in the gym to anyone else, McCluer reached out to Westminster's military alumni, stating, "We are eager to have Westminster men from the armed forces present on this occasion. I hope you will write me that you will be here in your uniform and that you would like a reserved seat." That same day, he also composed a letter to the rest of Westminster's former students, informing them that if they acted quickly they could obtain two tickets to this "program of worldwide interest."[38] He sent formal invitations to the Westminster trustees on February 4, requesting their presence at lunch with Churchill, Truman, and Governor Donnelly at noon on March 5. As the McCluers' campus residence was a modest dwelling, the wives would eat in Reunion Hall and then join their husbands for a reception after the meal.[39] Unsurprisingly, every invitee soon accepted.

In addition, McCluer set aside seating for all Westminster students, trustees, faculty members, staff, and their spouses, as well as for state government officials and ministers of the local churches. So that a wider audience could see Churchill and Truman up close, he planned a pre-speech procession across the campus for the afternoon of March 5.

One of the many applicants for nonreserved tickets was seventeen-year-old Tennessee high school junior John David Marshall. In addition to writing to McCluer, this industrious lad, who was enamored with Churchill's wartime exploits, petitioned the White House as well as Democratic Tennessee senator Kenneth McKellar. His diligence was duly rewarded—an ecstatic Marshall received a coveted ticket.[40]

While planning for the Churchill visit, McCluer readied Westminster College for the upcoming spring semester and worked alongside four fellow Missourians on a commission studying child welfare in the state. They presented the report and their recommendations for improved child services to Governor Phil Donnelly in the last week of December.[41]

To effectively juggle his state political duties, family responsi-bilities, college business, and the C-T Day preparations, McCluer honed his organizational skills. He kept his desk clear, except for a writing pad, a pair of pens crossed in their stand like dueling sabers, and the important letters and telegrams delivered from the mailroom each afternoon. Even the dozens of books on the long cherry wood shelf behind his chair were arranged in neat, horizontal rows. Dorothy Canada, his secretary, maintained a tight calendar for her boss, enabling McCluer to devote just the right amount of his time to maintaining each aspect of a daily life that could easily have become fragmented and overwhelming without careful monitoring. It also helped that Joe Humphreys's office was just next door in the Administration Building, enabling the two to collaborate in person any time they saw the need.

Ida Belle also provided balance in Bullet's world. Though they seemed at first glance so different in appearance (she was six inches taller and slender next to his stocky frame) and manner (he outgoing, she reserved), the McCluers had an effortless, sym-biotic relationship.[42] With his days ever more crowded, Bullet leaned on his wife of twenty-four years to provide emotional respite as the visit of Churchill and Truman drew closer.

Bullet had come to the end of 1945 in a blur. Even for him, a man who had brought renowned speakers to Westminster and was well known by the president of the United States, the coup of landing Churchill was far beyond his most ambitious hopes. The following year promised the realization of this dream, but chal-lenges also loomed as McCluer readied his small town for the biggest day in its history.

CHAPTER 4

FINDING A KETTLE DRUM: THE SPEECH TAKES SHAPE

We should fortify in every way our special and friendly relations with the United States, aiming always at a fruitful association for the purpose of common protection and world peace.

—Winston Churchill to the House of Commons
(November 7, 1945)

A S MCCLUER WAS BUSYING HIMSELF with preparations for Churchill's visit, his future guest was trying to maintain control of the battered Conservative Party. The youthful group Churchill led bore little resemblance to the group of political veterans he had inherited from Baldwin and Chamberlain, with holdovers from the prewar contingent comprising fewer than a third of its meager 189 MPs in 1945.[1]

Some long-standing members of Parliament had retired; many others were booted from their seats by a dissatisfied public. Though they respected Churchill's wartime leadership, the new blood in the party had little tolerance for his spotty attendance in the Commons and deferral of many leadership duties to his

deputy, Anthony Eden.[2] Churchill had delivered a commanding
speech on the Communist threat in August but it was an exception, and he had yet to recapture the dynamism of the war
years.

Frequent heavy colds, such as the one that laid him low from
October 14 to 21, made him even more apathetic.[3] Still, on the
latter date he was well enough to visit Bancroft School in his constituency to receive the Freedom of the City—a ceremonial
British award often given to prominent citizens.

Despite his continuing malaise, Churchill did show glimpses
of his previous verve—as in late October, when he delivered a
powerful speech at his old school Harrow, which had long been
associated with shaping the country's elite. Founded in 1572,
the boarding institution was graced by imposing red-brick
buildings, manicured lawns, and thickets of evergreen trees that
made it look more like a country estate than a school in northwest London. Churchill had spent four years there as a full-time
boarder, becoming the Public Schools Fencing Champion, winning a poetry recital contest after memorizing more than a thousand lines, and developing into a crack shot in the School Rifle
Corps. Despite these highs, he was far from an accomplished
student and was often lonely, as his parents rarely visited despite
living in the capital.

Seeing the boys going in and out of his old haunts in their
distinctive straw boater hats likely brought back bittersweet
memories for the ex-Harrovian. Once in the Old Speech Room,
with light streaming through the stained-glass windows and reflecting off the hardwood wall panels, the school's most celebrated alumnus addressed the pupils, who were seated in quiet
awe in neat rows of reading desks. Churchill revealed that his
own school teachers had dissuaded his ambitions to play the
kettle drum and conduct a band. He then drove home his inspiring message:

[E]ventually, after a great deal of perseverance, I rose to be the conductor of quite a considerable band. It was a very large band and it played with strange and formidable instruments, and the roar and thunder of the music resounded throughout the world. We played all sorts of tunes, and we finished up the concert with "Rule Britannia" and "God Save the King."

Even with his command performance of World War II behind him, Churchill was not ready to pack up his "music." He told the boys and their masters that he was "looking for a new orchestra, and thought perhaps I might find one here." But if he could not "keep the position of conductor I at least hope to find a kettle drum."[4]

Churchill had revealed the pitch and tone of his planned performance when he had met with Canadian Prime Minister Mackenzie King at the Churchills' newly purchased London townhouse on a rainy October 26, five days before the Harrow appearance. The latter, a devoutly Christian bachelor who had offered unwavering support to Churchill in World War II despite the conscription debacle that split his nation, was in his third term and twentieth year as Canada's premier.[5] King, who stood two inches shorter than Churchill and was the same age, took small, purposeful steps down the narrow sidewalk toward Churchill's three-story red-brick residence, past the pointed wrought-iron fence and up to the black double doors of 28 Hyde Park Gate. Randolph and Mary Churchill met him, and Winston came down the hall and onto the steps to greet his friend. The butler took his umbrella, coat, and hat and ushered him into the drawing room to see Clementine. "My dear Mr. King. How glad we are to have you with us again," she said with a warm smile.

Churchill showed him the white hardwood bookcase in the room he was converting into a library, though, to his chagrin, his books were not yet on the shelves. He then retrieved a crystal decanter and two glasses, and poured sherry for each of them. After Randall and Mary left, King, Winston, and Clementine went downstairs to a small dining room that looked out onto the modest garden, with vines creeping up its brick walls and a crystal globe on a small statue. They dined on caviar and snipe, a long-billed wading bird that Clementine had picked out at a market earlier that day. When the butler offered the threesome vodka sent as a gift from Moscow, Clementine asked him to throw it out and bring brandy instead. King would soon discover the symbolism of this.

The two men first talked about the lamentable influence of far-left politics on certain members of the Labour Party, most notably Stafford Cripps, who had served as Churchill's ambassador to Moscow and was now Attlee's president of the Board of Trade, a powerful economic position. In addition, Churchill had told King of Labour's intention to pursue wealth redistribution by "destroying the rich to equalize the incomes of all," which would disincentivize hard work. They wished to "govern the actions of men," Churchill feared. The election loss had surprised Churchill and "come as quite a blow," he told King. Though he planned to attack the Attlee government for its failures, particularly the hash he thought they were making with demobilization, Churchill admitted that he had given up hope of ever returning to 10 Downing Street.

Churchill then swiftly redirected the conversation to the Russian conundrum.[6] As King wrote in his diary:

He said that Russia was grabbing one country after another. . . . [H]e said that all these different countries, naming a lot of the Balkans, including Berlin, would be under their control. He thought they should have been stood up to more than they were. He spoke about the Russian regime as being very difficult but said there was nothing to be gained by not letting them know we were not afraid of them. . . . He said that they would be as pleasant with you as they could be, although prepared to destroy you. That sentiment meant nothing to them—morals meant nothing. . . . [Y]ou must remember that with the Communists, Communism is a religion. . . . He felt that the Communist movement was spreading everywhere.[7]

King and Churchill agreed that only a strong alliance of the English-speaking peoples would be a successful tonic to what Churchill had previously called the "disease" of Communism. King recalled:

I said to him that I did not think the British Commonwealth of Nations could compete with the Russian situation itself, nor did I think the U.S. could. That I believed that it would require the two and they must be kept together. He said to me, "That is the thing you must work for above everything else . . . if you can pull off a continued alliance between the U.S. and Britain . . . if you can get them to preserve the Joint Chiefs of Staff arrangement . . . you will be doing the greatest service that can be done the world."[8]

Churchill would air these views, he confided in King, during his trip to the United States early in the new year. In addition to affording him a speaking opportunity on "the conditions of the world," the nine-week stay would "give him a chance to talk with Truman and he might be helpful to British and American relations in that way." This in-depth conversation shows that Churchill's views of the Soviet challenge were clearly defined at this time, that he had correctly predicted the Communist threat to Berlin, and that his intentions for the Fulton engagement were concrete. In his diary, King also noted that Churchill made a distinction between the Russian people and their Kremlin masters' "militarist regime."[9] Churchill often talked publicly and privately about the great sacrifice of the Soviet populace, and rued their great losses in World War II. He was also aware, however, of the grievous toll of

Stalin's forced collectivization-induced famine, purges, and labor camp interments, which, though Churchill may not have known the numbers, took the lives of at least 5 million others. Churchill also believed the time was nigh to expose Communism's true malevolence to the world.[10]

Less than twenty-four hours after King's visit to Churchill, twenty-nine nations, including Russia, Britain, and the United States, ratified the United Nations pact, leading to the official inception of the United Nations Organization (UNO). However, flying in the face of international cooperation, the Soviets prevented Chinese Nationalist forces from landing at two ports, leading to new accusations that Moscow was supporting the Chinese Communist Party in their continued war against Chiang Kai-Shek's government. Meanwhile, famed American columnist Walter Lippmann reported that despite evidence of some changes in Politburo policy, rape, pillaging, and looting were still believed to be common practices among the Red Army troops who had supposedly "liberated" Eastern and Central Europe from Hitler's Wehrmacht.[11]

Churchill's dark appraisal of the Communist specter was compounded by the events of November 1945. On September 17, 1941, the Allies had invaded Iran, which bordered Azerbaijan, to prevent it from falling into German hands. Britain and Russia agreed to withdraw their forces but, as of late 1945, the Red Army and a bevy of heavy-handed administrators remained, setting up a Soviet-Iranian oil company as a foil to the Anglo-Persian Oil Company and placing Communist leaders at the head of the Tudeh Party. With Russian oil reserves increasingly taxed by Stalin's ongoing military buildup and Britain's need to protect its trade interests, the region had become a testing ground for increasing tension in Anglo-Russo relations.[12]

This animosity came to a head in the first week of November 1945, when the unjustly named Democratic Party overthrew the rulers of Azerbaijan, established a Communist regime, and declared sovereignty in Tabriz, the nation's capital. In exchange for a half-hearted "commitment" to withdraw the Red Army from central Iran, Stalin duped the beleaguered Iranian government into giving him oil dividends and formal recognition of the now Soviet-controlled Azerbaijan as a legitimate independent state.

Puppets of Stalin were also exerting power through dubious means in Eastern Europe. In the November 1945 election in Hungary, the Smallholders Party garnered 57 percent of the vote. As they did not have enough seats for majority rule, the Smallholders formed a coalition administration with the Hungarian Workers' Party, which was Communist and had earned just 17 percent at the ballet box. Under pressure from the Red Army, which had taken over Budapest the previous February, Smallholder Party leader Ferenc Nagy ceded control of the Interior Ministry (the most important government branch) to Communist chieftain Matyas Rakos. This gave Moscow domain over all internal affairs and, just as importantly, left the Smallholders impotent.[13] A country that had lost a million lives in the war and almost half its national wealth had little chance of resisting Soviet pressure to move leftward. In his autobiography, leading Communist Party member Zoltan Vas explained his party's ascendancy in 1945 and 1946: "In Hungary, political as well as economic power is completely in the hands of Moscow."[14]

The picture was equally grim in Poland. The sixteen leaders of the Polish Underground State, who had led the resistance against Nazi occupation, were lured to Moscow in June 1945 by the promise of "talks" with the Politburo, but were soon tried as traitors and imprisoned.[15] Throughout 1945, the Polish Communists continued to send political opponents to prisons at Skobow, Lubartow, and Rembertow, as well as to former German concentration camps. London received intelligence reports indicating that as many as 25,000 Polish prisoners were being held in the Russian gulag.[16]

Churchill eyed these developments warily. His experience with Stalin's broken promises had been bitter, and the wounds he suffered at the wartime summits still smarted. While satisfied with British Foreign Minister Bevin's wily negotiating attempts to preserve British influence in the Middle East, he feared that the Azerbaijan situation would merely be the beginning of a Russian power grab in the region. Such an eventuality, he knew, would put Britain in an unacceptable position of weakness, economically more so than militarily. The tightening Communist grip on Eastern and Central Europe also unnerved him.

The Commons debate on November 7 presented a perfect opportunity for Churchill to share these concerns with his countrymen, though, ironically, his son Randolph was in Moscow reporting on the twenty-eighth anniversary of the October revolution that had created the Soviet government. Parliament had been in session since early August, but this day saw the first lengthy discourse about the role of Russia in the postwar world. With Russian Foreign Secretary Molotov claiming a day earlier that Russia would soon obtain nuclear warheads and match other advances in Allied weapons technology, Prime Minister Attlee knew it was now high time to discuss British policy toward the aggressive posturing of its former ally.[17]

After several perfunctory Labour speeches, the Speaker of the House motioned the Leader of the Opposition to speak. Churchill rose from his position on the front bench of the Opposition side of the aisle, slowly positioned his black reading glasses, and removed several small note cards from his coat pocket. He paused for dramatic effect (a stage direction he often wrote in the margins of his notes) and launched into a blistering attack on the Labour Party's domestic policies, which he claimed were holding back British recovery from the war effort. Churchill then switched his attention to Soviet ambitions. In keeping with his wartime efforts to keep the Big Three united, he praised Stalin as a "great man" and asserted that his former Big Three counterpart would never pursue an anti-British policy for its own sake.[18]

However, he quickly changed tack, petitioning Prime Minister Attlee (and, indirectly, Truman, who no doubt received a report) to rebuff any Russian requests for insight into America's nuclear program. "I am sure that were the circumstances reversed and we or the Americans asked for similar access to Russian arsenals, it would not be granted," Churchill stated.[19] He had approved the use of America's nuclear arsenal on Nagasaki and Hiroshima just months earlier, but now Churchill, peering at his fellow MPs with utmost gravity, proposed that atom bombs be used as a deterrent to prevent a third worldwide conflict, rather than for aggressive purposes. Keeping these "dire, superhuman weapons" within the Anglo-American alliance would, Churchill asserted, "help the United States and our Allies build up a structure of world security."[20] He then pledged unequivocal support of Truman and his "12 Points" on foreign policy, which had been announced the previous month.

With the fight against Nazi tyranny so recently concluded, few of the assembled MPs could have argued persuasively against their wartime leader's statement: "I cannot bring myself to visualize another World War." As he had frequently done in his inspiring oratory of the previous five years, Churchill then used the binary opposition of darkness and light to contrast potential war with Russia with a lasting peace.

"The valley is indeed dark and the dangers most menacing," he said, using the familiar biblical image of the Valley of the Shadow of Death from Psalm 23. "Yet we know that not very far away are broad uplands of an assured peace. Can we reach them? We *must* reach them. It is our sole duty."

Without giving his ministerial colleagues on either side of the aisle time to ask the rhetorical question "How?" Churchill moved quickly to answer it with several distinct points of his own. The first concerned the Atlantic partnership: "[W]e should fortify in every way our special and friendly relations with the United States, aiming always at a fruitful association for the purpose of common protection and world peace." Instead of being a confrontational alliance, he believed, it should "lead the victorious powers ever more closely together on equal terms." Next, he advised Attlee's government to support the United States in helping to "guard this weapon [nuclear bomb] as a sacred trust for the maintenance of peace." The strong ties between his mother's homeland and Britain should be used to "strengthen and promote" the fledgling United Nations Organization for the good of all countries, Churchill then affirmed. Finally, he told the Commons that Britain should build up a nuclear armory as the basis for strong diplomacy with potential adversaries. If Attlee and his Cabinet could put these principles into action, Churchill believed, they could help prevent the devastating consequences of another "aggressive war."[21]

At least one person in the House was unimpressed by Churchill's rhetoric. The Communist William Gallacher, predictably, recoiled at the former prime minister's remarks, stating that Churchill wanted "a declaration of war against the progressive forces in Europe and the rest of the world." His condemnation met with a clamor of disagreement from both sides of the House, and loud shouts of "No!" rang out as he took his seat.[22]

Churchill found a more willing listener in Ernest Bevin, a man who wielded far more influence than Gallacher. Though Bevin downplayed the role of the atomic bomb in the postwar world, he echoed Churchill's support of Truman's foreign policy pronouncement and bristled at Molotov's attack the previous day on the "Western bloc." In a strong riposte, Bevin asked rhetorically, "What am I doing wrong?" He proceeded to provide the retort: "I am doing nothing to injure anybody and I am not prepared to accept that position from any country in the world." Britain should be allowed to have "good neighbors as any other country," he contended. Bevin then emphatically completed his argument: "You may think I am a little energetic about this, but I am a little resentful and I think the House will agree I am entitled to be." Certainly Churchill concurred, as he did with Bevin's comment that Russia's aggressive foreign policy was "coming right across the throat of the British Commonwealth."[23] All in all, with the minor exception of Gallacher, the House had presented a united position to Molotov and to Moscow—specifically, that Britain would continue to stand with America, support Truman, and vocalize its objections to Soviet misdeeds and misstatements. The day had also been a resounding success for Churchill, and his best parliamentary performance since VE Day.

Churchill had little time to celebrate his Commons resurgence and, instead, prepared more speeches on foreign affairs for his November 15 trip to Belgium. People began milling about in the cobbled streets of Brussels at dawn, and by the time Churchill's motorcade came into the city center in late morning there were tens of thousands on hand, clamoring to catch a glimpse of the wartime prime minister and his daughter Mary. Churchill's first stop was at the Palais des Académies, where he was made an Associate. At that point, he spoke briefly of British soldiers fighting alongside their Belgian counterparts to liberate Belgium from Nazi occupation: "The fight has been long, hard, and victorious. The night is passed and there is light again. May every man and woman work always to consolidate the freedom that we gained." From there, it was on to a ceremony in which Churchill received honorary Belgian citizenship, the first time the award was bestowed on a Briton. En route, a girl burst through the police ranks guarding Churchill's open-top car and pushed a bouquet of flowers into his hands, as the crowd chanted as one: "Churchill, Churchill, Churchill!" Soon afterward, Belgian Prime Minister Achille van Acker anointed his guest as nothing less than "the savior of civilization." Churchill then delighted the throng by giving a brief, impromptu speech in an error-filled, yet spirited flourish of French, which he ended by bellowing "Vive la Bruxelles!" to uproarious applause.[24]

Following the jubilant event, during which Churchill was also given diamonds and a tapestry on behalf of the Belgian people, he paid his respects at the tomb of Belgium's Unknown Warrior. From there, it was on to Brussels University, where students received him with Beethoven's Fifth Symphony, the opening notes of which closely resemble the Morse code for "V," in recognition of his famous hand gesture.[25] Churchill responded in kind by showing them the two-fingered victory salute. After receiving the honorary degree of the Faculty of Law, he told the student body that the school's mission to promote "the free examination of thought and ideas" would again flourish now that the Nazism which had tried to suppress it was no more. He spent much of the speech celebrating this victory, but, in a subtle acknowledgment of the looming Communism specter, also cautioned his listeners to be wary of forthcoming threats to their liberty: "Yet, the champions of freedom can never afford to sleep. Intolerance and persecution are no sooner overcome than they return in new shapes. . . . Always be on your guard against tyranny, whatever shape it may assume. Remember the cause of Freedom for which heroes died."

Just a couple of hours later Churchill was again called on to speak—this time, by a Louvain University delegation that conferred his second honorary degree of the day. The ceremony took place at the British Embassy instead of at the campus, owing to the great material damage the university had suffered during the Nazi occupation.

The following day, Churchill strode beneath the eight towering Grecian pillars at the Palace of the Nation in Brussels and into a joint meeting of the Senate and Chamber. Once situated in the hemicycle, daubed green in imitation of the House of

Commons with which he was so familiar, he again praised Belgian determination in the face of Nazi oppression, declaring that "[t]he restoration and rebuilding of Europe, both physical and moral, is animated and guided by the kindred themes of Liberty and Democracy." He described the tenets of true democracy in detail and concluded with a simple question: "Do the Government own the people, or do the people own the Government?"[26]

Churchill next remarked that, in his opinion, "the affairs of Great Britain and the British Commonwealth and Empire are becoming ever more closely interwoven with those of the United States, and that an underlying unity of thought and conviction increasingly pervades the English-speaking world."

He was also quick to point out that the bond between Britain and the United States did not in any way hamper the possibility of continuing friendly relations with Russia. In fact, London and Moscow shared the Twenty Years Treaty, which he stated was "cherished by us as one of the sure anchors of world peace."

In his most pragmatic musing of the day, Churchill proposed a new organization within the framework of the United Nations: a "United States of Europe, which will unify the Continent in a manner never known since the fall of the Roman Empire, and within which all its peoples may dwell together in prosperity, in justice and in peace."[27]

This was the first time Churchill had used this phrase in a speech, but he had pondered such a principle for more than fifteen years. In a *Saturday Evening Post* article published on February 15, 1930, he stated that Britain supported "a richer, freer, more contented European communality."[28] However, he also was clearly against a federation that would involve any diminishing of British sovereignty, writing: "But we have our dream and our own task. We are with Europe, not of it. We are linked but not compromised. We are interested and associated but not absorbed." Churchill maintained a similar stance throughout World War II, with his beliefs about European union encapsulated in a 1941 conversation with his assistant, Jock Colville. Churchill told the young man that Britain must be the forerunner of a United States of Europe, but that "while Britain might be the builder and Britain might live in the house, she would always preserve her liberty of choice and would be the natural, undisputed link with the Americas and the Commonwealth."

Churchill's central position on this matter—namely, closer ties between European nations without Britain losing its right to chart an individual course—had changed little by the time he took the podium at Brussels fifteen years later. However, his motive in calling for the creation of a new pan-Continental organization in late 1945 *was* different. He now saw a defeated Germany and a weakened France as best able to resist the march of Communism if they were part of a multinational body, and believed that peaceful settlement with Stalin depended on a reinvigorated and rebuilt Western Europe.[29]

Such early-winter prognostications on foreign policy emboldened Churchill to work ever more diligently behind the scenes to impress his concerns about Communism upon Bevin and Attlee. To keep the Soviet Union in check, Churchill needed to keep the Labour Party on side when it came to foreign policy. He was reminded of this necessity in mid-November, when the British ambassador to Russia, Frank Roberts, sent alarming reports about the Soviet press relentlessly attacking British actions abroad, particularly in Turkey, India, and Greece.[30]

Iran was another continued source of strained relations between Britain and Russia. The Red Army refused to allow Iranian government troops into its occupation zone in the north of the country, and, as a result, Azerbaijani insurgents continued their violent southward advance and conflict with nationalist forces in three northwest provinces.[31]

There was also the growth of Communist Party membership across Europe to reckon with—1.7 million members in Italy, over a million in Czechoslovakia, and several hundred thousand in Hungary and France.[32] These numbers fueled British fears that Communism would spread beyond the Kremlin-dominated Eastern and Central European nations. War-ravaged, unstable Germany—particularly the Soviet occupation zone—was also a worry. Looking to find its way within the postwar power vacuum, the nation was on the brink of plunging into the depths of Communism, Churchill feared.

To bring the Foreign Office and State Department closer together, Bevin was strongly considering accepting the American proposal to create joint Anglo-American bases in the Pacific. He wanted Churchill's input on this, as the ex–prime minister had long been in favor of ongoing military collaboration with the United States. In response to Bevin's request for advice, Churchill dictated a letter on November 13, suggesting that the Labour government maintain close ties with Washington and encouraging him to go ahead with the joint bases proposal. Churchill urged Bevin to "have our affairs so interwoven with those of the United States in external and strategic matters that an idea of war between the two countries is utterly impossible." He hoped that a stance of unity would help foster "friendly and trustful relations with Soviet Russia." His suggestions for cooperation with Truman's administration included "military and scientific information . . . weapons . . . inter-related plans for the war mobilization of civil industry and finally, interchange of officers."[33]

Such communications did not mean that Churchill and the Labour Party were unified on all matters, however. On November 27, Churchill, at the urging of Tory backbenchers, proposed a motion of censure on the Attlee government.[34] By failing to privatize industries that were nationalized during the war, Churchill claimed that Labour showed "a desire to have every economic detail of the social life of our country held in a wartime grip indefinitely, and obviously for purposes far beyond those of the transition from war to peace." He also charged the government of aggressive partisanship "for faction's sake" and of failing to confront the challenges of a "grave" economic crisis. In summary, Churchill stated, "I believe profoundly that the attempt to turn Great Britain into a Socialist State will, as it develops, produce widespread political strife, misery, and ruin at home."[35]

Churchill was no stranger to haranguing the government, even when it was his own party that was at the helm. In the late 1930s, he had assailed Conservative Prime Minister Neville Chamberlain for his appeasement of Hitler and lack of military preparedness. Though now in his seventies, Churchill still relished the verbal jousting of the Commons as much as he had then or upon entering Parliament in his twenties, and the sweeping reforms proposed by his opponents provoked in him as strong a reaction as did Stalin's continued advance across Europe. On this occasion, however, his censure motion—although it temporarily silenced the calls for him to resign as Tory leader—failed to gain the required traction among his fellow MPs, who voted it down 381 to 197.[36]

On November 29, Churchill wrote a letter to Truman that echoed the sentiments he had expressed to Bevin two weeks earlier. He also made plain his desire for the two of them to be in accord about Churchill's message in Missouri: "Naturally I would let you know beforehand the line I propose to take in my address on World affairs, so that nothing should be said by me on this occasion that would cause you embarrassment. I do not however think that this is likely to happen, as we are so much agreed in our general outlook."[37]

Churchill then emphasized the great responsibility he felt lay with Truman and his countrymen:

The United States has reached a pinnacle of glory and power not exceeded by any nation in the whole history of the world, and with that come not only opportunities literally for saving misguided humanity but also terrible responsibilities if those opportunities cannot be seized. Often . . . I think of you and your problems as I did of those of our dear friend F.D.R. I am most thankful you are there to fill his place.

He also revealed to the president that he had labored with "many colds and sore throats already this winter" and that Lord Moran was looking forward to the benefits he would accrue from the warm air in Miami—which would be a far cry from the damp cold of the British late winter.[38]

The day after writing to the president, Churchill celebrated his seventy-first birthday. Later that week he received the perfect birthday gift: his friend Lord William Camrose had formulated "a princely plan for making Chartwell a national possession."[39] Churchill's beloved country home in the tranquil Kent countryside, where he took up residence in 1924, had become a source of solace from the bustle of London and a gathering place for his wide and eclectic social circle.[40] Although Clementine at first loathed the draftiness of the vast Victorian red-brick structure, her husband's love of the property was contagious and she soon came around. Churchill once remarked to one of his secretaries, Grace Hamblin, that "[a] day away from Chartwell is a day wasted."[41] In addition to entertaining and spending late nights pacing his study, Churchill spent a great deal of time in the grounds, where there was a heated swimming pool, an orchard of fruit trees, and a terrace for entertaining the many visitors. A hands-on owner, he laid the wall around the south garden, landscaped the ponds that were home to his beloved black swans and goldfish, manicured a grass tennis court for Clementine, and built a playhouse.[42]

His most ambitious project was the three-bedroom Orchard Cottage, which he had spent several years constructing and had finished by nailing down tiles on the roof just before the outbreak of World War II. Chartwell also provided the natural beauty that inspired Churchill to paint, and he could often be found among the chestnut, beech, and oak trees, or on the lawn with a paint-splattered smock staring intently at his easel.[43] Hamblin described the scene when her boss left his labors for the distractions of his garden with childlike exuberance: "All the papers would go flying . . . the dog would be pushed aside, the secretary pushed aside, everything pushed aside, ready to leap out. And he'd say, 'Ah, Chartwell.'"[44] So it was with great relief that he learned of Camrose's scheme to buy Chartwell with a consortium of other Churchill associates and then sell it to the National Trust for permanent safekeeping.

On December 10, another Churchill secretary, Kathleen Hill, wrote to the head of Scotland Yard's Special Branch to inquire about another detail of the U.S. trip. She requested that "any representative of Scotland Yard who goes with Mr. Churchill will have to be in close relations with the United States police, who will take special pains to protect Mr. Churchill from any disturbance of his rest and leisure at Miami, and otherwise safeguard his movements. He considers therefore that you would probably wish to send with him at least one officer capable of establishing good relations with the American security personnel." She went on to convey Churchill's personal liking for Sergeants Davies and Stratton, though Canning would instead dispatch an Inspector Williams to take care of Britain's preeminent "private citizen" on his transatlantic voyage.[45]

As Christmas approached, Churchill received a card from King George VI featuring a black-and-white photograph of Churchill standing with the Royal Family on the Buckingham Palace balcony on VE Day. The next evening, the Churchills enthusiastically watched their friend, civil servant John Carr, perform a puppet show at a Christmas party held at 28 Hyde Park Gate. They hosted another dinner party on Christmas Eve and, on December 26 (Boxing Day in England), watched Shakespeare's *Henry IV, Part II* at the theater. Then it was on to Chartwell to see out the last days of the year.[46]

Despite the crushing disappointment of losing the General Election in 1945 and the physical and mental toll of his wartime leadership, Churchill came to the end of 1945 firmly focused on addressing the challenge of Soviet Communism and ready for his three-month sojourn in America. The prospect of developing his burgeoning friendship with Truman, of seeing old friends Frank W. Clarke and Bernard Baruch, and of having weeks to paint and write in the tropical Miami climate beckoned invitingly. With meetings set over a proposed new U.S. loan to Britain, a trip to Cuba planned, and the Fulton address waiting, he would need all of his persuasiveness, experience, and endurance.

CHAPTER 5

PREPARATION IN EARNEST:
A BANNER DAY IN FULTON HISTORY

Bullet McCluer, Joe B. Humphreys, and Neal S. Wood review the route map for "Churchill-Truman Day." CREDIT: NATIONAL CHURCHILL MUSEUM ARCHIVES, CHURCHILL, TRUMAN, MCCLUER DAY COLLECTION, FOLDER 07, IMAGE 07026

A s Fulton entered 1946, preparations for Churchill's impending visit continued to weigh heavily on Bullet McCluer
and his corps of volunteers. In addition to overseeing the practical considerations—such as providing food, lodging, and parking
for a crowd of thousands—the McCluer family dealt with some
less predictable challenges. "Several Secret Service men came
about two weeks after the announcement to look over the college
and our home," Ida Belle McCluer recalled. "I found that there
would be needed a bedroom and bath for Mr. Churchill and a
bedroom and bath for President Truman. They wanted to know
exactly where they would be at all times."[1] Ida Belle was impressed by the diligence of Truman's protectors, though their
methods were somewhat lightweight compared to the security
measures enacted following the assassination of John F. Kennedy,
after which open presidential motorcades were strongly discouraged. The Secret Service was also acting without the background
checks, satellite surveillance, and other state-of-the-art tools that
make it easier to safeguard the dignitaries of today, instead rely-
ing on intuition and experience to protect Truman and Churchill.

To alleviate stress, Bullet kept up his favorite pursuits: going
for long drives through the tree-lined, lake-dotted southern

Missouri countryside with Ida Belle, tending his ruby roses, pink snapdragons, and prize-winning kaleidoscope of dahlias in the small garden outside the window of his administration building office, and playing tennis and golf. Bullet also continued attending events on the Westminster campus, such as the basketball team's home opener against Drury College on January 7, and went to debates hosted by the school's forensics club—debates in which he had earned his nickname for rapid-fire rhetoric thirty years before.[2]

At the same time as overseeing the spring semester and maintaining his local political commitments, McCluer was mulling over how to maximize the impact of Churchill's arrival in Fulton. For example, Bullet wanted to honor Churchill and Truman with a special ceremony in which Doctor of Laws degrees would be given to them.[3]

On January 15, the American Telephone and Telegraph Company arrived in Fulton to make preparations for telecasting Truman's upcoming national address, which would share news of Churchill's visit with the nation. McCluer recommended to A. P. Green, who was overseeing this project, that technicians run their lines "a short distance only to the Chapel and maybe a church or two. It would give them good publicity as well as us."[4] The work crews battered sidewalks and roads with picks, carving man-made ravines to run their lines through before burying them in concrete and asphalt.

Bullet had hoped to make further use of this burgeoning technology for the big day itself, and received requests from CBS and Paramount for exclusive rights, but he was forced to change this plan. Churchill was intimately familiar with radio broadcasting, having made many speeches via the BBC studios in his long parliamentary career, including dozens during the war years. However, he was very suspicious of and uncomfortable with television. TV was very much in its infancy (fewer than 10,000 American homes had sets and far fewer in austere postwar Britain), with coverage restricted to major metropolitan areas. Viewing hours were limited, as the fledgling networks struggled to add quality programming options.[5] To reach a larger audience, newsreels were still often tagged onto the tail end of movies.

Despite the limitations of television distribution, McCluer's office received numerous overtures from the TV networks as well as from various Hollywood studios. In late January, Mc-Cluer wired an inquiry to Churchill requesting his permission to schedule a television broadcast. Suspecting that the Briton would like to maximize his audience, Bullet pitched the TV coverage on the grounds that it "would permit several thousand people to see as well as hear the program." Though he wished Churchill to approve the use of TV, McCluer deferred to his guest's wishes, stating, "Your decision in this matter will, of course, be final."[6]

A few days later, McCluer sent Churchill a box of the finest Missouri apples and another to Truman. McCluer asked when Churchill would finish the speech, which Bullet wished to study before he distributed it to the press on March 5. He also conveyed the mounting excitement among Missourians about Churchill's visit, which "testifies to recognition of your great leadership, and to the appreciation of the great ideals which Great Britain and the United States hold in common."[7]

On January 30, McCluer received a note from Churchill thanking him for the "welcome and delicious gift" and stating that he would not finish his speech until the end of February. He did, however, give Bullet some insight into his preparations for the Fulton address, in which Truman would play a part: "I hope to see the President . . . and I will discuss with him the arrangements for the time and subject matter of my address. In the circumstances, it will be a political pronouncement of considerable importance."[8]

Five days into February and exactly one month before his big day, McCluer was disappointed to receive a curt Western Union telegram communicating Churchill's decision to forbid live TV coverage of his speech: "I will discuss the matter with the President in the near future. I deprecate complicating the occasion with technical experiments."[9] Not wanting to offend his soon-to-be guest, McCluer turned down the requests of the TV networks for live footage, throwing them the "carrot" of recording the event with newsreel cameras for posterity's sake.

McCluer also sent an event program and supplementary information to Churchill: "The academic procession will move from the building next to the gymnasium into the gymnasium. We hope it will be convenient for you to bring your own academic costume but if it is not we can provide appropriate costume for you. The four major [radio] networks are carrying the program, which will go on the air at three thirty in the afternoon." Before signing off, McCluer indicated that he would add the title of the speech to the program once Churchill had finalized it.[10]

A. C. Huber, Joe Humphreys, and Bullet McCluer devoted a significant part of their time to managing the media coverage of Truman and Churchill's appearance. The prospect of seeing Truman in his home state introducing Churchill for his first major international speech after the election calamity was too much to resist for scribes from local, city, and international publications. McCluer's final list of reporters included 146 names from 57 organizations—and many more would show up unannounced. There was to be no preferential access—industrious reporters from local dailies such as the *Fulton Sun-Gazette* and student writers from Washington University's *Student Life* would be fighting for space in a cramped media staging area alongside luminaries like David Brinkley from CBS, James Bell from *Time*, and Harold Hinton from the *New York Times*. No matter what their name or reputation, each would barely have requisite elbow room to put pencil to paper as they recorded their impressions of the president and ex–prime minister's speeches in the cramped press box.[11]

Indeed, even representatives from the major print, radio, and TV outlets were not shoo-ins for places in the gym. Huber, the Westminster College publicity department manager, replied to an inquiry from William Newton in the BBC's New York office, informing him that "[s]ince our demands for seats from the working press are extremely heavy I cannot promise you definitely that you will have a seat."[12] Newton eventually received two tickets, but this uncertain wait by one of the world's premier networks illustrated the extent of demand for media passes.

Magazines and newspaper editors were anxious to enhance their written coverage of Churchill's visit with lush pictorials. To this end, almost every publication that planned to dispatch writers to Fulton also asked McCluer's permission to send at least one photographer, and many of them far more than that. The Associated Press submitted eight names for approval, and archrival Acme Photo one-upped them with nine.[13]

After enduring six months of fervent lobbying from national and local radio stations, McCluer gave St. Louis's KWK radio station and the Mutual Broadcasting System (with its 279 affiliates) the nod to originate the broadcast of Churchill's speech and supporting material. Kansas City–based KMBC was the first to be awarded rights to cover the buildup to the speech. CBS would be broadcasting nationwide on March 4 at 4:00 P.M. and on the speech day at 8:30 A.M., 10:00 A.M., and noon. Humphreys also received notice that ABC planned to cover the event in its entirety.[14]

With copious radio, TV, magazine, and newspaper coverage ensured, McCluer and Huber looked to a further medium in which to memorialize Churchill's visit for posterity—photography. The print publications would be sending "snappers" with their writers and the White House was sure to bring at least a couple along, too, but Bullet was eager to get plenty of shots for the Westminster College archives. As was his way, he looked for a local option, and he and Huber quickly selected Terry Savage, a well-respected photographer from St. Louis. On Valentine's Day, Savage notified Huber that he would be available, could provide prints and negatives as McCluer had requested, and would be bringing his fifteen-year-old son to assist him. Huber reserved two rooms for the Savages at the Daniel Boone Hotel in Columbia, Missouri (where the college had a thirty-room block for March 3 through March 5), and checked another to-do off his list.[15]

The same day that Savage signed on, McCluer received a note from Churchill's North Bay Road residence in Miami. The Briton told him, "I fear I have not yet come to a final conclusion about the title of the speech I am to deliver, but I think it will probably be 'World Peace.'"[16]

As Churchill was composing this note, Fulton's Accommodation Committee members were agonizing over how to house so many potential guests in their small town with its population of just 8,297 (including the inmates of the local asylum). Evidently, the two small hotels—the fifty-room Palace, with now-outdated features such as claw-foot tubs and a hand-crank cash register, and the slightly larger Seminole, with its faded-glory dining room—wouldn't pass muster for the scale of this event.[17]

Those lucky enough to receive tickets to Churchill's address had to move quickly, as lodgings all the way to St. Louis, nearly a hundred miles away, filled up within weeks of the announcement. Bullet wrote to Westminster College trustee Neal Wood, asking him to "reserve all the hotel rooms you can in Mexico [Missouri] so that we can give them to some of our visitors." Wood secured a hundred beds for the event, but with thousands of visitors expected, many more were needed.[18] Private residents in Fulton came forward to offer hospitality, and neighboring townsfolk made a similar gesture.

Westminster College also opened its doors. Bullet's assistant, Joe Humphreys, arranged for five members of the KWK broadcasting team to stay at Westminster College's neo-Tudor Beta Theta Pi fraternity house on the corner of Westminster and Sixth. The regular inhabitants would soon squeeze in many more visiting broadcasters and journalists who had failed to plan accommodations in advance. Among the other guests would be writers, editors, and photographers from the Associated Press.

The school also made its Delta Tau Delta house (located adjacent to the Beta Theta Pi residence across the street from the campus) available for the March 5 event; among the new temporary residents would be the team from St. Louis's KMOX radio station, which would relay CBS's broadcast. They would share accommodations with the famous *Time* reporter James Bell.[19]

During the latter half of February, McCluer and his staff were still scrambling to make last-minute preparations, including finalizing the program. As the college president could not very well just cancel all college-related activities, on February 22 he drove two hours east to St. Louis to attend the inauguration of a good friend as the new president of Washington University–St. Louis. When work called him out of town, as on this occasion, he left matters in the capable hands of Joe Humphreys, A. C. Huber, and the organizing committees.[20]

Of all the logistical challenges presented to McCluer's helpers by the imminent arrival of Churchill and Truman, providing food and drink for the expected multitudes was probably the greatest. The *St. Louis Globe-Democrat*'s Margaret Maunder asked a question on the minds of many Fultonians: "Where will the people eat? Fulton has three large cafés with a capacity of about a hundred each and seven small ones, each accommodating less than a dozen people." Local churches made plans to bake around the clock in the week preceding the event, with Fulton Methodist Church offering to feed the parents of Westminster's students.

McCluer also enlisted the help of several Fulton organizations, including the Women's Society, the Women's Council, and the Evangelical & Reformed Women's Guild; the latter, with its newly installed gas range, could feed up to seventy guests. Yet even with all this local goodwill, the meals committee recognized a shortfall in provisions and asked St. Louis catering companies to provide sandwiches and drinks after the noon parade.[21]

Westminster College received more than 15,000 requests for 2,500 nonreserved tickets and finished processing this deluge less than three weeks before Churchill and Truman arrived. McCluer retrieved eight tickets from the final seating block and sent them to Joseph Pulitzer II, who had continued as publisher of the *St. Louis Globe-Dispatch* following the death of his father (in whose honor the Pulitzer Prize was created).[22] Bullet also gave three seats to Major General James Lester Bradley, a hero of the bloody Battle of Okinawa (April–June 1945) and other precious seats in the gymnasium to two representatives from the Missouri Senate and two from the House. A pair of the remaining tickets went to Clarence Cannon, a Democratic congressman from Missouri whom Bullet had known for years, and his wife, Ida. In acknowledging receipt of the tickets, Cannon predicted that on March 5 "Westminster [College] will be the most noted geographical position on the globe." Fittingly, as he furthered his relationships with politicians from his home state, McCluer received the Missouri Bronze Medal from Governor Donnelly in recognition for his role in the new Missouri Constitution.[23]

With the seating problem now alleviated, McCluer took some time to speak with local journalists, who were devoting ever-increasing column inches to Fulton. Churchill's imminent appearance had national and international ramifications, but Mc-Cluer was quick to remind people of his personal aim in inviting the ex–prime minister to his campus—the enrichment of his students and of Fulton residents. "It will certainly be a stimulation to their interest in political affairs and it is expected to enlarge the service the college will be able to render to the general public through the Green Foundation," he told a writer from the *Jefferson City News and Tribune*.[24]

One more problem for Bullet was the travel itinerary for Truman and Churchill's large entourage. The grass and gravel runways at the Fulton Municipal Airport were fine for the 680-pound, 65-horsepower J-3 Piper Club and Piper L-4 Grasshopper that trainee pilots flew, but they could not safely accommodate Truman's "Sacred Cow" plane (an early precursor of Air Force One), which was comparatively colossal at 80,000 pounds.[25] The nearest appropriate site was at Vichy, but as this was a two-and-a-half-hour drive from Fulton, Churchill and Truman would have had to get up before dawn to maintain the schedule. Also, the size of the presidential party for the trip had become too great for Westminster trustee A. P. Green to accommodate at his home as originally planned, even if there had been closer suitable airfields. With Truman scheduled to speak in Columbus the day after his Fulton appearance, his staff changed the plan: he and Churchill would take a more leisurely journey aboard the presidential train from Washington to Jefferson City and then go on to Fulton by car.[26]

Despite his personal despondence over this news, Green remained an important contributor to Fulton's preparations, assisting Bullet with much of the faculty, staff, and trustee participation. On February 26, Green sagely suggested to McCluer that Neal S. Wood and John Raeburn Green send their speeches for the honorary degree presentations to alternates, in case fortune misled them out of attending.[27]

That same day, Huber informed Governor Donnelly that Arthur Hardimen, a longtime friend of Bullet's, would drive Truman and Churchill in the new black Packard coupe that the governor had offered for Truman and Churchill's Jefferson City–to–Fulton motorcade. Finalizing the driving assignments coincided with McCluer's completion of the agenda:

12:00 P.M.: a parade through the streets of Fulton

1:00 P.M.: luncheon at the home of Dr. F. L. McCluer

1:15 P.M.: the campus opens to ticket holders to the gymnasium where the lecture will be given

2:45 P.M.: the doors to the gymnasium close

3:00 P.M.: the procession begins

3:30 P.M.: the program will go on the air[28]

McCluer was not the only busy person in Fulton as Churchill's visit approached. At Fulton High School, band director Taylor Hagen called his young musicians to rehearsals on the school's wide-planked theater stage at 1:00 P.M. each day, following the students' lunch hour. There was more practice late into every evening to ensure that each note was on key for Truman and Churchill. Hagen had also ordered new military-style uniforms in black, and though he had to make do with dark blue owing to the vendor's short supplies, at least the yellow sashes matched the school colors.[29]

The early days of March were no less frenetic for other Fultonians, as they put the finishing touches on every conceivable detail for the event, which had grown in scope beyond anything Bullet McCluer could have imagined at its inception the previous autumn. Ida Belle recalled: "There were many hurried preparations going on—new bath fixtures in one of our bathrooms, three phones were put in our house, and Western Union ran 35 lines behind our house into the gymnasium next door. Bell Telephone worked for about 3 weeks putting in a new cable containing 600 circuits from the local telephone company to the college campus." These wires were designed to carry newspaper and magazine dispatches relaying the speech from Westminster's gymnasium.

As the phone company noisily dug up the pavement outside, Ida Belle McCluer was toiling to finish the elaborate meal for Churchill, Truman, and fifty-plus guests. To help her organize it, she had enlisted the expertise of Mrs. Zula Trigg, the hostess from the Fulton Country Club.[30] The club boasted the best recreational facilities in the area—an immaculately manicured, nine-hole golf course, grass tennis courts, and a croquet lawn.[31] Fulton resident O. T. Harris recalled gathering with friends to eat hearty meals prepared by the curly-haired, full-figured Zula: fried chicken, green beans, mashed potatoes, and gravy was a favorite, costing seventy-five cents a plate. Though it offered comfortable dining and lounging, the country club, with its log exterior and expansive covered porch with white pillars, lacked air conditioning. Harris remembered seeing Zula laboring in the club's unventilated kitchen, "red-faced, copious perspiration, with a towel around her head."[32]

With much of the college campus resembling a construction site and the unlikely assortment of Secret Service agents, workmen, and community volunteers turning the campus into a whirlwind of activity, it's a wonder that Zula and Ida Belle were able to finalize preparations for feeding the large group at the McCluer house and the adjacent Reunion Hall. After attending the Sunday-morning service at the red-brick Fulton Presbyterian Church, the two ladies hightailed it back to the kitchen at the McCluers' campus home, which was chock full of cooking supplies.[33]

"I had a busy time hunting up enough Callaway County ham to feed about 275 people," Ida Belle recollected. "As to the silver and china, if it had not been for friends, some of the guests would have had to eat off cardboard boxes and use sticks for forks. Sugar was another problem—it was still rationed. Somehow the story was carried in the local paper, and if we had not stopped them, we would have had to build a larger house to take all that sugar."[34]

The gymnasium built in 1928 by McCluer's predecessor, President Marion Melvin, was also bustling. A corps of workers from the Boekesh Chair Company in St. Louis, sweating in the 78-degree heat, ferried in a thousand chairs from several large trucks. They then arranged them in neat rows according to Mc-Cluer's detailed floor plan and carefully affixed white covers. Around the Boekesh team bustled myriad volunteers from the college and Chamber of Commerce, testing the lighting, placing seating-section signs, and ensuring that the four microphones on the podium were in place and operational.[35]

As dusk enveloped Fulton on March 3, there was still much to do before the biggest event in the hamlet's history. Streets needed to be swept, police checkpoints set up, and the giant ham for Churchill and Truman's lunch to be cooked. In less than forty-eight hours, 20,000 visitors, 2,800 ticketholders, 200 journalists, and the world's two most famous politicians would turn the town into a hub of activity. To add to Bullet McCluer's many concerns, the local Weather Bureau predicted rain.

CHAPTER 6

A MESSAGE TO A BAFFLED WORLD: CHURCHILL'S SPEECH CALLS FOR SHARP FOCUS

I have a message to deliver to your country and to the world and I think it very likely that we shall be in full agreement about it. Under your auspices anything I say will command some attention and there is an opportunity for doing some good in this bewildered, baffled and breathless world.

—Winston Churchill in a letter to President Harry Truman
(January 29, 1946)

NEW YEAR'S DAY 1946 USHERED IN the first year in the previous seven without world conflict. Churchill also received more good news: his name was included in the King's New Year's Honors List, which read "Winston Churchill: Order of Merit"— the highest civilian award other than a knighthood.[1]

On the morning of January 8, as Churchill prepared to receive the honor from King George VI, the dailies carried a disturbing report. Dr. Raphael Armattoe, a leading biologist, claimed in an interview that Russia had developed an atomic weapon "which renders the Anglo-American bomb obsolete."[2] Though not an atomic physicist, Armattoe said he had infallible sources, and his comments were aired on both sides of the Atlantic—to the concern of British and American leaders.

Less than twenty-four hours later, Churchill, Clementine, Inspector Williams from Scotland Yard, Churchill's valet Frank Sawyers, and Jo Sturdee, his trusty secretary, set sail from Southampton on the *Queen Elizabeth* liner, bound for New York. The impressive ship, its two colossal funnels belching gray plumes into the sky, was under the command of Sir James Bisset, whom Churchill met during World War II when Bisset ferried him to four meetings with Roosevelt as skipper of the *Queen Mary*. Now the commodore of the Cunard White Star Fleet, the unflappable, white-haired Bisset—Churchill's equal in height, build, and who also loved the sea—was the perfect choice to convey his former commander in chief across the Atlantic in peacetime.[3]

Four days into the voyage, Churchill addressed the 12,000 Canadian soldiers traveling with him. Ralph Allen, writing for the *Toronto Globe and Mail,* reported that Churchill drew loud cheers as he told the assembly: "[O]ur future is in our own hands. Do not be too anxious about the future. The old flag flies; the task is accomplished, and the duty done." If transatlantic unity was maintained, Churchill believed, "the British Commonwealth, glorious and free, will form a structure and an organization in which there will be room for all and a fair chance for all."[4]

With the warmth of such sentiments still buzzing among the Canadians and a U.S. Army band's uplifting rendition of "Hail, Hail, the Gang's All Here" ringing in his ears, Churchill braved a bitter northerly wind as he walked down the gangplank of the *Queen Elizabeth* after it landed at Pier 90, in West Manhattan, at 8:30 P.M. on a rainy January 14.[5] Behind him, the squall churned the Hudson River, with whitecaps bulging up from the surface and eddying menacingly around the anchored liner.

Churchill had come to America with several clear objectives in mind. The first, which was also the top priority of Clementine and Lord Moran, was to get more rest. Despite being invigorated by the Communist challenge, he was still distracted by domestic politics and had been plagued by an irregular heartbeat in recent months.[6]

This three-month trip was not to be a mere holiday, however. Churchill would meet with top-ranking U.S. officials, including Secretary of State James F. Byrnes and their mutual friend Bernard Baruch—the seventy-five-year-old finance magnate and presidential counselor who *Time* declared "has an almost mystic reputation as The Man Who Can Solve Anything"—to press Britain's claims for a low-interest, long-term postwar loan.[7] With more than a quarter of the country's wealth sapped by the war effort, rations stayed in place and industry struggled. British trade with continental Europe was significantly weakened, as the Germans, French, and Italians were also enduring the financial strain of the all-consuming armed conflict. The British Commonwealth nations, such as Canada, Australia, and New Zealand, had also suffered heavy casualties, as well as loss of money and military equipment, and Britain struggled to fulfill its obligations. In the wake of preeminent British economist John Maynard Keynes's persuasive September 1945 trip to Washington, America seemed poised to offer a significant loan, but since December many politicians in Britain deemed the terms too harsh.[8]

Indeed, before the parliamentary Christmas break, Churchill pulled his party's dissenting MPs into line at the last minute, preventing them from voting against the deal that month. Churchill won out, and the Commons voted in favor of the $3.75 billion package. Despite this assent, isolationist Democratic and Republican congressmen refused to ratify the deal. The most notable detractors were fiscal conservatives who balked at the idea of sending hundreds of millions of dollars across the Atlantic without punitive interest, an unrealistically brief repayment schedule, or both—not least because Britain had received hundreds of millions in aid and armaments during the war. Churchill was determined to advocate for the British position, in the hope of lowering the interest rate and extending the repayments when the debate came up again in Congress and the Senate. On his 1946 trip to the United States, he was not an official emissary of Attlee, but the prime minister in no way dissuaded him from using his strong personal ties in the United States to Britain's advantage in trying to secure the approval of a fair assistance package.[9]

The third, and arguably most important, aim of Churchill's visit was to make an impact from the Westminster College podium. He had informed Truman and McCluer that he would speak about world peace, and as he strode onto American soil, jaw jutting and stick relentlessly tapping the ground ahead as he moved down the dock, Churchill thought about how to deal rhetorically with the issue of Russia. Part of the challenge involved condensing a turbulent four-decade relationship into a few memorable phrases, none of which could be wasted. Should he sound the alarm bell to warn of the abuses and increasingly anti-Western rhetoric of the Kremlin, or take a more stealthy approach? Churchill had no need to play nice with Stalin, now that the wartime coalition was separated, and was determined to use the full force of his voice once more.[10]

He got the opportunity right from the get-go, meeting the American and Canadian press for a thirty-minute conference in the waiting room at the end of the dock.[11] There, Churchill sat at a great hardwood desk, placed his hat and glasses on the desktop beside three radio-station microphones, and asked for questions from the reporters, who pressed in on him from all sides. Speaking about politics at home, he dismissed questions about his retirement, stating his determination to "lead the Conservative Party until they can make arrangements for other leadership." On

Britain's appraisal of its Labour Government, he quipped, "I never criticize the government of my country when I'm abroad, and I rarely leave off criticizing them when I'm at home."

Next, Churchill fielded a question about the status of American financial aid to the U.K. "I ought to say nothing about the loan, which is entirely for the American nation to decide," he tactfully replied. When reporters moved on to the inevitable topic of nuclear weapons, Churchill's voice became slow and deliberate as he took a dig at the Soviets: "I think it would be a grave mistake to share the secret of the atomic bomb unless proper controls are established."

The thirty-minute press briefing closed all too quickly for the reporters, with many a hand still aloft, waving for Churchill's attention.[12] Yet, despite their need for more editorial fodder and Churchill's enjoyment of bantering with them, there was a schedule to keep to, and it was time for him to move on to the next phase of the journey—the two-day train ride down the Eastern Seaboard to Miami, Florida.

Accompanying him as he bade the American press corps farewell were Clementine, his secretary Jo Sturdee, the British Consul General, Frank Sawyers, Inspector Williams, and Churchill's soon-to-be host, Canadian Colonel Frank W. Clarke, whom Churchill had visited after the second Quebec conference in September 1944 for what the Briton described as "some wonderful trout fishing."[13] The party arrived in Florida on the warm morning of January 16, traveling by car to 5905 North Bay Road, the six-bedroom summer home that Clarke had purchased in 1945. A prime piece of coastal real estate, North Bay Road was located on a thin spit of land that poked out from eastern Miami into the Atlantic, affording it spectacular ocean views on both sides.

Clarke brought his valet, secretary, driver, cook, and two maids from Quebec. The colonel's son, William, who had endured four years in a Japanese prison camp in Hong Kong, his wife, Tolly, and their infant son, Frank William, would join them later that day. In preparation for hosting Winston and Clementine, Clarke instructed decorators to paint the master bedroom on the second floor pink and turquoise, likely more for her benefit than for his. The room also offered them an awning-covered veranda, on which Churchill could set up his easel to capture the seaside panorama. To ensure that the guests were not disturbed by the marauding mosquitoes that accompanied the Florida heat, the gardener liberally sprayed the foliage surrounding the patio with insecticide.[14]

An editorial published in the *Miami News* on the evening the Churchills arrived in South Beach implored Miamians to allow Winston to enjoy this palm tree-shaded patio and the other pleasures of his visit unmolested: "Let us leave him to steep himself in our sun and sea and sky, if he so pleases. Let us grant him equal freedom, if restless energy takes command, to transfer a seascape to canvas, or, to book plates, the memories of earth-shaking years."[15]

The next morning, Churchill channeled some of that energy into his initial public-relations push for the postwar loan by addressing local and national reporters, who had assembled en masse in Miami Beach to cover every detail of his stay. Though Churchill looked relaxed in a loose-fitting light-tan suit as he puffed away in a lawn chair, he had solemn words for the journalists: "We suffered far more than any country during the war. Some other countries were overrun but were not fighting. We were fighting and using up our credit. We borrowed all we could. If we're not given the opportunity to get back on our feet again, we may never be able to take our place among other nations."[16]

That afternoon, Churchill stationed himself at his easel in a white painter's smock that billowed in the breeze, before succumbing to the charms of his sea-facing deck chair under the shade of palms and a fragrant melaleuca, the rough-barked Australian tree that yields potent-scented and medicinal tea tree oil.[17]

Though interested in his political proclamations, many local reporters devoted the majority of their column inches to apprising Churchill the man. He received enough fawning coverage during the war to achieve mythic status, and Florida "beat" writers were eager to draw a more representative picture than this caricature offered. In January 17's *Miami Daily News,* reporter Walter Locke described how the new resident of North Bay Road differed from his presuppositions about the fearsome "British bulldog" who had defied Hitler: "A round-faced, round-headed, benevolent, almost jolly gentleman, without a vestige of a front. The collar of his shirt spreads open. A soft hat with brim upturned in front gives him a look of genial impishness. . . . [T]he humor which has lubricated his life flashes in his face and sparkles on his tongue."[18]

It was not just Florida reporters who were taken by Churchill. Lorraine Bonar, Frank Clarke's secretary, whom he assigned to help Sturdee with Churchill's administrative tasks during his South Beach stay, told her parents on January 17: "Well, the great man has arrived and he's just wonderful—he entirely captivated me with his lack of pretentiousness and is really charming to everyone. Today Mr. Churchill and I had a little chat about the goldfish, of which I am the keeper. He is very fond of them and thought he may try to take some back with him."[19]

Churchill was eager to enjoy the local wildlife while in Miami, which differed greatly from the domesticated menagerie he had left at Chartwell—dogs, cats, swans, and a pot-bellied pig. When Clarke mentioned the nearby Parrot Jungle Gardens, the Briton insisted that they go. Founded by burly Austrian immigrant Franz Scherr in 1936 after the Great Depression crushed his construction business, this leafy estate featured a bevy of delights for the avian enthusiast—rainbow-hued parrots, large-beaked macaws, and elaborately coiffed cockatiels. As they made their way through the foliage, a cockatoo perched on Churchill's shoulder and "kissed" him on the cheek several times. Churchill grinned like an awed five-year-old, and Clarke arranged for the owner to bring some of the birds to North Bay Road later that week so that Clementine could see them.[20]

When Churchill returned to Clarke's home, he received a Western Union telegram from Florida Senator Claude Pepper, welcoming the Briton to the state. The two had met in London, and Pepper conveyed his "gratitude for your incomparable contribution to the freedom which the world today enjoys." He also expressed a "fervent hope that you may find in our state refreshment from your great labors and new strength for those tasks which challenging causes will lay upon you."[21]

Clementine summed up the first few days at North Bay Road in a letter to her daughter, Mary, on January 18:

> We arrived here 48 hours ago in tropical heat, rather much but delicious—And lo and behold in the same night it changed and we are shivering amongst rustling palm trees and gray skies. . . . Papa has not yet settled down to painting and is a little sad, poor thing. I hope he is going to begin writing something.
>
> *Later in the day:* The weather has slightly improved and Papa has now started a picture of palms reflecting in the water. I visited him, and draped a knitted Afghan round his shoulders as he was sitting under a gloomy pine tree in a particularly chilly spot.[22]

The following day, an atypical wintry spell forced the Churchills inside and Winston, who was supposed to be in Miami for the good of his health, to bed with a heavy cold. Bellicose Senator Homer Ferguson wanted Churchill to testify in Washington before he returned home, but a congressional committee that was investigating the response to the Japanese bombing of Pearl Harbor voted down this proposal by six votes to two as Churchill convalesced.[23]

January 21 saw the usual humidity and warmth return, a welcome respite from the frigidity of English wintertime and the chilly Chartwell, which, like most Victorian houses, lacked insulation. Clementine wrote to Mary again the next day, describing how the change in weather coincided with the improved health and temper of the patient:

> Papa, thank God, has recovered or nearly so. We had a wretched 36 hours. . . . [T]he temperature, tho [*sic*] not very high, simply would not go down and Papa was very nervous about himself, & yet very obstinate and would take either no remedies at all or several conflicting ones at the same time.
>
> But today he bathed! And loved it. The weather is now perfect but tropical. Crickets chirp all night—there are lovely flowering hedges of hibiscus pink lemon and apricot. . . . The sea is heavenly, water about 70°. . . .
>
> Papa has learnt a new card game "Gin Rummy" and plays all day and all night in bed and out of bed. He has started 2 not very good pictures.
>
> Tender love (I must fly, Papa is calling).[24]

Though Churchill met with his literary agent Emery Reves about the composition of his war memoirs and planned for his upcoming meetings with Bernard Baruch and Secretary of State James F. Byrnes, the *Palm Beach Post* described how (as Clementine had written) he spent most of his time painting rather than politicking during his first week in Miami: "From a vantage point near Colonel Clarke's Miami Beach home, Churchill transferred

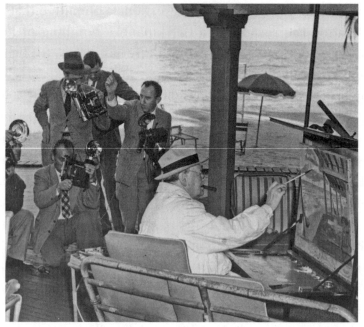

Winston Churchill paints at the Miami Surf Club, watched by reporters and photographers in January 1946. CREDIT: MIAMI NEWS COLLECTION, HISTORYMIAMI, IMAGE 1989–011–19793

the riotous colors of the evening sky to canvas, as the sun sank over Biscayne Bay and the Miami skyline."[25]

Such leisurely social engagements would not have been possible if Churchill had been distracted by the three hundred or more letters that Lorraine Bonar and Jo Sturdee processed each day—of which fewer than ten were presented to their boss. Indeed, the volume of autograph requests was such that British Ambassador Lord Halifax sent one of his secretaries to Miami to assist them. Despite Sturdee's diligence, Churchill (who Bonar revealed "invariably had a little smile on his face and seemed to be secretly amused that he had caused such a sensation") seemed intent on keeping her in a constant state of readiness. Bonar described a typical scene in another letter home:

He just loved to shout at the top of his lungs for Miss
Sturdee despite the fact that we had buzzers installed in his
room and maids and telephones. . . . Miss Sturdee would
very calmly reply—"I'm coming," which really broke me up
because I was so much in awe of him.

Others in the house felt the full force of Churchill's well-
trained vocal chords, too. According to Bonar, "He wasn't above
being very difficult and contrary and even had his little spats with
Mrs. Churchill when he screamed 'Clemmie' at her from across
the hall. Once they went for about two days with only the very
necessary speaking between them."[26]

Since arriving in Miami, Churchill had been the subject of
daily American newspaper reports, particularly those in
Florida that enthusiastically recorded his every move. On January 25, Churchill was in the news for another reason. In the
first of a series of exclusives, *Life* published a previously secret
speech he had given to the Commons on April 23, 1942. Such
addresses were presented behind closed doors to protect the
fragile confidence of the British public from demoralizing
news. In the oration published in *Life,* Churchill had revealed
the embarrassing and devastating defeat of 100,000 British
troops at Singapore by a much smaller Japanese force. He also
told MPs about the heavy loss of British naval shipping in the
Pacific and Atlantic and admitted that with the damage to the
Queen Elizabeth and *Valiant* there was, at least temporarily, no
British seafaring presence in the Mediterranean. There was
also the risk, Churchill believed, of the Japanese making inroads into or even taking over the "jewel of the British Empire," India. Finally, Churchill reiterated his long-held desire
that the United States enter the war, but hoped this could be
achieved without hostilities between the Allies and Japanese
Emperor Hirohito's nation.[27]

Four years on and with Japan defeated, Churchill still hoped for greater unity between the United States and Britain. Though he was supposed to be resting body and mind on Miami's sun-drenched shores, Churchill's daily habit of reading newspapers with breakfast ensured that he was not insulated from troubling international developments. Before they had disembarked, he had asked Jo Sturdee to ensure he received each edition of the *Times, Daily Express,* and *Daily Herald* and their Sunday versions via airmail from London for the duration of his stay.[28]

The day after Churchill got to Miami, these newspapers and their American counterparts informed him that Iran had lodged the first complaint in the brief history of the United Nations Orga-nization, over Russia's refusal to withdraw troops from north Iran. To the United States and Britain, this signaled a further betrayal of the promises Stalin had made at Yalta and Potsdam—pledges he was breaking, one by one. James F. Byrnes, the former lawyer from South Carolina and now U.S. secretary of state, thought that the Kremlin's actions were a direct affront to the legitimacy of the UNO.[29] Churchill was likely inclined to agree.

In Britain's case, Iran was pivotal to preserving its strong trad-ing relationships in the Middle East, not least the powerful Anglo-Iranian Oil Company established in 1935. There was fear on both sides of the Atlantic that if Russia wrested control of Iran, the entire region may be overrun by Communism and Britain's economic interests imperiled. Stalin needed oil from northern Iran, as domestic output had fallen precipitously to just 5 million tons per year, yet Churchill did not consider it reason-able for Red Army troops to secure it by illegally occupying a country beyond an exit date ratified in a treaty.

Such troubling developments, plus newly released reports of voter intimidation and other irregularities in the Bulgarian elec-tions held two months prior, were on Churchill's mind when he wrote to Truman on January 29. He told the president: "I need to talk with you a good while about our Fulton date. I have a message to deliver to your country and to the world and I think it very likely that we shall be in full agreement about it. Under your auspices anything I say will command some attention and there is an opportunity for doing some good in this bewildered, baffled and breathless world." It was becoming increasingly clear that whatever Churchill said, though it came from his vantage point as a private citizen of Great Britain, would match the viewpoint of Truman and many of his top advisers.[30]

The day after writing Truman, Churchill gave his mind a brief rest from political matters as he, Clementine, and Frank Clarke headed out to the Hialeah race course, with its distinctive palm tree–lined entry road and famous pink flamingos that lived on an island in the middle of the infield lake. Churchill put a couple of bucks on Cedar Creek, son of the Derby-winning Bahram. Much to Churchill's delight, jockey Eddie Arcaro (who had won the Triple Crown five years before) brought Cedar Creek home first, and later in the event Wee Admiral (aptly named, as Churchill had twice been First Lord of the Admiralty) brought Churchill his second success of the day, racing clear to give the Briton another payout on his wager.[31]

Early the following morning, Churchill—dressed in a gray suit and black-and-white polka-dot bow tie—took full advantage of the private plane and pilot lent to him by the president and flew with Clementine, Frank Clarke, and Jo Sturdee to Havana, Cuba. The Associated Press recounted the enthusiastic welcome that awaited the party: "Thousands cheered the ruddy-faced British war leader at the airport, where his silver-painted B-17 bomber, 'The Mary Win II' landed shortly after 3:00 P.M. . . . [I]t was 15 minutes before strong-armed police and army guards could guide him through huge throngs which overran barriers and flooded onto the field surrounding Churchill and the plane."[32]

Once Churchill freed himself from the crowd, a motorcade conveyed him and his group through narrow winding streets,

lined by thousands more cheering Havanans. After dropping off
his luggage at the white stone Hotel Nacional, with its two red-
tiled towers rising above accommodations that gave residents of
the north-facing rooms an unimpeded view of the Gulf of Mexico's endless blue, Churchill was whisked away to the palace of
Cuban President Ramón Grau San Martín for an introductory
conversation. The Presidential Palace, constructed just east of the
hotel in 1920, was a neoclassic wonder, and Churchill marveled at
the elaborate white stonework façade—including the great arches
on either side of the main entrance—and the gleaming interior,
which was lavishly decorated by New York's Tiffany & Co.[33]

Churchill took his easels, brushes, and oils with him and finished several tropical scenes over the following days. Even during
his repose he egged on the American reporters who had followed
him from his Miami base to Havana. Churchill engaged in jovial
banter until one writer asked whether Russia's current foreign
policy was in keeping with the Big Three wartime alliance.
Churchill's smile vanished as he pondered a diplomatic response
that would not give away the element of surprise he desired for
the Fulton address. "That is a very difficult question," he finally
replied. The reporters had silenced their scribbling pencils as he
paused to consider how much to reveal and what to leave unsaid.
After a few moments, he opted for positivity over pessimism, expressing the hope that "unity among the Allied powers during the
war will continue." Asked whether the atom bomb would be used
as a deterrent or an aggressive weapon, Churchill responded
more quickly: "May God permit there won't be any further reasons for its use!"[34]

There is little doubt, given his previous and subsequent
speeches and writing, that Churchill wholeheartedly believed in
his second statement that day. But while he may have aspired
toward an ongoing partnership with Russia, he knew that the
sentiments of his first answer were by now based on little more
than fading hope. Though diminished, such hope would not be

extinguished in Greece, Churchill explained, because British troops were intervening to "insure the present government." Without such action, Churchill told the press corps, the country would have fallen to "communist masses and tyranny." Russia had wrongly accused the British of interfering in Greek governmental matters, Churchill believed, and he invited a "full, public airing" of such claims before the UNO. These were his strongest statements about Soviet foreign policy to date, and he was eager to share further fears with the White House.

On the following morning of February 2, Churchill received an encouraging telegram from Truman, in which the president wrote, "I know you have a real message to deliver at Fulton, and, of course, I shall be most happy to talk with you about it." Truman seemed to have an inkling of what Churchill would focus on in Missouri and was eager to contribute.[35]

Churchill's concerns about the Soviet Union surfaced again in a letter to Eisenhower four days later, on February 6. "I am worried about the way things are going. There is only one safe anchor; wh[ich] both you and I know." Churchill was referring to the unbreakable bonds between the United States and Britain, which he and Eisenhower had given their all to defend, and which must now, in early 1946, act as a bulwark against the rampant expansion of Communism.[36]

On February 7, R. Henry Norweb, U.S. ambassador to Cuba, wrote a revealing note to Truman describing how Churchill might articulate such thoughts in Fulton. The previous evening, as Norweb's dinner guest at the U.S. Embassy, Churchill was "deeply apprehensive as to the future of the United Nations Organization." The reasons were twofold. First, Churchill told Norweb that military backing for the UNO was inadequate, just as it had been with the doomed League of Nations established by the victors of World War I. Second, and more troubling, was the changing dynamics between the United States and Britain and Russia, "the ever-threatening 'Bear who walks like a man.'"

Norweb relayed Churchill's gloomy assessment that the power base of the UNO "depends on the political relations between the three great powers around which the whole structure is built, and these relations he feels are now neither clear nor promising."

Churchill had evidently conveyed his fear that Moscow would soon have the atomic bomb and, when that time came, would "not hesitate to employ it for her own ends in this atmosphere of postwar friction and confusion." The Briton believed it was his "lifetime fate to issue 'clarion calls' regarding the danger he fore-sees," which Norweb tied to Churchill's visionary warnings against Nazism in the 1930s.

The solution to the Russia problem, as Churchill saw it, was for "development over the years of some definite working agree-ment between the American and British governments." He rec-ognized, Norweb wrote, that "any formal merger or alliance would doubtless now be impractical, untimely and unpopular on both sides of the Atlantic—but he holds that the sheer pressure of events will . . . force our two great commonwealths to come to-gether in some workable manner if the peace and order of the world are to be preserved from chaos."[37]

It was clear to Truman and his closest advisers why Churchill wanted to speak at Fulton and what his central messages would be. They were also aware of the negative response Churchill had pre-dicted and his conviction to press on regardless. In the mid-1930s he had stood almost alone (with the exception of a group of young Tory rebels), and his prophecies about Hitler were derided in the House of Commons and by the majority of the British press. Now, at least, he had the ear of the U.S. president and his inner circle both in preparing another grave warning about the intentions of an aggressive foreign power and in proposing solutions.[38]

Such proposals found a receptive audience in Truman. From the beginning of 1946, Truman realized, as Churchill had all along, that a tougher approach toward the Politburo was needed if the geographical and ideological spread of Communism was to be arrested. This newly hardened position was partly the result of the ineffective New York conference among the "Grand Alliance" foreign ministers. On January 5, Truman had sounded positively Churchillian when he told the sixty-four-year-old Byrnes, "Unless Russia is faced by an iron fist and strong language another war is in the making. Only one language do they understand: 'how many divisions do you have?' . . . I'm tired of babying the Soviets." Two days later, Truman showed his mettle by telling the White House press corps that he would defend the rights of sovereign states in Europe. Felix Belair, Jr., writing for the *New York Times,* stated that Truman also "reserved the right to withdraw recognition of Rumania, Bulgaria, and Yugoslavia if they fell short of the Yalta provisions for freedom."[39]

As Norweb conveyed Churchill's concerns to the White House, Russia continued to confound its former allies. While Churchill was in Havana, news broke that Canadian authorities had arrested Russian spies alleged to have infiltrated Canadian government with the intention of stealing nuclear arms secrets. The breathless news coverage this incident received stirred Churchill's fears over the security of the Western allies' nuclear program (or, rather, lack of security), amid news that Russia had successfully achieved uranium fission.[40]

Furthermore, the Soviets shuttered their newly acquired Eastern European satellite states, refusing to admit Western diplomats or journalists. Poland, which Churchill had tried in vain to pull out of the fire at Yalta and Potsdam, was by now lost to Communism, he feared. In France and Italy, which were still reeling from the tremors of war, Communist groups tried to consolidate power by first inviting and then coercing other left-leaning parties to join with them. In the Soviet-controlled Eastern Berlin zone, the Communist Party forced a merger with the more powerful and, though still independent, democratically legitimate Social Democratic Party. It would not be so for long.

The power of the Soviet Military Administration in Germany left the more moderate Socialist Party with little choice. Though Churchill would not have known it, East German Communist leader Walter Ulbricht told his party members, "It's quite clear— it's got to look democratic but we must have everything in our control." Albania was also a trouble spot. Once the United States and Britain had officially recognized the administration of left-wing premier Colonel-General Enver Hoxha, he had abandoned any trace of the moderation used to win such an endorsement. In addition to establishing a secret police, persecuting the minority Catholic population, and eliminating political opponents, Hoxha invited Red Army officers into the country to aid in his establishment of an iron-fisted dictatorship.[41] In short, Churchill's fears about the German capital and Eastern Europe were justified and had progressed beyond what he had envisaged.

Returning from Cuba, Churchill was eager to share with Truman his fears about the mounting Iranian crisis and the Soviet stranglehold on Eastern Europe. To this end, Churchill braved heavy snow during his journey to Washington on February 10 for an 8:30 P.M. meeting at the White House. The four-and-a-half-hour flight took him from a balmy evening in Miami into the middle of the worst storm to hit Washington that winter. As the plane flew into the edge of the squall, the turbulence sent Churchill, Frank Clarke, Jo Sturdee, and Inspector Williams, all of whom had shunned seatbelts, out of their chairs and onto the unforgiving metal floor of the B-52 Stratofortress. Climbing slowly back into their seats, they buckled themselves in to avoid further bruises.

As an antidote to their troubles, the quartet received a rousing welcome from thousands of cheering Washingtonians oblivious to the arctic blast.[42] Following Churchill's customary, yet atypically rushed, display of appreciation for his encouragers, White House staff bundled him and his companions into a town car for the short drive to the White House.

Charles Ross, Truman's press secretary and fellow Missourian, claimed that the Fulton speech was the main topic of conversation between the statesmen, but asserted that they did not discuss any political matters. The second part of Ross's statement seems unfathomable, given the opinionated nature of both men, the increasing international tension, and the fact that Truman had been mulling over Norweb's memo about Churchill's mindset on Russia for three days before the Briton arrived in Washington.[43]

Churchill was also opaque about his visit with Truman when he returned to Miami on February 12. "No comment," he gruffly responded when asked during a news conference if he had discussed the Soviet Union with the president while in Washington.[44]

Admiral William D. Leahy, Truman's top naval adviser, shed some light on the White House meeting in his diary entry for February 10: "The subject of that [Fulton] address will be the necessity for full military collaboration between Great Britain and the U.S. in order to preserve peace in the world until the United Nations Organization is fully able to keep the peace. . . . Mr. Churchill believes it necessary to our safety that the combined British-American Staff be continued. . . . I can foresee forceful objection by the Soviets to our having a bilateral military association." After the White House meeting, Leahy took Churchill back to the British Embassy, where the two men and Lord Halifax, the British ambassador, talked about the Soviet conundrum until midnight. Leahy told Halifax that Truman was "more than happy about his [Churchill] making the kind of fraternal speech that he has in mind to deliver."

Halifax also played a role in shaping the latest iteration of the address, discussing it with Churchill each day of his Washington stay at the British Embassy. On February 10, the ambassador wrote in his diary, "I can see that it is the one thing on which all Winston's thought and willpower and dynamic nature are concentrated." The following day, Halifax noted the focus of Churchill's work-in-progress. "He wants to speak very frankly about the importance of maintaining very close Anglo-American cooperation . . . and thinks he can do this without upsetting Uncle Joe." On the last day of his stay, Churchill performed an emotional reading of his Fulton address for the ambassador. "He rehearsed to me a great deal of the speech . . . with tears almost rolling down his cheeks as he thought of the great strategical [*sic*] concept of the future which was the cottage home of happy, humble people, and quoted 'Childe Harold' to reinforce his elegance."[45]

Several days after Halifax hosted Churchill, the latter's suspicions about Soviet intentions again proved valid. Since the London meeting of foreign ministers in September 1945, when Bevin rebuffed Russian Foreign Minister Molotov's request for bases in Constantinople, the request had become a demand. On February 16, Bevin met with the Turkish foreign minister, who revealed mounting Soviet pressure on his country and Moscow's claim that a treaty between the U.K. and Turkey that gave Britain exclusive rights to military bases there was "obsolete."

Bevin, sensing the need to bide his time with Russia—not least due to the severe weakening of the now demobilized British armed forces—refused to create a formal Western alliance against Russia, preferring to pin his hopes on Churchill's proposed solution to the Communism conundrum: forging even closer ties with the now economically and militarily preeminent America.[46]

On the same day as Bevin's meeting with his Turkish counterpart, February 16, U.S. Secretary of State Byrnes and Bernard Baruch flew to Miami to confer with Churchill about the American loan and, unofficially, Churchill's upcoming trip to Fulton. Baruch, with his six-foot-three-inch frame and immaculate pin-striped suit conveyed a statesman-like air.[47] He was not easily swayed, even by a persuasive rhetorician such as Churchill.

Though Baruch refused to answer reporters' questions about the dialogue, it is unlikely that he opposed Churchill's firm stance on Communism. A few weeks earlier, the financier wrote to Herbert Hoover: "Certainly Statism marches westward. It beats upon all shores. There lies the greatest fight to preserve our form of government which is the only one where men still have some freedom and some dignity." These lines could only have galvanized Churchill's opinion that, with Nazism in ruins, Communist ideology and Russian military expansionism were the next great threats to democratic nations.[48]

Baruch's reservations stemmed from the instability of the American economy. True, the war effort had kindled an inferno in the furnace room of American industry, resulting in unemployment of a mere 2 percent, production of goods and services in 1945 that doubled 1939's output, and a similar increase in the average wage relative to the preceding six years. And yet, these statistics masked myriad underlying struggles born of the transition from the heady illusion of wartime vigor and unity to the harsh economic, social, and cultural realities of an uneasy peace.[49]

Now that production of military supplies had dwindled and demobilization was in its latter stages, unemployment was certain to rise sharply—to as many as 8 million out of work in 1947 (5.5 percent, almost triple the wartime figure), according to the prediction of a pessimistic Secretary of Commerce Henry Wallace. Those who kept their jobs were not always willing to man their posts: with labor unions pushing for higher wages, tens of thousands of workers in all the main industries staged regular walkouts to press their demands. There was also the grim housing shortage to contend with: reportedly more than 100,000 veterans were homeless in Chicago, just one of many cities with far more people than dwellings to accommodate them.[50]

In an effort to overcome objections on such grounds, Churchill presented a strong case for aiding England to Baruch and Byrnes, asserting that "the failure of the Loan at this stage would bring about such distress and privation in our island as to play into the hands of extremists of all kinds, and lead to a campaign of extreme austerity, detrimental alike to our speedy recovery and to our good relations."

After the meeting, Churchill wrote to Attlee to request specifics of the loan proposal so that he could be better prepared for the follow-up meeting in New York. Churchill turned to the Westminster address next, writing that it "will be in the same direction as the one I made at Harvard two years ago, namely . . . the buildup and maintenance of the UNO [United Nations Organization], and . . . mutual safety in case of danger, in full loyalty to the [Atlantic] Charter. Byrnes said that he could not object to a special friendship within the Organization, as the United States had already made similar special friendships with the South American States. There is much fear of Russia here as a cause of future trouble." Attlee, like Truman, now had full knowledge of Churchill's intentions for his Fulton engagement.[51]

Byrnes favored such a position. He "seemed to like it very well," Churchill told Attlee. The diplomat later wrote that he was also impressed by Churchill's diction, despite the latter being confined to bed with a heavy cold: "When I commented on a phrase he had used, he said a man should not be 'a slave to phrases but should make phrases his slaves.'"[52]

Attlee's reply arrived at North Bay Road on February 25, by which time Churchill had returned from his stint in New York. The prime minister thanked Churchill for his work on securing favorable loan terms and told him, "I am sure your Fulton speech will do some good." If Attlee or Bevin, who was also aware of Churchill's letter, had strongly disagreed with Churchill's assessment that Russia would cause future headaches for Britain, this memo was their chance to take such a stand. Similarly, if the two had wished to distance Britain from the United States, Attlee would have made the point during this letter. The fact that they did neither shows that, despite their war of words in the 1945 election campaign and frequent jousting in the House of Commons, Churchill, Attlee, and Bevin shared a common view on the present and future of Britain's relationships with Russia and America—a firmer tone with the former and a closer alliance with the latter. Their interpretation differed somewhat, with Attlee less concerned about Russia's intentions than the other two, yet, in practical terms, it was the more proactive and forceful Bevin who would take the lead in talking with Moscow.[53]

Churchill shared these opinions with a wider audience the day after receiving Attlee's note. On the morning of February 27, Churchill strode into the Burdine Stadium (aka the Orange Bowl) at the University of Miami, with Clementine and Sarah alongside him and Inspector Williams in tow. Before them, students filed onto the lush green turf in fours, splitting off into pairs when they reached center field and filing up into the stands of the cavernous arena. Just before 10:30 A.M., three police officers led Clementine and Sarah up onto the stage, following the black-robed faculty, former University of Miami president William P. Dismukes, and Churchill. As the Briton walked up the wooden steps, he waved to acknowledge the warm ovation from the students. The crowd remained standing as the university band played rousing renditions of "God Save the King" and "The Star Spangled Banner."

Following the invocation and a greeting from the American Association of Colleges, Dr. Bowman F. Ashe, longtime president of the University of Miami, conferred an honorary degree upon Churchill, saying, "Except for the staunchness of these people, the rest of the world should have faced a degradation too awful to contemplate." Dr. Ashe handed him the diploma as the students applauded enthusiastically, and he placed a green, orange, and white cap on Churchill's head to signify his acceptance of the award and the school's colors.

Churchill approached the microphone, taking off the ceremonial cap and putting on his reading glasses as he placed his
note cards on the podium. He got a long and loud collective
laugh when he told the students that "no one ever passed so few
examinations and received so many degrees." Churchill got to
his main point for the day: the natural and strong bond between
his country and theirs. Churchill noted that a common language
"unites us [Britain and the United States] as no such great com-
munities have been united before . . . but is also a powerful instrument whereby our conceptions of justice, of freedom, of fair
play and good humor may make their invaluable contribution to
the future progress of mankind." Even Bismarck, the mighty
German leader, had stated in the nineteenth century that "the
most important fact in the world was that the British and American peoples spoke the same language," Churchill reminded his
listeners. This theme of unity would form one of the pillars of
his subsequent address at Fulton and shape the sunset years of his
political career. The working title of his next speech was, as of
that day, still "World Peace."[54]

As Churchill spoke in Miami, the Soviets refused to enter into
the international monetary union that was a key part of FDR's
original plan for the UNO. At first they were supposed to be the
third-largest contributor to the organization's general fund but
quickly decided to withdraw. The State Department's top brass
were miffed and confused by the Russian position, and desper-
ately needed expert insight to help them formulate a response.

They also sought an explanation of Stalin's recent "election"[55]
speech, in which he had restated the Marxist theory of inherent
incompatibility between the capitalist West and Communist Russia, and announced a new five-year plan for Russian industry.
This blueprint proposed dramatic increases to the production of
petroleum, coal and steel, and electrical output. The motivation
for this, Stalin stated, was "chance happenings," which implied

that increased raw materials would be needed for a potential armed conflict with Russia's ideological antagonists in the West.[56]

Charles "Chip" Bohlen, a U.S. State Department official at the time and later U.S. ambassador to Moscow, echoed Stalin's appraisal of the void between the autocratic communist East and the democratic capitalist West when he reflected: "After Potsdam, there was little that could be done to induce the Soviet Union to become a reasonable and cooperative member of the world community. Discrepancies between the systems were too great, the hostility of the Soviet Union toward capitalist countries too deep."[57]

George F. Kennan, a veteran American diplomat who was considered the most able-minded man in the State Department's Moscow embassy, took it upon himself to make an even deeper analysis that explained Stalin's saber rattling and refusal to enter the new international monetary union. Kennan poured his years of Soviet experience into the "Long Telegram," which he dispatched to his superiors in Washington on February 22.

In it, Kennan revealed the extent of Soviet oppression at home—under what he called "a police regime par excellence"— as well as expansionist aims and the desire to weaken capitalism abroad. To counter these developments, Kennan urged the Truman administration to adopt a position of "cohesion, firmness, and vigor." He vowed that America "will not and cannot stand aloof if force or the threat of force is used contrary to the purposes and principles of the [United Nations] charter." He concluded, "If we are a great power, we must act as a great power, not only to ensure our own security but in order to preserve the peace of the world."[58] Kennan later described the response of the State Department and White House to his exposition: "If none of my previous literary efforts had seemed to evoke even the faintest tinkle from the bell at which they were aimed, this one, to my astonishment, struck it squarely and set it vibrating with a resonance that was not to die down for many months."[59]

Kennan was not alone in urging Truman to adopt a stronger position on Russia. Admiral William Leahy had dubbed Stalin a "liar and a crook" after Potsdam, and believed in maintaining the wartime power of the U.S. military to show the Politburo that America would not stand down in the face of Russian saber rattling. Assistant Secretary of War John J. McCloy, U.S. Ambassador to Britain Averell Harriman (who later married Pamela, the ex-wife of Churchill's son, Randolph) and several other top-ranking State Department officials also favored a harder line with Moscow. It was Harriman who, upon receiving Kennan's Long Telegram, was so convinced of its merit that he passed it on to James Forrestal immediately. As secretary of the Navy (and, later, the first U.S. secretary of defense), Forrestal had Truman's ear, so when he made a copy for everyone in the Cabinet and Truman himself, and personally delivered it to their desks, the impact was significant. Harriman observed, "In a matter of days the official Washington attitude [toward Russia] hardened considerably."

The conciliatory stance of Henry A. Wallace, FDR's vice president from 1940 to 1945, and Truman's secretary of commerce opposed the views of Averell Harriman and Admiral William Leahy. However, Truman was now convinced that the Soviets would not push the United States around, and Wallace's soft position on Russia, and indeed tenure, was increasingly precarious.[60]

Against this backdrop of political turmoil and international crises, Churchill revised the Fulton speech in earnest. He was notoriously diligent in his preparation, and the composition of this address would be no different. Though verbose and spontaneous when in conversation, Churchill informed Lorraine Bonar during his Miami stay that he favored a more measured approach in even his longest speeches, in keeping with his mantra "Don't Waste Words."[61]

Churchill had brought twenty-six-year-old Jo Sturdee, by far the youngest of his secretaries, to North Bay Road so that she could capture, as she put it, his frequent "alterations and additions on the spur of the moment." With Sturdee there to transcribe his thoughts in real time, Churchill pursued his typical late work hours. As he paced the bedroom overlooking the Atlantic, pausing only to relight one of the many Cuban cigars he had procured while visiting Havana, he spoke in soaring, metaphor-filled sentences while Sturdee's pencil scratched furiously to record her boss's rapid-fire, stream-of-consciousness remarks. Churchill's prolific use of dictation as a tool of speech craft had always created an uncanny connection with his audiences, and it was this method, as much as the content and delivery, that was to again make such an impact at the podium in Missouri.[62]

Despite the intimate nature of his speechwriting, Churchill in no way composed the Fulton message in isolation. He was always eager to hear the opinions of others and not too proud to incorporate their suggestions when he thought them valid. Attlee, Truman, Byrnes, and Bevin knew of his sentiments weeks or even months before his appointment with Bullet McCluer, and encouraged them. With the near-bankrupt state of Britain in 1946 and the need for U.S. fiscal support to remedy this, he was more apt to listen to his American hosts than ever before.[63]

Such meetings would have been commonplace had Churchill been in power, but for the Leader of the Opposition they were atypical. Yet personal diplomacy, even when outside the lines of government protocol, had always been Churchill's modus operandi. From the start of his political career, he had acted upon the belief that private meetings between men of influence could achieve as much as the parliamentary debates he so relished.

Like a well-conditioned athlete, Churchill trained daily in the art of conversation, whether at his Chartwell dinner table, in the Commons, or at the social gatherings of friends such as

Max Beaverbrook who were almost his equal at verbal sparring. He was utterly convinced that his powers of rhetoric and articulation could convince any audience, particularly one or two of his political counterparts at a conference. Churchill had applied this thinking to the wartime summits and, despite Stalin's repeated betrayals of his confidence, still held on to such a belief in 1946. This is evident from the primacy he placed on tête-à-têtes with Truman, Baruch, and Byrnes during his trip. For any other British politician who was not prime minister, meetings with these statesmen would have been extraordinary—but for Churchill they were merely everyday business.[64]

With the day of his Fulton engagement drawing near, Churchill continually honed his speech, carefully inspecting each phrase, reading every line aloud to see how it resonated when vocalized, and scribbling furiously in the margins like a formidable newspaper copyeditor.

Churchill had now changed his speech title to "The Sinews of Peace." Roman senator, lawyer, and orator Marcus Tullius Cicero had declared that "[t]he sinews of war are infinite money." Churchill included this phrase verbatim in his 1899 book *The River War*, but for the title of his Fulton speech he inverted it. By turning a classic idiom on its head, he was deliberately alluding to the wording and sentiments of the original, while making it clear that his purpose was to push for peace, not war.

On February 28, two American politicians gave him indirect encouragement to retain the more confrontational aspects of the address. First, Michigan Republican U.S. Senator Arthur Vandenberg, who had just returned from the London Conference of Foreign Ministers, told a packed Senate that the supreme conundrum of the time was "What is Russia up to now?" He went on to echo Stalin's sentiments that Communism and democracy were incompatible, using the phrase "two great rival ideologies." Vandenberg concluded, hopefully yet cautiously, that "we can live together in reasonable harmony if the United States speaks as plainly upon all occasions as Russia does; if the United States just as vigorously sustains its own purposes and its ideals upon all occasions as Russia does . . . if our candor is as firm as Russia's is. . . . [T]he situation calls for patience and goodwill, but not for vacillation."[65]

The same evening, Secretary of State Byrnes built on the themes Vandenberg had introduced when he addressed the Overseas Press Club in New York. While Byrnes stated that only "an inexcusable tragedy of errors could cause serious conflict between this country and Russia," he warned that "we must make it clear that we do intend to act to prevent aggression" in a time when "all around us is suspicion and distrust."[66] He did not name a specific country but was clearly rebuking Russia over its encroachment in Iran and Eastern Europe when he stated: "No power has a right to help itself to alleged enemy properties in liberated or ex-satellite countries before a reparations settlement has been agreed upon by the allies. We have not and *will not* agree to any one power deciding for itself what it will take from these countries." Byrnes also insisted, in a comment he later confirmed was intended "for the benefit of the Russian leadership," that "[w]e have no right to hold our troops in the territory of other sovereign states without their consent."

To emphasize the severity of such actions, Byrnes recalled that Hitler "wanted the world to accept the domination of a totalitarian government under his direction. He wanted that without war if possible. He was determined to get it with war if necessary." And then, he hammered his point home: "To banish war, nations must refrain from doing the things that lead to war." Byrnes finally reasserted that the United States would play an active role in defending the principles of the United Nations Organization Charter: "We cannot allow aggression to be accomplished by coercion or pressure or by subterfuge such as political infiltration."[67]

It was becoming increasingly evident to Churchill that Washington shared his concerns about Russia's dubious undertakings in the Middle East and across Europe, and that the White House was prepared to take a tougher stand.[68]

As Vandenberg and Byrnes aired their views, Churchill telephoned his friend, confidant, and fellow statesman Canadian Prime Minister Mackenzie King. He asked King if he could make it down to Washington before March 3 to discuss his Fulton speech, but owing to his concern about the ongoing spy scandal, King demurred, suggesting instead that Churchill mail him a copy of the draft. Now it was Churchill's turn to be wary: if his message was intercepted, the consequences would be disastrous. Realizing that this long-distance conversation would have to suffice, Churchill revealed that, while in Missouri, he would call for "closer American-British relations and [the] question of bases." He then told King that his message would be agreeable to him.[69]

Even as Byrnes spoke and Churchill shared his intentions for the Fulton oration with King, the Iranian problem grew in complexity. As February gave way to March, the Red Army defied the deadline for withdrawal, continuing its maneuvers in Persia as if an agreement for standing down had never been made. After meeting with Stalin in Moscow the previous December, Byrnes had sent a memo to the State Department communicating the marshal's claims that he had "no territorial or other designs against Iran" but was merely maintaining troops there to secure Russian interests in the Baku oil fields. These were, Stalin claimed, threatened by the "hostility" of the Iranian government toward the Kremlin.

Now, four months later, with thousands of Red Army troops encamped and Soviet puppet governments installed in the Iranian districts of the Azerbaijan People's Republic and the Kurdish Republic of Mahabad, Soviet involvement in Iran seemed more like an indefinite occupation than a temporary deterrent to oil field sabotage.

Byrnes later revealed that the White House was incensed by Russia's extraordinary claim that "Iran did not have the right to present its case to the United Nations." Having now served two presidents committed to the UNO, Byrnes took it upon himself to tell a Security Council session in New York: "If the United Nations is to endure there must be no excuse or need for any nation to take the law into its own hands." He then urged Russia to withdraw all troops from Iran. When the Iranian ambassador to the UNO stood to bolster this case, Andrei Gromyko, his Russian counterpart, symbolically turned his back and stalked out of the chamber. That same day, the United States issued a strongly worded rebuke to Russia for its attacks on two U.S. Navy fighters off the Manchurian coast. Such developments gave Churchill even greater confidence that the message he would soon share with the world in Missouri was timely and just.[70]

On the night of March 2, Churchill attended a farewell celebration in his honor in the ornate dining room of the exclusive Miami Beach Surf Club, which looked out onto a broad deck, a turquoise pool, and, through a deliberate gap in the palm trees, the pearl-white sands of South Beach. While enjoying this panoramic view through the club's windows, Churchill stayed for almost an hour to greet several hundred members invited for the occasion. Then it was on to the train station for the thousand-mile trip to Washington, from which he and Truman would journey to Fulton. In his mind, he had already reached the destination of the speech he would deliver in Missouri.[71]

CHAPTER 7

THE NEW MISSOURI GANG: FINAL PREPARATION ON THE LONG JOURNEY

I have a suggestion to make. The head should be on a swivel so that it can turn from the talons of war to the olive branch of peace as the occasion warrants.

—Winston Churchill, commenting on the eagle's head on the *Ferdinand Magellan* presidential seal (March 4, 1946)

A T 7:53 A.M. ON MARCH 3, 1946, a bleary-eyed Churchill, who had worked on "The Sinews of Peace" long into the night, emerged from the Miami train at Washington's cavernous Union Station, with Sarah, Clementine, Jo Sturdee, his aide Frank Sawyers, Dr. Robert M. Harris (the former U.S. Navy officer who had served as Churchill's physician in Miami), and Colonel Frank Clarke (their host in South Beach). They were met by Churchill's only son, thirty-four-year-old Randolph. He had followed his father's path into 4th Queen's Own Hussars and was now a columnist for the New York *World Telegram* and a frequent contributor to Britain's *Daily Telegraph*. Several inches taller than his father, endowed with the same piercing blue eyes, and with his red-brown hair impeccably combed into a side parting, he cut a dashing figure on the platform.[1] Randolph would remain with his mother and sister in Washington, D.C., while his father accompanied Truman to Fulton, and the family would be reunited in the capital on March 7.

Before departing for Missouri, Churchill enjoyed fine hospitality again from Lord Halifax and his staff at the red-brick, U-shaped British Embassy, whose sprawling green lawn, symmetrical walled garden, and grand courtyard resembled those at English country estates. This was no coincidence—the building was designed in the late 1920s by prominent British architect Sir Edwin Lutyens, whose combination of Classical and Arts and Crafts styling gave his projects a distinctive appearance that made the residence of Britain's emissary stand out from the white stone construction of the capital's other government buildings.[2]

Once he had settled into Lutyens's fine accommodations, Churchill summoned Halifax and the two pored over every word of his upcoming speech. The ambassador, towering above Churchill, stared at the text with small, intent eyes. After reading the copy in his typically cautious, analytical manner, Halifax implored his countryman to cushion his Soviet indictment by adding a passage "showing that we recognize the propriety of Russia's desire for security on her frontiers and also her desire to be interested in all parts of the world as we were."[3]

Though the two had often been at loggerheads, most famously when Churchill lambasted Halifax for being one of Prime Minister Neville Chamberlain's "Men Of Munich" who allowed Hitler to acquire the Czech Sudetenland in September 1938, it was Halifax who declined Chamberlain's offer to take over the premiership, clearing the way for Churchill to assume power. Churchill, partly in ridicule but mostly in respect, had long ago dubbed his counterpart "The Holy Fox" for the combination of piety and political guile he displayed (not to mention the irresistible play on words). Whatever their differences in philosophy, personality, and delivery—Churchill the emotional, commanding speaker, Halifax rational and softly spoken—Churchill respected his colleague's keen intellect and measured approach. In addition, he felt that the ambassador had a unique ability, having been in Washington for several years, to appraise the potential reaction of the White House and the American public to his Fulton address.[4]

That evening, the two men dined with Clementine, Sarah, and Randolph in the majestic dining room in the Ambassador's Residence, its walls lined with twelve prints of the verdant English countryside painted by famed British artist Clare Leighton. Also present was Secretary of State James Byrnes, who, although used to the finery of official dinners, had not been in many settings that were more luxurious. As they talked about Churchill's trip to Missouri, the party sat on green leather chairs handmade in Brazil and ate with nineteenth-century gilded silverware from gold and cream Minton chinaware.

Following dinner, Churchill ushered Byrnes up the double-spiral staircase, past a Sir George Hayter coronation portrait of an eighteen-year-old Queen Victoria in her regal robes, and into his suite.[5] There he handed Byrnes the speech manuscript, complete with Halifax's suggested edits, for review. The next day, Byrnes regaled Truman with the details. At this point, Byrnes later revealed, Truman did not want to read Churchill's words, so that he could distance himself from them later if necessary (specifically, if the Russians were to accuse Britain and America of "ganging up" on them).[6]

As Byrnes briefed Truman, Churchill entertained Admiral Leahy, whom he wanted to peruse the speech that the Navy man had reviewed in its formative state back in early February. Leahy found Churchill in bed puffing away at a cigar, which deposited ashes all over the bed clothes and the discarded pages of the speech draft. Leahy wrote in his diary:

I could find no fault in his proposed address to the people of
America which will be of high interest also to the people of the
world. He told me that for the past week he has been distressed
by a vertigo that was at first severe and that still persists to a
much lesser degree. He is assured by his doctor that the trouble
is due to a digestive disorder and that it is not serious.[7]

Truman presided over a White House ceremony the following
morning, endorsing the proposed $3.75 billion loan to Britain
and calling for Congress to approve it because it represented "a
cornerstone in the world's structure of peace."[8] By making his
case for bolstering the U.K.'s foundering finances on this particular day, Truman reinforced Churchill's calls for continued and
closer Anglo-American solidarity. Indeed, *what* he was saying was
in some ways secondary to *when* he was saying it. He could have
picked any day to reveal to the world his position on the British
loan but chose the very one on which he would accompany England's most recognizable statesman to Truman's home state.

For Britain, congressional assent would provide a financial life-
line, and Truman's public support was of no little influence in the
congressional debate. For Churchill, gaining Truman's advocacy
was a diplomatic triumph that showed his commitment to putting
the national interest above all else, as he had always done.

The content of Truman's announcement fit well with unnamed
sources referred to in several American newspapers, which predicted that Churchill would call for common defense policy and
greater unity between the United States and Britain when he
spoke in Missouri. The Associated Press cited information from "a
strategically-placed British official" who revealed Churchill's
intention to appeal for "closely-welded Anglo-American solidarity
to guard the peace by continuing the cooperation of the war
years." A *New York Times* reporter had similar thoughts, speculat-
ing that Churchill's oratory "would contain a frank discussion of
the international tension created by Soviet diplomatic tactics."

And a writer in the *Kansas City Times* made an even bolder prediction, sharing his belief that Churchill would make "an anti-Red Plea."[9]

A few hours after the press conference, Truman dispatched a chauffeur on the two-mile drive to the British Embassy at 3100 Massachusetts Avenue to collect Churchill. The car then returned to the White House via Pennsylvania Avenue, where the unseasonably warm weather had coaxed out vibrant red pansies and purple-tinged white magnolias.[10] The Man from Missouri climbed into the back seat next to Churchill for the short first leg of their journey, and soon after, the black limousine pulled into Union Station.

In his enthusiasm, Churchill bounded out of the car first but went the wrong way across the asphalt until two Secret Service agents guided him back to the correct train platform. There stood the majestic, navy-blue *Ferdinand Magellan* presidential car, hooked to the end of more than a dozen other more modest ones and a great black locomotive engine. The *Ferdinand Magellan* had been built by the Pullman Company in 1928 and was acquired fourteen years later by the government for FDR's use, making it the first private railroad car assigned to a president. It would now convey Churchill and Truman's party 850 miles on the Baltimore and Ohio Railroad to St. Louis.[11] The train would then switch to the Missouri Pacific line on Tuesday morning for the quick jaunt to Jefferson City, Missouri.

Before getting under way, Churchill and Truman posed for photographers and three hundred onlookers on the observation deck at the back of the train—Truman looking dapper as an ex-haberdasher should in a gray suit, overcoat, and matching fedora. Churchill struck his familiar pose—black bowler hat, Havana framed by a broad grin, right arm aloft signaling "V" for victory. They then retired to their walnut-paneled coach and settled in for the trip to St. Louis as the locomotive puffed purposefully out of the station.

Winston Churchill, Major General Harry Vaughan, and Harry
Truman wave to the crowd at Union Station, Washington, D.C., on
March 4, 1946. CREDIT: NATIONAL CHURCHILL MUSEUM ARCHIVES,
CHURCHILL, TRUMAN, MCCLUER DAY COLLECTION, FOLDER 07,
IMAGE 07120

As the train pulled out, Truman asked Vaughan, "What do you
have to do to get a drink on this thing?" Vaughan called for a stew-
ard, who rushed in and presented the president and Churchill
with whiskey tumblers. The Briton held his glass aloft and,
swirling its golden brown contents meditatively, said, "You know,
when I was a young subaltern in the South African War, the water
was not fit to drink. To make it palatable, we had to put a bit of
whiskey in it. By diligent effort I learned to like it." Truman
laughed long and loudly.[12]

While Churchill, Truman, and company sipped their drinks,
the president said, "Now, Mr. Churchill, we are going to be together on this train for some time. I don't want to rest on formality
so I would ask you to call me Harry." Churchill smiled and
replied, "I would be delighted to call you Harry. But you must call

me Winston." It was Truman's turn for amusement. "I just don't know if I can do that," he said. "I have such admiration for you and what you mean, not only to your people, but to this country and the world." Churchill, feigning embarrassment, insisted, "Yes, you can. You must, or else I will not be able to call you Harry." Truman quickly assented. "Well, if you put it that way, Winston, I will call you Winston."

Naming conventions now agreed, the men moved on to more substantial matters. Truman told Churchill that he intended to demonstrate to Moscow the United States' commitment to preserving Greek and Turkish sovereignty (which was under threat from Communism) by sending the USS *Missouri* to return the body of the recently deceased Turkish ambassador, Mehmet Munir Ertegun, to his motherland.

Churchill affirmed this decision, telling Truman that it was "a very important act of state," which he believed would encourage Russia to "come to reasonable terms with the Western democracies."[13]

Meanwhile, in Fulton, a trailer for KXOK, the St. Louis ABC radio affiliate for whom Bullet had recorded several political commentary spots back in 1939, rolled slowly to a halt in front of Fulton's courthouse and parked on the lawn as permitted by city officials. To set the scene for Churchill's speech, the station's four-person crew would begin interviewing Fulton residents that evening and continue their coverage the following day. A few hundred yards down Court Street, organizing committee volunteers hung the last few pieces of bunting from storefronts, with town stenographer Margaret Sanders clambering up a step ladder to fix the banner of an eagle perched atop the Stars and Stripes on the brickwork of a Court Street store. Fulton barber Fred Carr had a full chair all day, ensuring that as many of Fulton's men as possible would have trimmed hair and clean-shaven chins to match their freshly pressed suits.[14]

Members of the Food Committee unloaded eight trucks of
bread and buns from St. Louis food distributors enlisted to help
Fulton's nineteen eateries, whose proprietors had quickly realized that the assistance offered by six church groups, three community clubs, and two civic clubs would not be sufficient to feed
the expected 20,000 visitors. Footsteps clanged heavily onto the
pullout metal gangways that led from the trucks to the pavement
below, as the volunteers groaned under the load of heavy food
crates.[15] With 8,000 pounds of hot dogs and 3,000 pounds of
hamburgers on hand, the food preparation team and the St.
Louis lunch vendors would need all the bread products they
could get, not to mention vats of mustard and ketchup, and
more pickles than the townsfolk themselves could consume in a
decade.

A cadre of Secret Service agents, who had arrived in town on
Friday, March 1, eyed the concession stands warily as they
strode past them, checking out the parade route one last time
with some of the five hundred state guardsmen sent to Fulton
for the occasion and the town's seven police officers. There were
also six detectives—three from Kansas City and three from St.
Louis—in the city to combat petty theft, though such a small
number faced a seemingly impossible task with the thousands of
onlookers who would soon line the streets. In case of emergency
during the parade, five medical stations were on hand, each with
its own ambulance. A mile north of the city, the farmers of Callaway County gathered as usual for their weekly livestock sale,
the only people in the area not consumed with the preparations
for Churchill and Truman's arrival.[16]

That morning, Southwestern Bell ran a full-page advertise-
ment in the *Fulton Sun Gazette*, informing residents about the
new telephone circuits that were installed in readiness for
Churchill's visit and reassuring them that plenty of operators
(such as the smiling, curly-haired young woman in the photo next
to the ad copy, about to plug a line into the switchboard) would

The day before her guests arrive, Ida Belle McCluer places name cards on the table where Churchill and Truman will be seated in her home. CREDIT: NATIONAL CHURCHILL MUSEUM ARCHIVES, CHURCHILL, TRUMAN, MCCLUER DAY COLLECTION, FOLDER 07, IMAGE 07023

be on hand to get calls through quickly, despite the expected surge in volume.[17]

At Westminster College, a local painter braved a rain shower and applied a fresh coat of whitewash to the McCluers' front porch. Inside, Ida Belle bustled around with a small army of volunteers, putting six angel food cakes in boxes, overseeing seating arrangements, and frequently checking on the Callaway County ham that would be the focal point of the main meal. Fulton grocer John Renner had delivered boxes of food for the big day, and Ida Belle's helpers were busy unloading the haul.[18] As his flustered wife bustled past, Bullet McCluer made the mistake of asking her to sit for a picture. With ham grease on her hands, a stained apron covering her floral print dress, and a thousand things still to get done, surely he was joking? "Not for seven billion dollars and five cents. I'm going to have a hot bath. I'm tired!" she said hurriedly. Then, fearing she had been too harsh with her husband, she added softly, "Tomorrow, alright."[19]

In the gymnasium where Churchill would speak in less than twenty-four hours, no detail was overlooked. The most elaborate preparations were the construction of an eighteen-by-six-foot wooden cubbyhole deck (originally built for Pathé, Universal, Fox, and Paramount newsreel cameras) positioned high above the floor at the south end and a second elevated platform brought from the Priest Field football pitch and modified for radio correspondents at the gym's east side. Volunteers had also spent weeks tinkering with less obvious intricacies. On the day before Churchill and Truman arrived, these helpers were everywhere, folding freshly ironed white linen on the dignitaries' chairs on the stage, placing bunches of greenery shipped from Atlanta under the two-story arched windows, and setting long-stemmed Roman roses and white- and pink-flowered huckleberry shrubs in sturdy pots to the back and side of the stage. Against a blue fabric backdrop, a lady carefully placed a large vase of vividly pink snapdragons. Above the clamor, some noble soul perched precariously atop an almost impossibly tall ladder performed the tiresome task of checking each light bulb, replacing duds, and polishing the reflectors.[20]

On the thin-planked wood stage from which Churchill would soon speak, the Westminster College choir tested the gym's PA system, newly installed by Fultonian Don O'Neill for the princely sum of $350. Their powers of concentration were tested by workmen making loud, last-minute adjustments to the stage. "The hymns could be heard blocks away, and the sound of a hammer rapping on a board . . . easily could have been mistaken for the reverberations of an 8-inch artillery piece," reported the *Kansas City Times*.[21]

Below them in the basement, Bell Telephone Company engineers tested and retested the direct lines for the press corps that they had spent the previous three weeks installing. Across the room, newly arrived operators for Western Union, some who had traveled from as far away as Denver, also sent trial communications.[22]

In the adjacent Administration Building, dozens of newly arrived reporters and photographers inundated Joe Humphreys's modest office to pick up their press credentials, with Humphreys checking each one off on his four-page list as he handed out laminated passes. They then joined more than 150 of their peers from local, national, and international media outlets, many of whom had been camped out in Fulton for more than a week, at the Fulton Country Club for a media luncheon arranged by the Fulton Chamber of Commerce. As the press corps ate, workmen

On March 4, 1946, Mrs. Zula Trigg checks on the Callaway County ham that will be served to Churchill and Truman the following day.
CREDIT: NATIONAL CHURCHILL MUSEUM ARCHIVES, CHURCHILL, TRUMAN, MCCLUER DAY COLLECTION, FOLDER 07, IMAGE 07060

scrubbed and spray-washed the six main campus buildings, including the buff brickwork and columns with Corinthian capstones at the front of the gymnasium, where opportunistic thieves took advantage of the frenetic preparations and stole two telephones and a microphone.[23]

Back on the *Ferdinand Magellan,* the president and ex–prime minister had quite an entourage with them on Truman's first railway trip back to his home state since assuming the highest office in the land the previous spring.

Accompanying Churchill were his trusty aide Frank Sawyers, Inspector Williams, British Embassy communications director Charles Campbell, Dr. Harris, and Jo Sturdee, who had transcribed Churchill's initial draft of "The Sinews of Peace," worked tirelessly to revise version after version, and would now help perfect the final iteration. Sturdee revealed in a letter to her parents that she almost stayed behind in Washington:

> As neither Mrs. C nor Mrs. Truman were going, as the President preferred a male party for such dos, I naturally assumed that Churchill would not take me. So there I was, scurrying as fast as possible through *the* speech, trying to get it typed up in time for him to take away—and grouping the piles of correspondence strewn all over the place to greet us at the Embassy.

Sturdee then reconstructed the exchange between herself and Churchill that led to her accompanying him to Fulton:

> MR. C: "Come along, come along, where are all my telegrams? Hasn't anything come from England? Surely there is a newspaper I can look at? What have you done with that red pen? Tell the Ambassador I want to see him. Where's Sawyers! Haven't you opened the post yet?" and so on.

ME: "I don't know, but I have to get your speech ready before you leave."

MR. C: "Why?"

ME: "Because I'm not coming."

MR. C: "What are you talking about?"

ME: (feeling like saying, "I don't know.") "Because the President doesn't like females."

MR. C: "What are you talking about?"

ME: "Oh, I thought you knew."

MR. C: "Of course you must come" (and various reasons why).

In the end it came to pass that after having flung office papers and a toothbrush into a suitcase that hadn't been unpacked or thought about since Miami, I tapped along feeling like another piece of baggage and looking like something emptied into the dustbin. I was very self-conscious about the fuss caused by my being added at the last minute and about being the only female and all that. But it's funny how one survives these things and quite enjoys them in the end. As a matter of fact I had a wonderful time.[24]

Truman was a little less madcap with his logistics, although he brought a much bigger group along, including legal counsel Clark Clifford, Admiral Leahy, press secretary Charles Ross, and the man who had helped McCluer and Truman facilitate the trip, their mutual friend Major General Harry Vaughan. The latter shared the sleeping quarters nearest the back of the train with Matthew J. Connelly, Truman's appointments secretary. Truman's cabin was next, with a bathroom separating him and Churchill. Admiral Leahy was in the car next to Churchill's. Then came the rooms for Ross, Churchill's party, and the seventeen aides and four communications assistants from the White House. They were joined by a large Secret Service detail, who occupied the middle cars as a buffer between the politicos and the media

correspondents—thirty-three reporters, thirteen radio broadcasters, ten newsreel photographers, and four print photographers.[25]

This large contingent had accommodations far different from
the luxurious appointments enjoyed by Churchill, Truman, and
company. David Brinkley, the veteran reporter who was on assignment from NBC, later recalled: "I and the other press were
put into cars up forward—a Pullman with roomettes, an ingen-
ious and highly uncomfortable space-saving invention of the
Pullman Company. At night, the seat folded down into a narrow
bed, and what was now the foot of the bed rested on the toilet
which, if needed during the night, required folding the bed back
up and then down again."[26] Despite their privations, the press-
men had unprecedented access to Truman and Churchill, which
was more than adequate compensation for a few hours of personal discomfort and missed sleep.

Less than an hour after disembarking from Washington on March
4, Truman took a tour of the train, shaking hands with writers,
photographers, and his Secret Service protectors as he worked his
leisurely way from his quarters near the back of the train to the
front.[27] With a wry grin, he told the writers that he was investigating "if there was any drinking or gambling going on." Once he had
reached the other end, Truman delighted the crew by borrowing
engineer J. L. Rock's hat and cotton gloves and taking a turn at the
controls of the diesel locomotive for a few minutes as the train
puffed through the rolling, verdant West Virginia countryside. After a few minutes he stood up and, as if striking a deal at a used-
car lot, told Rock, "I like it so much I think I'll buy it!"[28]

A few miles further down the track, with Truman seated
back in his cabin alongside Churchill, the Briton surprised the
president with his command of Civil War history by retelling
the tale of unlikely heroine Barbara Fritchie, who, according to
folklore, defiantly waved the Union flag as Stonewall Jackson

marched his Confederate troops through her home town of Frederick. Churchill proceeded to show off his skills of memorization by reciting the first stanza of the John Greenleaf Whittier poem written in her honor:

> *"Shoot, if you must, this old gray head,*
> *But spare my country's flag," she said.*
> *A shade of sadness, a blush of shame,*
> *Over the face of the leader came;*
> *The nobler nature within him stirred*
> *To life at that woman's deed and word;*
> *"Who touches a hair of yon gray head*
> *Dies like a dog! March on!" he said.*[29]

Churchill's recollections of the Civil War were far from perfect, though. When the train continued its rhythmic, almost hypnotic rumbling through Harper's Ferry, West Virginia, he remarked, "That's where Jackson seized McClellan's stores." He was correct in saying that it was the Confederate general who took the provisions, but the stores were actually under General Henry Halleck's command. Truman, graciously, did not risk offending his guest by pointing out the minor mistake.[30]

Later that afternoon, Churchill left Truman's party to work on the last iteration of "The Sinews of Peace" undisturbed, while Truman greeted onlookers from the rear platform (under which hung a banner with the white silhouette of the Washington Capitol Building dome) at the rural stations the train trundled through. When Charles Ross conveyed Churchill's diligence to the press corps, Brinkley recollected, he met with surprise and skepticism. "Most of us had barely ever heard of a politician writing his own speeches," Brinkley wrote. "Politicians did not write speeches, they read them. They hired people to write them." Harold B. Hinton, covering the event for the *New York Times*, spoke for all the assembled when he asserted, "Writes his own speeches? Maybe that's why they're so good."[31]

Hinton's assertion was bolstered by the positive reactions of the president, White House counsel Clark Clifford (another member of Truman's "Missouri Gang" of old home-state contacts who had received top posts), and Admiral Leahy to Churchill's final version. Clifford was "deeply impressed by its sweep and sense of history." Truman had told his staff that, just as with earlier drafts, he would not read the last revision for the sake of deniability after Churchill had spoken in Missouri; but according to Clifford, his curiosity got the better of him as his team sat around mulling over the text.

Clifford recalled Truman's prediction that Churchill was going to make "a brilliant and admirable statement" that would "create quite a stir." However, wary of escalating the tension with Moscow, Truman asked Clifford to insert some flattering comments about Stalin into the president's introduction for Fulton. In Clifford's opinion, Truman was conflicted by his hope to improve relations with Russia and his ever-growing mistrust of the marshal's intentions and methods. Yet, regardless of these mixed feelings and his concerns about how Churchill's speech would be received, it is evident that Truman read every word of Churchill's address and did not suggest or demand last-minute revisions. By inviting Churchill and sharing the platform with him in his home state, Truman endorsed the message, whatever Stalin or anyone else would make of the ex–prime minister's position.[32]

For Churchill, the chance to spend two full days with the president was invaluable. They had met only once before the Briton came to America, and their brief time at the Potsdam Conference, while endearing them to each other, was dominated by plenary sessions and noisy dinners with the Russian delegates that offered little occasion for substantial conversation. Though he was no longer prime minister, Churchill was still at his best when matching words and wits with another statesman, and now, after their February 10 conversation at the White House, he had an even better chance to develop his relationship with Truman— which he hoped could match his friendship with FDR.

The opportunity to spend uninterrupted time with Churchill was also useful for Truman. He had been vice president for a mere eighty-two days when FDR passed away and was just eleven months into the presidency as his train rumbled through the Midwest. Churchill, on the other hand, had occupied high office since 1908, when he became president of the Board of Trade (the British equivalent of secretary of commerce) and had held almost every Cabinet position since, except deputy prime minister and foreign secretary.[33] He had successfully led the Western democracies to victory and managed a fractious coalition government during his five years as prime minister, and Truman was eager to learn from him as he faced the prospect of a new conflict with Soviet Russia, tackled labor strikes and a dire housing shortage, and prepared for a fierce fight with the Republican Party in the forthcoming midterm elections.

As part of a tour of the train, Truman proudly showed Churchill that great symbol of American patriotism, the presidential seal, on the wall of the train car. "This may interest you," the president said. "We have just turned the eagle's head from the talons of war to the olive branch of peace." Churchill observed the fearsome bird for a moment and then quipped, "I have a suggestion to make. The head should be on a swivel so that it can turn from the talons of war to the olive branch of peace as the occasion warrants." He then remarked that the olive branch berries reminded him of atomic bombs. These comments revealed Churchill's mounting concern about American passivity in the face of Russian aggression and foreshadowed the contents of the speech he would give less than twenty-four hours later.

With the *Ferdinand Magellan* continuing its steady westward progress across the green arable land of northern Kentucky on the evening of March 4, Churchill turned to Truman and said, "Harry, I understand from the press that you like to play poker." Truman flashed a wry grin. "That's right, Winston, I've played a lot of poker in my life." Churchill claimed he had started playing the game some forty-five years earlier during the Boer War, and despite Truman's caution that his aides were all "serious poker players," a lengthy game ensued. Before it began, Truman took advantage of Churchill's brief departure to change his clothes by telling his men, only half in jest, to play hard, as "[t]he reputation of American poker is at stake."

Churchill soon returned, having swapped his formal attire for his blue "siren suit" (a soft cotton garment that, his family had often joked, resembled a baby's one-piece outfit, with a full-length zip running down the middle). Once Churchill took his seat, Truman, Vaughan, Ross, and Truman's physician Wallace Graham clustered around the dining table with him, to cut cards on a green baize that attendants had hastily laid down following dinner.

It was soon evident to all that Churchill had exaggerated his poker prowess, and when he again left the room for a moment, Truman admonished his countrymen for not going easier on the ex–prime minister: "I fear that he may already have lost close to three hundred dollars." Harry Vaughan, ever the joker, piped up: "But Boss, this guy's a pigeon. If you want us to play our best poker for the nation's honor, we'll have this guy's pants before the evening's over."

"I don't want him to think we're pushovers, but at the same time, let's not treat him badly," Truman implored. From then on, Churchill's "luck" improved enough that he actually won a few games. In a telling exchange, with Churchill and Charlie Ross the last two players in, Churchill wagered close to $100 and waited for Ross to respond. Ross had an almost unbeatable hand and yet, after pausing for a moment, decided to throw in his cards and allow Churchill the victory.

Despite taking this pot, Churchill was down $250 by the time the party turned in for the night.[34]

Just after daybreak on March 5, the *Ferdinand Magellan* crossed the Mississippi River that marks the Illinois/Missouri border, left the rural fields behind, and chugged past several miles of red-brick and concrete buildings. The train then arrived on time at St. Louis's Union Station at 8:45 A.M. As the crew readied their charge to switch lines, Truman, Churchill, and St. Louisian John W. Snyder (now Truman's director of reconversion) came out onto the rear balcony of their car to greet the well-wishers on the platform, Truman waving his fedora and Churchill temporarily holstering his smoking stogie in his left hand as he beamed at the cheering crowd.

After a few minutes, Truman stepped down onto the concrete platform to enthusiastically greet some old friends. Behind them in the front row of the crowd, a lady who had driven from Illinois to see Truman told her three-year-old grandson, "Wave to the President." The toddler demurred, despite persistent urging from his embarrassed grandmother. Truman leaned over the rail and said to Aloys Kaufmann, St. Louis's Republican mayor, "That little boy refuses to wave at me. He must be a Republican!"[35]

As the locomotive chugged along, the morning papers delivered to Missouri homes and newsstands reported that Iranian premier Ahmad Qavam had returned from Moscow burdened by six harsh demands issued by Stalin, the first being that the Teheran government "invite" the Red Army to remain in the country indefinitely. This occupation would end, Moscow insisted, only when Qavam and his Cabinet gave in to the other six requirements: recognizing the Soviet puppet regime in Azerbaijan, giving oil rights to the Kremlin, signing an alliance treaty with Russia, "coordinating" foreign policy, allowing the Red Army to organize Azerbaijani troops, and enabling Russia to station its troops in "strategic" positions throughout the country.[36] With Moscow's continuing bellicosity and seeming disregard for international opinion or national sovereignty, Churchill's impending speech, it seemed, could not have come at a more appropriate hour.

CHAPTER 8

"C-T Day":
Welcome to Fulton

Thousands lining the streets of Fulton, Missouri, cheer Winston Churchill and Harry Truman as their motorcade passes through the city on March 5, 1946. Credit: National Churchill Museum Archives, Churchill, Truman, McCluer Day Collection, Folder 07, Image 07141

My only worry when I'm preparing a speech—what to put in and what to leave out.

—Winston Churchill, explaining his speech-writing process to Ida Belle McCluer on March 5, 1946

ON THE MORNING OF MARCH 5, 1946, Fultonians looking at the front page of the *Fulton Sun-Gazette*'s extra edition found no date but, instead, "C-T Day" in a sweeping serif in the top-right corner. At 9:00 A.M., Bullet McCluer said good-bye to Ida Belle, opened his front door, and stepped out into bright sunshine that defied the Weather Bureau's gloomy, rain-filled forecast. Looking typically dapper in a tailored, three-piece gray suit and matching fedora with a thick black ribbon, he turned right, strolled along the narrow sidewalk past budding trees, and after three minutes came to Westminster Hall. There to meet him were his friend Tom Van Sant, who had encouraged his plan to invite Churchill; organizing committee chairman Truman Ingle; and Walter Head, president of Westminster's Board of Trustees. With them were the mayors of Jefferson City and Fulton among a group big enough to fill the thirty cars parked around the college's crescent driveway.[1]

At 11:20 A.M., the *Ferdinand Magellan* pulled into the Jefferson City station, located just west of the Mississippi and half a block north of the red-brick Governor's Mansion, instantly recognizable for its unusual, near-vertical Mansard roof. Churchill's attire was simple, if nonmatching—black jacket, waistcoat,

At Westminster College, Franc "Bullet" McCluer opens the door of his car on the way to greet Churchill and Truman, March 5, 1946. CREDIT: NATIONAL CHURCHILL MUSEUM ARCHIVES, CHURCHILL, TRUMAN, McCLUER DAY COLLECTION, FOLDER 07, IMAGE 07051

bowler hat, pin-striped trousers, and polka-dot bow tie, accented with a gold chain across his waist that was attached to his ever-present Breguet pocket watch, which he referred to as "the turnip" because of its great size.[2] Truman's brightly patterned tie gave a dash of color to his gray, double-breasted suit and matching fedora.

As the welcoming committee approached the train along the wide concrete platform, Secret Service agents checked McCluer's credentials and then welcomed him and the rest of the party aboard the president's train car to meet their guests. Five lucky students, each representing one of Westminster's fraternities and main student groups, also stood there, smiling nervously in the presence of the two dignitaries. Though neither Churchill nor Truman would ever be described as tall, they stood almost a head above McCluer as he came alongside them.[3]

Bullet grinned broadly as he shook hands with Churchill. After months of late nights and working weekends, not to mention his initial worries over Churchill's response to the Green Foundation invitation, the two unlikely partners had finally come together on the biggest day in McCluer's career. Against all odds, the man who symbolized the victory of the democratic West over Nazism was here, in little Jefferson City, Missouri—a place previously unknown to him.

With the entire town and thousands of visitors eagerly awaiting Churchill and Truman's arrival, Phil Donnelly proudly presented the two statesmen with the first gifts of the day. They were appropriate choices: a twenty-pound hickory-smoked Cole County ham for the president and, somewhat predictably, a hinged box of H. De Cabana Cuban cigars, made with fragrant tobacco from the fine 1939 crop, for Churchill. To make sure his guest had plenty for the ceremonial duties that day, Donnelly asked local tobacconist Wallace Simpson to pack fifty stogies into the cedar box.[4]

With the parade about to begin, Churchill and Truman sat on the back seat of the open-top black car, facing forward. McCluer, delighted that his big day was finally here, then got in opposite them, with Harry Vaughan and Donnelly squeezing in on either side of him. Arthur Hardimen checked his rearview mirror to make sure his passengers were ready, put Governor Donnelley's newly waxed and polished black Packard coupe into first gear, and began the slow crawl through Jefferson City's modest downtown. The cars carrying the presidential party and Churchill's group followed his lead, as the White House press corps took their places among the milling crowd, notebooks and flashbulbs at the ready.[5]

Rifle-wielding state guardsmen lined Jefferson City's main street, poised to intervene if anyone from the cheering, 10,000-strong crowd broke through the cordon. As the motorcade passed the Missouri Hotel, Churchill made a special point of waving to an elderly man who frailly returned the motion. McCluer asked Churchill to make this gesture to buoy the spirits of the ailing Dr. W. A. Simpson, a resident of the hotel who had been bed-ridden for six weeks.[6] After the brief parade, the party switched to hard-top cars for the twenty-four-mile northeast ride to Fulton, but there was trouble ahead. As Churchill's car passed groups of by-standers waving flags on the outskirts of the city, smoke billowed from the hood, and the car—by now making an awful grinding sound—slowed to an inglorious halt. This was not what McCluer had in mind for his guest of honor. To his relief, all was not lost, Jo Sturdee recalled: "[O]ut we have to get & into the only spare car there, the open Presidential car. . . . [Then we went] along the roads at 70 mph—hair flying—until they decide they want their open car again for the crowds at Fulton. So out we get again, with looks from both of them [Churchill and Truman] as much to say 'What do you mean by riding in our car?' and into the closed Presidential car. And that is the closest I shall get to fame . . . poor me!"[7]

Fultonians and visitors who had come from across America in the preceding week assembled before Churchill and Truman even arrived in Jefferson City. Thankfully, the gloomy weather forecast proved incorrect, and even at 8:00 A.M. they were greeted by an unexpectedly temperate 59 degrees.[8] Once the out-of-towners parked or disembarked from Southwestern Greyhound buses that arrived hourly, they followed signs into the business district, which was closed to traffic for the day to ensure the parade route was clear.

In town, they encountered a lively group of traders offering commemorative pennants, pins, and other trinkets from hastily assembled stalls set up outside the two-story red and white brick stores. The "balloon men," dressed in their gaudy "Churchill-Truman Day" hats and sporting even brighter signs to advertise their wares, did a roaring trade with the town's children, whose obliging parents were too focused on the arrival of the great men to put up much resistance to their offspring's high-pitched demands.[9] Down Court Street and opposite the courthouse, a dapper forty-something gentleman clad in a gray three-piece suit, fedora, and matching overcoat stood underneath a "No Parking" sign tied to one of the black cast-iron lampposts that punctuated the sidewalk. Beside him was a sandwich board that mirrored the design of the triangular pennants he was offering— a black background with three lines of white serif text:

WELCOME TO FULTON
TRUMAN AND CHURCHILL
MARCH 5TH 1946.

The stores themselves were also ringing up their cash registers as fast as clerks could punch the buttons. Twelve staff members opened Mattingly's dime store on Court Street at 8:00 A.M., selling candy, coffee, and soda to lines of customers eager to stock up before the parade.[10] Fourteen-year-old Glenn Acree ran excitedly from his home on East 7th Street to the Old Spot Café a block away. Genial owner Conway Brown handed him several dozen ham sandwiches that he offered the entrepreneurial teen at cost so he could resell them to hungry visitors. Not wanting to waste time or potential sales, Acree hurriedly stuffed his wares into an ice-filled cooler. He was hoping to also obtain several kinds of soda, but Brown had only Dr. Pepper left, with its distinctive red swirling logo and "Good for You" slogan. Disappointed but undeterred, Acree bought as many eight-ounce glass bottles as would fit in his cooler, placing them carefully alongside the sandwiches and tightly closing the lid.

Bidding Brown good-bye, Acree left the café and a couple of minutes later reached the forecourt of the Skelly Oil gas station, which his father managed. Acree, wiping away the sweat from his eyes, set the cooler down near one of the three fire-engine red pumps, with the bold Skelly "S" stamped on a blue diamond in the center of each. Hailing passersby on the sidewalk in front of him, he yelled, "Ham sandwiches, 25 cents! Cold Dr. Pepper!" Down Court Street, catering companies' portable grills exuded the unmistakable smells of browning hot dogs and hamburgers, compelling those who inhaled them to indulge. Once finished with their char-grilled sandwiches, Fultonians and visitors besieged one drugstore selling "Churchill and Truman Sundaes."[11]

By mid-morning, the crowd had grown to several thousand. Bands from the two local military academies marched up and down the street, and the Fulton High band played well-known ditties, including "The Missouri Waltz." This was included in the set list wherever Truman went, to honor his home state; but, unbeknownst to Fulton's musicians, he detested the song.[12] People enjoyed the music but also continued to purchase goods from the street vendors. Bill Johnson, a newspaper boy for the *Fulton Sun-Gazette*, plied a thriving trade selling the extra edition for a nickel as he carried his rapidly diminishing stack up and down the sidewalk.[13]

As their car climbed Hockaday Hill just outside Fulton, Churchill tapped McCluer's arm and said, "Have them stop this car a moment. I can't light my cigar in this wind, and I know the people will be expecting it." Arthur Hardimen halted the Packard as Churchill fired up a Havana, and they were under way again.[14] The adornments of the open-topped car—British and American flags on the hood, with three gray-suited Secret Service agents and Inspector Williams on the running boards—made it easy for the crowd to identify the guests of honor. Churchill and Truman held on to the back of the car as they stood in the rear foot-well. To protect the statesmen, police motorcycles and two armored personnel carriers full of state guardsmen followed the procession, though the festive mood made their presence seem a little heavy-handed.[15]

When the ten-deep crowd caught sight of Churchill and Truman they cheered unreservedly, surely the loudest clamor the small town had ever created. People stood anywhere they could find a spot—in shop doorways, on the concrete wall outside the court house, and on previously well-manicured church lawns they would not dare defile on a Sunday. Fathers held giddy, wriggly children aloft on their shoulders for a better look as the motorcade came into view. Teenagers jostled each other for prime positions at the roadside. Fulton's older citizens favored slow, dignified waves.[16]

As in Jefferson City, people also jammed into second- and third-floor rooms above shops and businesses. Among them was Glenn Acree, who left his sandwiches and soda at Skelly Oil to get a better view from the window of the Wilson Overstreet Insurance Agency, above the Callaway County Bank on 5th Street. "I was so excited," he recalled. "After all, it's not every day that the President *and* Winston Churchill visit your little home town." Bill Johnson, his fingers blackened by newspaper, sought an even loftier view, clambering up a staircase at the back of the RexAll drugstore and onto the roof.[17]

The motorcade passed underneath the white-and-red-striped bunting strung across the road, which framed giant British and American flags and homemade signs—"Welcome Visitors," "Welcome President Truman," and "Welcome Churchill." The dignitaries waved as the car rattled across the cobblestones, moving slowly enough for two White House photographers jogging alongside to keep pace.

As they made their way east, the party passed through a residential neighborhood, with a gaggle of teenagers running helter-skelter along the sidewalk next to the cars.[18] The red-brick houses with white siding and big front porches likely reminded Truman of his hometown of Independence, Missouri, just a couple of hours away.

The motorcade drove past Westminster College's striking six Grecian columns, looming like giant sentries from a bygone age on the front lawn, and climbed the horseshoe-shaped driveway to the McCluers' two-story, yellow-brick home. They were just in time—dark clouds gathered threateningly overhead.[19] After pausing on the porch to give the photographers more fodder for the evening papers, Churchill followed McCluer to the front door. There to welcome him stood Ida Belle McCluer, who, despite the frantic preparations, had kept her new golden suit and red and white floral necktie spotless, her auburn hair pinned up just so. "May I bring this old stogy [sic] into your house?" Churchill asked her, grinning as he glanced lovingly at his Havana. Well used to the aroma of tobacco from her husband's pipe smoking, Ida Belle gladly assented.

She had expected to see Churchill with the familiar cigar and "that jutting jaw that . . . portrayed his Blood, Sweat and Tears [sic] character," but Ida Belle was not overawed by his presence: "I was surprised to find him a smaller man than I had always visualized him. With all the strength and courage he had shown toward England's dark days, I guess I was looking for a physical giant, too. When I shook hands with him, I thought how very soft his hands were, almost like a baby's."[20]

Churchill and Truman carefully picked their way through the McCluers' hallway, weaving between several drop-leaf tables that would seat sixty for lunch. As the party walked across the main floor, their noses were treated to a waft of the sweet-smelling cured ham. Ida Belle had reviewed every detail in the dining room countless times—the two black vases with matching floral prints on the mantel were evenly spaced, the simple brown oak chairs pulled out six inches from the white-clothed table, and the place settings and pink snapdragon centerpiece assembled with the precision of a royal butler. Small white cards, each folded into a peak, indicated where each guest should sit: Truman and Churchill on either side of Ida Belle, Bullet facing her, with John Raeburn Green (son of the Green Foundation Lectures benefactor) on his left and Phil Donnelly on his right.[21]

The meal began with a fine spread: Idaho potatoes twice-baked with cream, seasoning, and cheese, buttered asparagus tips, Missouri fried chicken, tomato aspic salad, and Mrs. Trigg's famed hot rolls. The guests did not know the pains to which Ida Belle had gone in acquiring this food despite postwar rationing, nor that they were eating from borrowed china and silverware.[22]

As he sat down, Churchill asked Ida Belle a question, but to her embarrassment she could not understand his accent. Truman intervened, telling her that Churchill was wondering if Fulton was considered part of the "Bible Belt." She wasn't sure and quickly changed the subject, asking him if he was nervous about the speech. "My only worry when I'm preparing a speech [is]— what to put in and what to leave out." He paused and, looking at Truman, added, "I am more anxious to know what that man across the table will think of it."

She then asked about politics in England, and in jest Churchill said: "You know, I am only a defeated candidate." A moment later, Truman announced the arrival of the meal's star attraction: "This is that famous Callaway County ham." The McCluers watched Churchill anxiously as he took a bite. He said nothing at first, but quickly polished off the rest of the helping. Indicating that he would like more, he told Ida Belle, "I believe the pig has reached its highest state of evolution in this ham."[23]

The main course soon over, Truman Ingle (Missouri School for the Deaf president and head of the day's organizing committee) and two of his female students presented a gold, four-by-three-inch card to Churchill. Underneath each letter of his name was a tiny hand with the equivalent sign-language symbol, and between "Winston" and "Churchill" was a bigger palm, its forefinger and middle finger spread in Churchill's trademark "V" for victory.

Churchill was so engrossed in studying the unique gift that he momentarily forgot to thank them. Realizing his omission, he smiled warmly and gave the "V" sign. Delighted, the girls returned the acknowledgment. After taking his fill of the angel food cake and ice cream dessert, Churchill leaned back, crossed one leg over the other, and lit a cigar. He then opened the box given to him by Governor Donnelly that morning and passed out Havanas to the other guests. Across campus, Jo Sturdee, Frank Sawyers, and Inspector Williams ate a less elaborate meal. Sturdee recounted washing down a sandwich with a bottle of Coca Cola, amid "a scrum with the hoard of Press men, cable men, broadcasting engineers & all the rest."[24]

Just after 1:15 P.M., as the day's guests of honor were still eating, Secret Service agents admitted the first ticketholders—the

A crowd of 2,800 people squeeze into the Westminster College gym to hear Winston Churchill deliver what became known as "The Iron Curtain Speech," March 5, 1946. CREDIT: McCLUER FAMILY ARCHIVES, PROVIDED BY RICHMOND McCLUER, JR.

men in fedoras and freshly pressed suits and the women sporting dresses and floral hats as they filed into the gymnasium in a jovial mood.[25] The small field house, with its "steel girders overhead, brick walls and athletic trophies in the vestibule" as an AP reporter described it, had completed its transformation into the staging ground for an international political event. On the four exposed brick interior walls were United Nations standards, American and British flags, and a large rectangular "Westminster" pennant, signifying the college's role in facilitating this unlikely event. A few hundred yards east, volunteers seated nine hundred ticketless people in the pews of Swope Chapel, where they would hear Churchill's address through two loudspeakers. The two-way audio connection would send organ music played by William Woods College music instructor Rachel Hinman into the gym during the processional hymns. Less than a mile away at Hinman's school, several hundred more packed the gym for the same purpose, with the scene repeated at Fulton's four churches. At the Missouri School for the Deaf, teachers readied themselves to interpret Churchill's oration to their students with sign language.[26]

Over at the McCluer house, Bullet showed Churchill into a bedroom borrowed for the Briton's customary post-lunch nap from his twenty-six-year-old son, Richmond, who was leaving town the next day for graduate school. McCluer then showed Truman and Admiral William Leahy into their rooms and joined the rest of the presidential party in the fourth bedroom, now a makeshift sitting area.[27] An hour later, Truman instructed Vaughan to find some scotch for Churchill. Vaughan dutifully went out to the crowded Westminster College lawn and asked a friend to obtain the liquor. The man dashed off toward town and returned a few minutes later with a pint bottle barely concealed by his bulging pocket. Going into the McCluers' kitchen, Vaughan grabbed an ice bucket and a glass, climbed the stairs, and rapped on Churchill's door. "Mr. Prime Minister, the President seems to think that you need a little sustenance before you go over to make the speech," he said.

"General, I am certainly delighted," Churchill replied with a grin as he opened the door. "You see, I was cogitating whether I was in Fulton, Missouri, or Fulton, Sahara!"[28]

Now refreshed, Churchill donned the red robe and wide black velvet tam-o'-shanter of a Doctor of Civil Law of Oxford University. He then bustled out of the room, leaving Vaughan in his wake, and clomped down the stairs after McCluer and Truman. His black overcoat, which he had cast aside before getting into bed, lay abandoned on an armchair. In the McCluers' living room, a photographer's flashbulb caught Churchill unawares and he recoiled from the noise. Gathering himself, he quipped, "There must be a Russian in the house."[29]

Missouri Governor Phil Donnelly, Winston Churchill, Harry Truman, and Franc "Bullet" McCluer share a joke at McCluer's home on March 5, 1946. CREDIT: HARRY S. TRUMAN LIBRARY

Meanwhile, at the gymnasium, Ida Belle prepared to take her seat. Suddenly realizing that she had left her hat and gloves in the guest room used by Admiral Leahy, she went to the door and was about to walk back to her house when a Secret Service agent informed her that he would soon close the doors. She aired her problem, and the kindly fellow ran to get her effects.[30]

Moments later, ticketless Westminster College alumnus Art Whorton, who had returned to his home town after serving in the U.S. Navy, followed a group of *Time* and *Life* photographers into the gym, slinging his camera around his neck and placing his military ID on his hat brim in place of press credentials. Somehow, he got past the security detail and found one remaining empty seat near the stage. Two hundred others who did have valid tickets were not so lucky, and were turned away from the overcrowded gym.[31]

Those who did get a seat were crammed together on bleachers and chairs, but it was an even tighter squeeze for the dozens of journalists and photographers in the media box. Below them in the basement, the locker room was now a staging area for thirty-five Western Union operators, with speakers on the wall to relay Churchill's words. Electrical wires snaked across the tile floor—a hazard for anyone careless with his or her foot placement. Alongside the Western Union employees sat typing teacher Helen Means, recruited the day before to transcribe Churchill's speech for the Fulton organizing committee. And across the room stood Howard Lange, a local court reporter who was poised to record Churchill's words in shorthand. He was the only one to handwrite the speech in its entirety, putting his version in great demand from reporters who found this out afterward.[32]

Just before 3:00 P.M., McCluer, Churchill, Truman, and the rest filed out of the college president's front door and took the short walk to Westminster Hall. Seeing them coming, college marshal Charles "Dog" Lamkin led the academic procession out of the double doors, down the concrete steps, and along the sidewalk. The two lines merged and continued toward the gym, walking two by two at a brisk clip behind students bearing the Stars and Stripes and the Union Jack on flagpoles and members of the school's Skulls of Seven society, clad in hooded black robes.[33] Standing behind a thick rope cordon, onlookers murmured encouragement to the passing dignitaries, respectfully lowering their voices so as not to interfere with the formal procession.

Entering the gym, Churchill and Truman were greeted by the hymn "How Firm a Foundation"—a fitting song given the transatlantic wartime partnership. Once they were situated on the white cloth–covered stage, the audience rose to sing "The Star Spangled Banner" and "God Save the King." Legal counsel Clark Clifford looked out from his vantage point beside Truman and saw a well-turned-out crowd: "professors in their academic robes, young clean-cut students, and well-dressed townspeople all squeezed together on wooden bleachers." Their only respite from the accumulated body heat and glare of the lights was the cool breeze from the gym windows, which had been opened several hours before.[34] Still, on the stage, Churchill and Harry Vaughan mopped their brows several times with white handkerchiefs.

Following the anthems, Reverend William Lampe from St. Louis's West Presbyterian Church rose to deliver the invocation. He reminded the audience of "the common ideal of justice which has bound our two countries" and prayed that God would give Churchill "insight into and an understanding of Thy will and courage to declare it." McCluer, with typical ease at the speaker's podium, then stated his hope that Churchill and Truman's visit would "emphasize the importance to all mankind of the ideals of political liberty cradled in England and nourished here as there."

As the president made his opening remarks, Churchill leaned over to Inspector Williams, the Scotland Yard detective appointed as his bodyguard for the America trip, and whispered, "I haven't

got my coat—I want it." Williams crept off the stage, trying not to
distract the crowd from Truman's address, and found Frank
Sawyers, who ran back to the McCluers' house and retrieved the
required article from the spare bedroom. Sawyers then sprinted
back to the gym, bounded up the steps, negotiated his way past
the Secret Service agents, and squeezed through the crowd,
which was "clapping and stamping" as Truman uttered the final
lines: "Mr. Churchill, a great Englishman, is half American. He
and I believe in freedom of speech. . . . I know he will have something constructive to say. . . . [I]t is one of the great privileges of
my life to be able to present to you that great world citizen, Winston Churchill." As applause for Truman echoed around the gym,
an out-of-breath Sawyers handed Churchill's coat to a relieved
Inspector Williams. Offering it to Churchill, Williams was dum-
founded upon being "pushed aside as if quite crazy" by his charge
as he strode toward the podium.[35]

CHAPTER 9

"THE SINEWS OF PEACE"

Winston Churchill stands at a podium in the Westminster College gymnasium to deliver "The Sinews of Peace," March 5, 1946. CREDIT: NATIONAL CHURCHILL MUSEUM ARCHIVES, CHURCHILL, TRUMAN, MCCLUER DAY COLLECTION, FOLDER 07, IMAGE 07058A

PRESIDENT MCCLUER, LADIES AND GENTLEMEN, AND, LAST, but certainly not least, the President of the United States. I am glad to come to Westminster College this afternoon, and am complimented that you should give me a degree. The name "Westminster" is somehow familiar to me. I seem to have heard of it before. Indeed, it was at Westminster that I received a very large part of my education in politics, dialectic, rhetoric, and one or two other things. In fact we have both been educated at the same, or similar, or, at any rate, kindred establishments.

It is also an honor, perhaps almost unique, for a private visitor to be introduced to an academic audience by the President of the United States. Amid his heavy burdens, duties, and responsibilities—unsought but not recoiled from—the President has traveled a thousand miles to dignify and magnify our meeting here today and to give me an opportunity of address-ing this kindred nation, as well as my own countrymen across the ocean, and perhaps some other countries too.* The Presi-dent has told you that it is his wish, as I am sure it is yours, that I should have full liberty to give my true and faithful coun-sel in these anxious and baffling times.**

---

* Indeed, were it not for President Truman's postscript on McCluer's invitation, Churchill would at that moment likely have been sitting on Frank Clarke's Miami patio in the heat and humidity, recording another brilliant Atlantic vista with brush, oils, and canvas.

** Here, Churchill was assuring his audience that his intentions were noble and his upcoming words reliable. His use of the phrase *anxious and baffling times* in-troduced tension to his listeners, as a herald of things to come.

I shall certainly avail myself of this freedom, and feel the more right to do so because any private ambitions I may have cherished in my younger days have been satisfied beyond my wildest dreams. Let me, however, make it clear that I have no official mission or status of any kind, and that I speak only for myself. There is nothing here but what you see.*

I can therefore allow my mind, with the experience of a lifetime, to play over the problems which beset us on the morrow of our absolute victory in arms, and to try to make sure with what strength I have that what has been gained with so much sacrifice and suffering shall be preserved for the future glory and safety of mankind.

The United States stands at this time at the pinnacle of world power. It is a solemn moment for the American Democracy. For with primacy in power is also joined an awe-inspiring accountability to the future. If you look around you, you must feel not only the sense of duty done but also you must feel anxiety lest you fall below the level of achievement. Opportunity is here now, clear and shining for both our countries. To

---

* Humor aside, this was a significant statement. Churchill was not on an Attlee-endorsed diplomatic quest, though the prime minister and the Truman administration knew full well the contents of his speech and had given their assent. The second sentence is the more significant, if only in subtext. What the audience saw was the former prime minister flanked by the president of the United States and his leading advisers. So, if they focused on "nothing" but what was in front of them, they, and Stalin, could not fail to behold unity between Churchill and Truman—and, ergo, Britain and America. (For this insight I am indebted to Larry P. Arnn, with whom I conversed on September 28, 2010.)

reject it or ignore it or fritter it away will bring upon us all the long reproaches of the after-time.

It is necessary that constancy of mind, persistency of purpose, and the grand simplicity of decision shall guide and rule the conduct of the English-speaking peoples in peace as they did in war. We must, and I believe we shall, prove ourselves equal to this severe requirement.*

When American military men approach some serious situation they are wont to write at the head of their directive the words "overall strategic concept." There is wisdom in this, as it leads to clarity of thought. What then is the overall strategic concept which we should inscribe today? It is nothing less than the safety and welfare, the freedom and progress, of all the homes and families of all the men and women in all the lands.** And here I speak particularly of the myriad cottage or apartment homes where the wage-earner strives amid the accidents and difficulties of life to guard his wife and children from privation and bring the family up in the fear of the Lord, or upon ethical conceptions which often play their potent part.***

---

* Churchill was giving the United States and Britain a simple choice: to be distracted by past achievements and thus let a dangerous malaise creep in, or to be purposeful in living up to the new tests of the present and future.

** This reference to homes and families transformed a politically focused statement into a personal, even sentimental appeal to all present in the gymnasium, and to millions not present. In short, Churchill was doing what he had done in his most effective wartime statements—connecting lofty goals with real people. This particular quote paraphrased the speech he had given in the House of Commons on August 16, 1945.

*** Here, Churchill paraphrased a verse from the book of Ephesians that this

To give security to these countless homes, they must be shielded from the two giant marauders, war and tyranny. We all know the frightful disturbances in which the ordinary family is plunged when the curse of war swoops down upon the bread-winner and those for whom he works and contrives. The awful ruin of Europe, with all its vanished glories, and of large parts of Asia glares us in the eyes.

When the designs of wicked men or the aggressive urge of mighty States dissolve over large areas the frame of civilized society, humble folk are confronted with difficulties with which they cannot cope. For them all is distorted, all is broken, even ground to pulp.

When I stand here this quiet afternoon I shudder to visualize what is actually happening to millions now and what is going to happen in this period when famine stalks the earth. None can compute what has been called "the unestimated sum of human pain." Our supreme task and duty is to guard the homes of the common people from the horrors and miseries of another war. We are all agreed on that.*

Presbyterian college audience would have been well acquainted with: "And here I speak particularly of the myriad cottage or apartment homes where the wage-earner strives . . . to guard his wife and children from privation and bring the family up in the fear of the Lord."

* At face value, the We here referred to "me, the speaker, and you, my audience." Yet, considering the beginning of the speech, the pronoun may have had a second meaning as well—namely, "I, Winston Churchill, and the President of the United States, who is sitting beside me on this stage."

Our American military colleagues, after having proclaimed
their "overall strategic concept" and computed available
resources, always proceed to the next step—namely, the
method. Here again there is widespread agreement. A world
organization has already been erected for the prime purpose
of preventing war. UNO, the successor of the League of Nations, with the decisive addition of the United States and all
that means, is already at work. We must make sure that its
work is fruitful, that it is a reality and not a sham, that it is a
force for action, and not merely a frothing of words, that it is
a true temple of peace in which the shields of many nations
can some day be hung up, and not merely a cockpit in a
Tower of Babel.* Before we cast away the solid assurances of
national armaments for self-preservation we must be certain
that our temple is built, not upon shifting sands or quagmires,
but upon the rock.** Anyone can see with his eyes open that
our path will be difficult and also long, but if we persevere together as we did in the two world wars—though not, alas, in
the interval between them—I cannot doubt that we shall
achieve our common purpose in the end.

I have, however, a definite and practical proposal to make for
action. Courts and magistrates may be set up but they can-

---

* Biblical allusion in this speech was powerful and compelling, and in Churchill's
hands created a vivid mental picture of what an impotent United Nations could
become. His use of the "Tower of Babel" metaphor was a powerful warning of the
potential divisions between the English-speaking peoples.
** In Churchill's version of this New Testament metaphor, inaction in the face of
new threats was the treacherous sand, and transatlantic unity of purpose and action the rock.

not function without sheriffs and constables. The United Nations Organization must immediately begin to be equipped with an international armed force. In such a matter we can only go step by step, but we must begin now. I propose that each of the Powers and States should be invited to delegate a certain number of air squadrons to the service of the world organization. These squadrons would be trained and prepared in their own countries, but would move around in rotation from one country to another. They would wear the uniform of their own countries but with different badges. They would not be required to act against their own nation, but in other respects they would be directed by the world organization. This might be started on a modest scale and would grow as confidence grew. I wished to see this done after the first world war, and I devoutly trust it may be done forthwith.

It would nevertheless be wrong and imprudent to entrust the secret knowledge or experience of the atomic bomb, which the United States, Great Britain, and Canada now share, to the world organization, while it is still in its infancy. It would be criminal madness to cast it adrift in this still agitated and un-united world. No one in any country has slept less well in their beds because this knowledge and the method, and the raw materials to apply it, are at present largely retained in American hands. I do not believe we should all have slept so soundly had the positions been reversed and if some Communist or neo-Fascist State monopolized for the time being these dread agencies. The fear of them alone might easily have been used to enforce totalitarian systems upon the free democratic world, with consequences appalling to human imagination.*

God has willed that this shall not be and we have at least a breathing space to set our house in order before this peril has to be encountered: and even then, if no effort is spared, we should still possess so formidable a superiority as to impose effective deterrents upon its employment, or threat of employment, by others. Ultimately, when the essential brotherhood of man is truly embodied and expressed in a world organization with all the necessary practical safeguards to make it effective, these powers would naturally be confided to that world organization.

Now I come to the second danger of these two marauders which threatens the cottage, the home, and the ordinary people—namely, tyranny. We cannot be blind to the fact that the liberties enjoyed by individual citizens throughout the British Empire are not valid in a considerable number of countries, some of which are very powerful. In these States control is enforced upon the common people by various kinds of all-embracing police governments.** The power of

---

* As George Kennan had done in his "Long Telegram," Churchill was contending that Stalin's desire to impose anti-democratic principles upon the free world was every bit as strong as Hitler's had been. Churchill was also issuing a retort to Foreign Secretary Molotov's recent claims that Russia would soon have atomic weaponry, while foreshadowing the forthcoming arms race. (See George Kennan, *Memoirs* 1925–1950 [New York: Pantheon, 1983], 303.)

** Here, Churchill contrasted the righteousness of liberal democratic values with the malevolent and all-consuming power of totalitarian rule. In the minds of some in the United States and in Britain in March 1946, the genial "Uncle Joe" Stalin was merely conducting an experiment in a new form of governance, and Communism was little different from the domestic form of socialism with which they were

the State is exercised without restraint, either by dictators or by compact oligarchies operating through a privileged party and a political police. It is not our duty at this time when difficulties are so numerous to interfere forcibly in the internal affairs of countries which we have not conquered in war. But we must never cease to proclaim in fearless tones the great principles of freedom and the rights of man which are the joint inheritance of the English-speaking world and which through Magna Carta, the Bill of Rights, the Habeas Corpus, trial by jury, and the English common law find their most famous expression in the American Declaration of Independence.*

All this means that the people of any country have the right, and should have the power by constitutional action, by free unfettered elections, with secret ballot, to choose or change the character or form of government under which they dwell;

---

familiar. However, they knew little of the purges, the gulag, or the famine caused by forced agricultural collectivization—which, all told, had claimed more than 5 million lives. This was not the right forum for discussing these horrors, yet Churchill wanted to make it clear that Communism was not benign. Rather, he knew it to be a brutal system under which freedom of the individual, the ballot box, and the press was forbidden.

* Churchill deliberately echoed Thomas Jefferson's 1801 inaugural address, which stated that all peoples are entitled to "freedom of religion, freedom of the press, and freedom of person under the protection of the habeas corpus, and trial by juries impartially selected." It was no coincidence that the 145th anniversary of Jefferson's inaugural address had been the day before Churchill spoke. Speaking in a town that had voted for the Democratic Party for generations, Churchill knew his audience would also be familiar with FDR's restatement of the "Four Freedoms" from January 1941. (See Thomas Jefferson, *The Papers of Thomas Jefferson, Volume 33: 17 February to 30 April 1801*, edited by Barbara B. Oberg [Princeton: Princeton University Press, 2006], 148–152.)

that freedom of speech and thought should reign; that courts of justice, independent of the executive, unbiased by any party, should administer laws which have received the broad assent of large majorities or are consecrated by time and custom. Here are the title deeds of freedom which should lie in every cottage home.

Here is the message of the British and American peoples to mankind. Let us preach what we practice—let us practice what we preach.

I have now stated the two great dangers which menace the homes of the people: War and Tyranny. I have not yet spoken of poverty and privation which are in many cases the prevailing anxiety. But if the dangers of war and tyranny are removed, there is no doubt that science and cooperation can bring in the next few years to the world, certainly in the next few decades newly taught in the sharpening school of war, an expansion of material well-being beyond anything that has yet occurred in human experience. Now, at this sad and breathless moment, we are plunged in the hunger and distress which are the aftermath of our stupendous struggle; but this will pass and may pass quickly, and there is no reason except human folly or subhuman crime which should deny to all the nations the inauguration and enjoyment of an age of plenty.

I have often used words which I learned fifty years ago from a great Irish-American orator, a friend of mine, Mr. Bourke Cockran: "There is enough for all. The earth is a generous mother; she will provide in plentiful abundance food for all her children if they will but cultivate her soil in justice and in peace." So far I feel that we are in full agreement.

Now, while still pursuing the method of realizing our overall strategic concept, I come to the crux of what I have traveled here to say. Neither the sure prevention of war nor the continuous rise of world organization will be gained without what I have called the fraternal association of the English-speaking peoples. This means a special relationship between the British Commonwealth and Empire and the United States.* This is no time for generalities, and I will venture to be precise. Fraternal association requires not only the growing friendship and mutual understanding between our two vast but kindred systems of society, but the continuance of the intimate relationship between our military advisers, leading to common study of potential dangers, to the similarity of weapons and manuals of instructions, and to the interchange of officers and cadets at technical colleges. It should carry with it the continuance of the present facilities for mutual security by the joint use of all Naval and Air Force bases in the possession of either country all over

---

* The phrase *special relationship* was a natural progression of Churchill's life-long fascination with the shared history and destiny of America and Britain—a fascination encapsulated by the press statement he composed on July 26, 1918: "In the community of interest & union of spirit & brotherhood in arms now being re-created between the American people and British race lies the most solid guarantee of our common safety, and in years to come, the general peace and progress of the world." As Churchill spoke in the Westminster College Gym, Truman retained a relaxed position, joining in the applause when it was given and appearing at ease with Churchill's sentiments. (See Martin Gilbert, *Churchill and America* [New York: Free Press, 2005], xxii; Winston S. Churchill, unreleased press statement, July 26, 1918 quoted in Martin Gilbert, ed., *The Churchill Documents, Volume 8: War and Aftermath: December 1916–June 1919* [Hillsdale, Mich.: Hillsdale College Press, 2008], 366.)

the world. This would perhaps double the mobility of the American Navy and Air Force. It would greatly expand that of the British Empire Forces and it might well lead, if and as the world calms down, to important financial savings. Already we use together a large number of islands; more may well be entrusted to our joint care in the near future.

The United States has already a Permanent Defense Agreement with the Dominion of Canada, which is so devotedly attached to the British Commonwealth and Empire. This Agreement is more effective than many of those which have often been made under formal alliances. This principle should be extended to all British Commonwealths with full reciprocity. Thus, whatever happens, and thus only, shall we be secure ourselves and able to work together for the high and simple causes that are dear to us and bode no ill to any. Eventually there may come—I feel eventually there will come—the principle of common citizenship, but that we may be content to leave to destiny, whose outstretched arm many of us can already clearly see.

There is however an important question we must ask ourselves. Would a special relationship between the United States and the British Commonwealth be inconsistent with our overriding loyalties to the World Organization? I reply that, on the contrary, it is probably the only means by which that organization will achieve its full stature and strength. There are already the special United States relations with Canada which I have just mentioned, and there are the special relations between the United States and the South American Republics. We

British have our twenty years Treaty of Collaboration and Mutual Assistance with Soviet Russia. I agree with Mr. Bevin, the Foreign Secretary of Great Britain, that it might well be a fifty years Treaty so far as we are concerned. We aim at nothing but mutual assistance and collaboration. The British have an alliance with Portugal unbroken since 1384, and which produced fruitful results at critical moments in the late war. None of these clash with the general interest of a world agreement, or a world organization; on the contrary, they help it. "In my father's house are many mansions." Special associations between members of the United Nations which have no aggressive point against any other country, which harbor no design incompatible with the Charter of the United Nations, far from being harmful, are beneficial and, as I believe, indispensable.*

I spoke earlier of the Temple of Peace. Workmen from all countries must build that temple. If two of the workmen know each other particularly well and are old friends, if their families are inter-mingled, and if they have "faith in each other's purpose, hope in each other's future and charity towards each other's shortcomings"—to quote some good words I read here the other day—why cannot they work together at the common task as friends and partners? Why cannot they share their tools and thus increase each other's working powers? Indeed they must do so or else the temple may not be built, or, being

---

* Knowing how committed Truman was to the UNO (and how important it had been to FDR), Churchill took great pains to explain that the "special relationship between the United States and the British Commonwealth" would not interfere with the world organization but, instead, would strengthen it.

built, it may collapse, and we shall all be proved again un-teachable and have to go and try to learn again for a third time in a school of war, incomparably more rigorous than that from which we have just been released. The dark ages may return, the Stone Age may return on the gleaming wings of science, and what might now shower immeasurable material blessings upon mankind, may even bring about its total de-struction. Beware, I say; time may be short. Do not let us take the course of allowing events to drift along until it is too late. If there is to be a fraternal association of the kind I have de-scribed, with all the extra strength and security which both our countries can derive from it, let us make sure that that great fact is known to the world, and that it plays its part in steadying and stabilizing the foundations of peace. There is the path of wisdom. Prevention is better than cure.

A shadow has fallen upon the scenes so lately lighted by the Allied victory.* Nobody knows what Soviet Russia and its

---

* Using the binary opposition of light and dark was hardly original and was somewhat playing to Churchill's predominantly Christian audience, but it was illustrative and effective—the Allies' triumph over the Axis powers in defense of democracy was good and Communism was evil. Churchill had used similar language to describe the consequences of Axis aggression on June 16, 1941, telling a radio audience: "Wickedness, enormous, panoplied, embattled, seemingly triumphant, casts its shadow over Europe and Asia." Though that particular shadow was now faded, it had been replaced by a macabre projection from Moscow, Churchill asserted. (See Winston Churchill, "The Birth Throes of a Sublime Resolve ['The Old Lion']," June 16, 1941, The Churchill Centre and Museum, available online at http://www.winstonchurchill.org/learn/speeches/speeches-of -winston-churchill/568-the-birth-throes-of-a-sublime-resolve-the-old-lion, accessed May 2011.)

Communist international organization intends to do in the immediate future, or what are the limits, if any, to their expansive and proselytizing tendencies. I have a strong admiration and regard for the valiant Russian people and for my wartime comrade, Marshal Stalin. There is deep sympathy and goodwill in Britain—and I doubt not here also—towards the peoples of all the Russias and a resolve to persevere through many differences and rebuffs in establishing lasting friendships. We understand the Russian need to be secure on her western frontiers by the removal of all possibility of German aggression. We welcome Russia to her rightful place among the leading nations of the world. We welcome her flag upon the seas.* Above all, we welcome constant, frequent and growing contacts between the Russian people and our own people on both sides of the Atlantic. It is my duty however, for I am sure you would wish me to state the facts as I see them to you, to place before you certain facts about the present position in Europe.**

---

* Churchill had inserted this comment at the urging of Lord Halifax, the British ambassador to the United States, who wanted to temper Churchill's criticism of Russia somewhat.

** Then came an unexpected hitch, which Churchill, with his full focus on his speech notes, didn't even notice—the speaker system went out. Fortunately, a quick-thinking observer with some technical know-how scrambled to the foot of the stage and, tucking himself in so as not to distract the audience or Churchill, kept the PA system working by holding two wires together for the remainder of the speech. Churchill continued speaking, and his words were duly recorded as if nothing had happened. (See James C. Humes, quoted in Bob Watson, "Churchill Expected Speech to Be Major Policy Statement," *Jefferson City News Tribune*, March 3, 1996, Callaway County Library, Fulton, Churchill Day Collection, accessed March 2011.)

From Stettin in the Baltic to Trieste in the Adriatic, an iron curtain has descended across the Continent.* Behind that line lie all the capitals of the ancient states of Central and Eastern Europe. Warsaw, Berlin, Prague, Vienna, Budapest, Belgrade, Bucharest and Sofia, all these famous cities and the populations around them lie in what I must call the Soviet sphere, and all are subject in one form or another, not only to Soviet influence but to a very high and, in many cases, increasing measure of control from Moscow. Athens alone—Greece with its immortal glories—is free to decide its future at an election under British, American and French observation. The Russian-dominated Polish Government has been encouraged to make enormous and wrongful inroads upon Germany, and mass expulsions of millions of Germans on a scale grievous and undreamed of are now taking place. The Communist parties, which were very small in all these Eastern States of Europe, have been raised to pre-eminence and power far beyond their numbers and are seeking everywhere to obtain totalitarian control. Police governments are prevailing in nearly every case, and so far, except in Czechoslovakia, there is no true democracy.**

---

* The use of *iron* made the curtain appear all the more impenetrable, implying that Stalin had something to hide in Eastern and Central Europe and wanted no outside light to illuminate the darkness. The choice of metal—iron—also alludes to military equipment, which is fitting given that Soviet munitions first "saved" the cities Churchill referenced from the German army and then imposed Moscow's controlling will on the citizenry.

** Bulgaria was a prime example of Stalin's misdeeds in Eastern Europe. On September 5, the Kremlin declared war on Bulgaria and, due to the Bulgarian Communists' power grab, marched into Sofia almost unopposed. The following February,

Turkey and Persia are both profoundly alarmed and disturbed at the claims which are being made upon them and at the pressure being exerted by the Moscow Government.*

An attempt is being made by the Russians in Berlin to build up a quasi-Communist party in their zone of Occupied Germany by showing special favors to groups of left-wing German leaders. At the end of the fighting last June, the American and British Armies withdrew westwards, in accordance with an earlier agreement, to a depth at some points of 150 miles upon a front of nearly four hundred miles, in order to allow our Russian allies to occupy this vast expanse of territory which the Western Democracies had conquered. If now the Soviet Government tries, by separate action, to build up a pro-Communist Germany in their areas, this will cause new serious difficulties in the British and American zones, and will give the defeated Germans the power of putting themselves up to auction between the Soviets and the

---

with Red Army troops still bolstering the new regime, the Communists sentenced Prince Kiril, former Prime Minister Bogdan Filov, and more than seventy other leading military officials and members of Parliament to death by a so-called People's Tribunal, for which there was no defense council or jury—only prosecutors. That night, Red Army soldiers frog-marched Kiril, Filov, and the rest to a cemetery, shot them, and threw the bodies in a mass grave. (See Yelena Valeva, "The CPSU, the Comintern, and the Bulgarians," in Norman Naimark and Leonid Gibianiski, eds., The Establishment of Communist Regimes in Eastern Europe, 1944–1949 [New York: Westview Press, 1997], 52; and "100 Death Sentences," Time, February 12, 1945, accessed May 2011.)

* This was a timely observation given the mounting tension and press coverage of the continued Soviet presence in Iran and Stalin's demands for bases in Turkey, which Churchill and Truman had discussed on the train ride to Jefferson City.

Western Democracies.* Whatever conclusions may be drawn from these facts—and facts they are—this is certainly not the Liberated Europe we fought to build up. Nor is it one which contains the essentials of permanent peace.

The safety of the world requires a new unity in Europe, from which no nation should be permanently outcast. It is from the quarrels of the strong parent races in Europe that the world wars we have witnessed, or which occurred in former times, have sprung. Twice in our own lifetime we have seen the United States, against their wishes and their traditions, against arguments, the force of which it is impossible not to comprehend, drawn by irresistible forces into these wars in time to secure the victory of the good cause, but only after frightful slaughter and devastation had occurred. Twice the United States has had to send several millions of its young men across the Atlantic to find the war; but now war can find any nation, wherever it may dwell between dusk and dawn. Surely we should work with conscious purpose for a grand pacification of Europe, within the structure of the United

---

* Churchill had entertained such fears at the birth of Bolshevism, writing to British Prime Minister David Lloyd George on May 5, 1919, that "[t]he overthrow of Bolshevism in Russia is indispensable to anything in the nature of a lasting peace and will cut off from Germany that refuge in Bolshevism which she may seek in her despair." On this day in Fulton, he also correctly predicted the long-term division of Berlin, which, little did he know, would be carried out by the embodiment of his "iron curtain"—the Berlin Wall. (See Winston Churchill to David Lloyd George, May 5, 1919, quoted in Martin Gilbert, *The Churchill Documents, Volume 8: War and Aftermath* [Hillsdale: Hillsdale College Press, 2008], 641; and Daniel J. Mahoney, "Moral Principle and Realistic Judgment," in James W. Muller, ed., *Churchill's "Iron Curtain" Speech Fifty Years Later* [Columbia, Mo.: University of Missouri Press, 1999], 71.)

Nations and in accordance with its Charter. That I feel is an open cause of policy of very great importance.

In front of the iron curtain which lies across Europe are other causes for anxiety. In Italy the Communist Party is seriously hampered by having to support the Communist-trained Marshal Tito's claims to former Italian territory at the head of the Adriatic. Nevertheless the future of Italy hangs in the balance. Again one cannot imagine a regenerated Europe without a strong France. All my public life I have worked for a strong France and I never lost faith in her destiny, even in the darkest hours. I will not lose faith now. However, in a great number of countries, far from the Russian frontiers and throughout the world, Communist fifth columns are established and work in complete unity and absolute obedience to the directions they receive from the Communist center. Except in the British Commonwealth and in the United States where Communism is in its infancy, the Communist parties or fifth columns constitute a growing challenge and peril to Christian civilization. These are somber facts for anyone to have to recite on the morrow of a victory gained by so much splendid comradeship in arms and in the cause of freedom and democracy; but we should be most unwise not to face them squarely while time remains.

The outlook is also anxious in the Far East and especially in Manchuria. The Agreement which was made at Yalta, to which I was a party, was extremely favorable to Soviet Russia, but it was made at a time when no one could say that the German war might not extend all through the summer and autumn of 1945 and when the Japanese war was expected to last for a further 18 months from the end of the German war. In this country you are all so well-informed about the Far East, and such devoted friends of China, that I do not need to expatiate on the situation there.

I have felt bound to portray the shadow which, alike in the west and in the east, falls upon the world. I was a high minister at the time of the Versailles Treaty and a close friend of Mr. Lloyd-George, who was the head of the British delegation at Versailles. I did not myself agree with many things that were done, but I have a very strong impression in my mind of that situation, and I find it painful to contrast it with that which prevails now. In those days there were high hopes and unbounded confidence that the wars were over, and that the League of Nations would become all-powerful. I do not see or feel that same confidence or even the same hopes in the haggard world at the present time.

On the other hand I repulse the idea that a new war is inevitable; still more that it is imminent. It is because I am sure that our fortunes are still in our own hands and that we hold the power to save the future, that I feel the duty to speak out now that I have the occasion and the opportunity to do so. I do not believe that Soviet Russia desires war. What they desire is the fruits of war and the indefinite expansion of their power and doctrines.* But what we have to consider here today, while time remains, is the permanent prevention of war

---

* This was almost a direct quote from Kennan's "Long Telegram," showing that though Churchill was in the minority in such thinking, he was by no means alone.

and the establishment of conditions of freedom and democracy as rapidly as possible in all countries. Our difficulties and dangers will not be removed by closing our eyes to them. They will not be removed by mere waiting to see what happens; nor will they be removed by a policy of appeasement. What is needed is a settlement, and the longer this is delayed, the more difficult it will be and the greater our dangers will become.

From what I have seen of our Russian friends and Allies during the war, I am convinced that there is nothing they admire so much as strength, and there is nothing for which they have less respect than for weakness, especially military weakness.*

For that reason the old doctrine of a balance of power is unsound. We cannot afford, if we can help it, to work on narrow margins, offering temptations to a trial of strength. If the Western Democracies stand together in strict adherence to the principles of the United Nations Charter, their influence for furthering those principles will be immense

---

* Churchill had made a similar argument for strength as a means of achieving enduring peace and avoiding another global conflict during his "Adamant for Drift" address in November 1936: "Thus I hope we may succeed in again achieving a position of superior force, and then will be the time, not to repeat the folly which we committed when we were all-powerful and supreme, but to invite Germany to make common cause with us in assuaging the griefs of Europe and opening a new door to peace and disarmament." A decade later, Churchill still believed that only superior weaponry and personnel, and the fortitude to put it into action, would discourage Russian bellicosity. Kennan and Truman advisers such as Admiral Leahy shared this belief. (See Winston Churchill, "Adamant for Drift" speech to the House of Commons, November 12, 1940, in Robert Rhodes James, ed., *Churchill Speaks 1897–1963: Collected Speeches in Peace & War* [Philadelphia: Chelsea House, 1980], 629.)

and no one is likely to molest them. If however they become divided or falter in their duty and if these all-important years are allowed to slip away, then indeed catastrophe may overwhelm us all.

Last time I saw it all coming and cried aloud to my own fellow countrymen and to the world, but no one paid any attention. Up till the year 1933 or even 1935, Germany might have been saved from the awful fate which has overtaken her and we might all have been spared the miseries Hitler let loose upon mankind. There never was a war in all history easier to prevent by timely action than the one which has just desolated such great areas of the globe. It could have been prevented in my belief without the firing of a single shot, and Germany might be powerful, prosperous and honored today; but no one would listen and one by one we were all sucked into the awful whirlpool. We surely must not let that happen again. This can only be achieved by reaching now, in 1946, in this year, nineteen hundred and forty-six, a good understanding on all points with Russia under the general authority of the United Nations Organization and by the maintenance of that good understanding through many peaceful years, by the world instrument, supported by the whole strength of the English-speaking world and all its connections.* There is the solution

---

* Churchill's repetition of the year "1946," which he added at the podium, made it clear that the time for action was *now*, and that there could be no delay in securing peace with Russia. (See "The Sinews of Peace," Jo Sturdee corrected version, Churchill Archives Centre, CHUR 5/4, accessed March 2011.)

which I respectfully offer to you in this Address to which I have given the title "The Sinews of Peace."*

Let no man underrate the abiding power of the British Empire and Commonwealth. Because you see the 46 millions in our island harassed about their food supply, of which they only grow one half, even in war time, or because we have difficulty in restarting our industries and export trade after six years of passionate war effort, do not suppose that we shall not come through these dark years of privation as we have come through the glorious years of agony, or that half a century from now, you will not see 70 or 80 millions of Britons spread about the world and united in defense of our traditions, our way of life, and of the world causes which you and we espouse. If the population of the English-speaking Commonwealths be added to that of the United States with all that such cooperation implies in the air, on the sea, all over the globe and in science and in industry, and in moral force, there will be no quivering, precarious balance of power to offer its temptation to ambition or adventure. On the contrary, there will be an overwhelming assurance of security. If we adhere faithfully to the Charter of the United Nations and walk forward in sedate and sober strength seeking no one's land or treasure, seeking to lay no arbitrary control upon the thoughts

---

* Mentioning the speech title was another ad lib for Churchill, who included it to reemphasize his desire for lasting peace with Russia. It also served as a signpost for his subsequent proposals in the address, which would act as the supporting ligaments of such a peace.

of men; if all British moral and material forces and convictions are joined with your own in fraternal association, the high-roads of the future will be clear, not only for us but for all, not only for our time, but for a century to come.*

---

* The most famous event in Westminster College's history was over. A new era of international relations had just begun. (Speech source: Winston Churchill, "The Sinews of Peace," March 5, 1946, courtesy of Curtis Brown, Ltd., on behalf of the Churchill family.)

Harry Truman applauds Winston Churchill in the Westminster College gym, as Admiral William Leahy and Major General Harry Vaughan look on.
CREDIT: HARRY S. TRUMAN LIBRARY

WESTMINSTER COLLEGE

The John Findley Green Lecture

BY

THE RT. HON. WINSTON CHURCHILL

INTRODUCTION BY

THE HON. HARRY S. TRUMAN

President of the United States

Fulton, Missouri
The College Gymnasium and Swope Chapel
Tuesday, March 5, 1946

Front page of lecture program for Winston Churchill's "The Sinews of Peace" speech at Westminster College, March 5, 1946. CREDIT: NATIONAL CHURCHILL MUSEUM ARCHIVES, CHURCHILL, TRUMAN, MCCLUER DAY COLLECTION, FOLDER 07, GREEN FOUNDATION LECTURE SERIES SCAN

CHAPTER 10

A FIREBRAND:
REACTIONS TO CHURCHILL'S MESSAGE
AROUND THE WORLD

I believe within three years you will agree that what was said here today should have been said.

—Winston Churchill to Franc McCluer, after delivering
"The Sinews of Peace" speech (March 5, 1946)

AFTER THE SPEECH, CHURCHILL, Truman, and their group returned to the McCluers' house, where Professor Danny Gage presented them both with gold watches on behalf of the faculty. Westminster trustee C. D. Smiley then gave Churchill a Thomas Hart Benton painting that he had requested in lieu of an honorarium. Fittingly, the twelve-by-nine-inch portrait of a Missouri farmer mending his white picket was entitled *The New Fence*.[1]

Ida Belle and her helpers had prepared another elaborate meal, including Churchill's favorite roast beef, but after Churchill and Truman greeted the families of the fifty-nine Westminster students who lost their lives in World War II, they were behind schedule and said their good-byes without even sampling the buffet.[2]

Back they went to the *Ferdinand Magellan,* which was idling at the Jefferson City station, the train's engine humming like a great beehive.[3] From there, the locomotive began retracing the route back to St. Louis, and on to Columbus, Ohio, where Truman was to address The Federal Council of Churches of Christ of America on "The Place of Religion in Democracy" the next day.[4] Churchill would continue on to Washington, before speaking to the Virginia General Assembly, and then would spend the remainder of his trip with Sarah, Clementine, and Randolph in New York.

As the train got under way, Churchill, Truman, and the others resumed their poker rivalry, which, predictably, ended with another Churchill defeat.[5] At this point, the president left the group for a brief snooze, eager to recover from the rigors of the trip before his Columbus appearance. Churchill continued his conversation with Clark Clifford and Charles Ross—Ross was a high school friend of Truman and his wife, Bess, and winner of a Pulitzer Prize in 1932—and the question arose as to where "The Sinews of Peace" would fit in Churchill's oratory canon. Without hesitation, Churchill dubbed it "the most important speech of my career."[6]

At a Washington press conference two days later, Truman stuck to his pre-Fulton plan of publicly separating himself from "The Sinews of Peace"—telling the White House press corps that he had not read the speech in advance. This was, of course, a fabrication—he had not only perused the final draft on the *Ferdinand Magellan* but had also wholeheartedly endorsed its contents. Indeed, Truman soon sent a telegram thanking Churchill for accompanying him to his home state and affirming that "the people of Missouri were highly pleased with your visit and enjoyed what you had to say."[7]

James Byrnes also presented a duplicitous stance on "The Sinews of Peace." In a news briefing, he denied that Churchill's words had anything to do with the State Department's position on Russia.[8] Yet he acted behind the scenes to support the former prime minister's Fulton proposals. On the very day Churchill spoke at Westminster College, Byrnes sent three high-impact communications to Moscow. In the first of these, he instructed chargé d'affaires George Kennan, author of the "Long Telegram," to obtain from the Kremlin copies of economic agreements between Russia and its Eastern European satellite states. In the second, he informed Molotov that America deemed Soviet financial demands from China to be unacceptable. Byrnes simultaneously released documents concerning Manchuria's economic matters that illustrated how the Stalinists were interfering with Chinese industry, thereby hampering Chinese Premier Chiang Kai-Shek's continuing fight against the Chinese Communist Party. Finally, in the third communication, the State Department issued its most pointed protest to date about the continued Red Army presence in Iran.[9]

Such communications are further evidence that, despite the Truman administration's efforts to deny any foreknowledge of Churchill's Fulton message, it was in fact very much in agreement with its content and was already putting into practice Churchill's call for strong diplomacy.[10]

Churchill received further validation from others in the president's inner circle. The same day as Truman and Byrnes delivered their disingenuous press conferences, Churchill received a message from U.S. Naval Secretary James Forrestal, communicating the view of veteran diplomat and Churchill's wartime confidant Averell Harriman: "I do not think you would find in him any profound disagreement with your observations." When Churchill met with Harriman in Washington later that week, the Briton revealed that he was "very gloomy about coming to any accommodation with Russia unless and until it became clear to the Russians that they would be met by force if they continued their expansion."[11]

Admiral Leahy emphatically endorsed Churchill's address, believing that it would "go down in history as one of the most powerful influences in bringing about close British-American collaboration to preserve world peace. It was a courageous statement of Mr. Churchill's belief in the inherent righteousness and power of the English-speaking world, and it was received by his audience with marked enthusiasm."[12]

At the British Embassy in Washington, Churchill composed a letter to Attlee and Bevin, informing them of how he gauged the White House's true position on Russia: "Having spent nearly three days in the most intimate, friendly contact with the President and his immediate circle, and also having had a long talk with Mr. Byrnes, I have no doubt that the Executive forces here are deeply distressed at the way they are being treated by Russia and that they do not intend to put up with treaty breaches in Manchuria or Korea, or pressure for the Russian expansion at the expense of Turkey or in the Mediterranean."

Churchill then reiterated one of his key points from the Fulton address: "I am convinced that some show of strength and resisting power is necessary to a good settlement with Russia. I predict that this will be the prevailing opinion in the United States in the near future."[13]

Opinion in Moscow was, predictably, quite another matter. On March 11, the United Press reprinted *Pravda*'s blistering denunciation of Churchill. The Politburo mouthpiece branded him (as well as Senator Arthur Vandenberg, whose speech had preceded the Briton's and had struck a similar chord) a "warmonger" who wanted an Anglo-American alliance to be "directed against the Soviet Union."

The diatribe continued: "Churchill forgets that freedom-loving nations have acquired, during the years of war, enormous political experience and have learned to distinguish the real defenders of peace from imperialists who under the mendacious flag of 'defense of peace' are making plans for new, unfettered, imperialistic wars." The fact that Truman was taking such great pains to distance himself from "The Sinews of Peace" suggests that he foresaw the Russian rebuke and wanted to minimize the damage to already fraying U.S. relations with Moscow.[14] Churchill anticipated such a reaction, too—after all, as *Pravda* had accurately stated, he *was* calling for a transatlantic alliance of principle against the perceived threat of the Soviet Union.

Two days later, the morning papers reported Stalin's stinging response to "The Sinews of Peace," which picked up where *Pravda* left off. He called Churchill a "firebrand" and alleged that his former Big Three ally had issued "a call to war with the Soviet Union," just as he had led the call for continued Allied support of anti-Bolsheviks after World War I. "History turned out to be stronger than Churchill's intervention," Stalin warned, implying that what he saw as the Briton's new saber rattling would be equally futile.

Stalin then bombastically compared Churchill with the man both had opposed in World War II—Adolf Hitler. The latter's warped mind had devised the Holocaust, but Churchill had an equally dangerous "racial theory," Stalin warned: that the English-speaking peoples "are . . . called upon to decide the destinies of the entire world." Russia had not sacrificed millions of lives in repelling the German advance eastward "for the sake of exchanging the lordship of Hitler for the lordship of Churchill." In a reversal of what Churchill had said at Fulton about the oppression of people living under Communist rule, Stalin asserted that those who did not speak English as a first language "will not consent to go into a new slavery."

In a slight directed at the British government, Stalin mocked British Foreign Secretary Ernest Bevin's offer to extend the twenty-year nonaggression pact between Britain and Russia to fifty years, and asserted that Moscow could nullify the original

agreement because "[p]roblems of the duration of a treaty have
no sense if one of the parties violates the treaty." Stalin evidently
put no stock in Churchill's assertion that he was speaking in
America as a "private citizen," nor did he acknowledge that
Churchill was the legitimate Leader of the Opposition in the
United Kingdom. To Stalin, it seemed, one Briton's words made
an entire nation culpable.

The Soviet leader claimed that Russia's neighbors needed
protection, and were receiving it and nothing more from his
country. He then skewered Churchill's claims about Soviet foreign ambitions, asking the pointed rhetorical question: "How
can one, without having lost one's reason, qualify these peaceful
aspirations . . . as 'expansionist tendencies?'" Churchill was aiming to "delude people" and "wander around the truth" when
claiming that Communism was spreading across Europe, Stalin
contended. He also maintained that the same type of "common
people" who now welcomed Communism in Russia had ousted
Churchill in the 1945 General Election. This latter accusation is
particularly odd, given that Stalin and Molotov were dumb-
founded about Churchill's defeat and that Stalin sulked in his
Potsdam villa for two days because of it, delaying the first plenary in which Attlee took Churchill's place at the negotiating
table.

When he lambasted Churchill's "ridiculous position" of
claiming there was no "true democracy" in the Soviet sphere,
the marshal was again on shaky ground. Stalin insisted that
Eastern European nations practiced stronger democratic principles than Britain because of their coalition governments.[15] He
appeared to have a short memory on this point—as Churchill
had presided over a coalition government during World War II
and had offered the Labour and Liberal parties the opportunity
to continue such an administration for as long as they would
want. Furthermore, nothing even closely resembling a free,
democratic election had taken place under Stalin's rule, and his

"coalitions" were made up of key government officials wrested by the Communist Party from other parties.

Churchill was also under fire at home, where Labour MPs Tom Driberg and William Warbey implored Prime Minister Attlee to "repudiate" "The Sinews of Peace" speech in the Commons. Attlee refused, insisting that Churchill had merely expressed his opinions "in an individual capacity." Warbey, proposing a motion of censure against Churchill signed by ninety-three Labour MPs, argued that the Fulton address had been "calculated to do injury to good relations between Great Britain, the USA, and Russia, and are inimical to the cause of World Peace."[16] The motion failed, but this was not the end of the criticism.

In his diary entry for March 5, Admiral Leahy had predicted "highly unfavorable comment from 'the vocal communists,' 'fellow travelers,' and 'pinkies' in the United States,'" and so it proved, even from those not fitting Leahy's disparaging description.[17] Democrats and Republicans alike bristled at Churchill's calls for a closer Anglo-American alliance and what they perceived as an attack on America's recent ally in the East. Republican Senator Joseph H. Ball thought such an agreement would force Russia into its own opposing alliances, while Southern Democrat Senator Walter George believed it would be a "body blow to the UNO." Liberal Senators Kilgore, Taylor, and Pepper, Democrats all, issued a joint statement condemning "the Tory clamor for war" and dismissing Churchill's speech as "new British-American imperialism."[18]

A British Foreign Office memo summed up the polarized reaction to Churchill's Fulton speech: "Profound as the uneasiness is about Soviet policies, there is still a reluctance to face the full implications of the facts and a timidity about the consequences of language as forthright as Mr. Churchill's."

One of the primary reasons for the overwhelmingly hostile response in the United States was that the title of "The Sinews of Peace" was not listed in the official pre-speech press release, thus undermining Churchill's focus on preventing war.[19] Despite the radio and newsreel coverage that McCluer had secured for Churchill's speech, most Americans who learned of its contents did so via newspapers. Though a few dailies reprinted the entire text, the majority omitted its title and framed the contents in critical editorials, distorting Churchill's words as a call to arms.

Walter Lippmann, one of America's most-read syndicated columnists, called the speech "an almost catastrophic blunder." The *Chicago Sun,* despite running a map highlighting nations of Eastern Europe that were behind the Iron Curtain alongside its write-up, claimed that Churchill's true intention was "world domination, through arms, of the United States and the British Empire." *The Nation*—often critical of Churchill—declared that he had "added a sizeable measure of poison to the already deteriorating relations between Russia and the United States."[20]

Negative sentiment also found its way into artists' studios. The *Chicago Tribune* ran a caricature sketch of Churchill in a black hat and the scarlet Oxford robe he had worn at Fulton, clutching degrees from Westminster College, the University of Miami, and Columbia University (the latter related to an event scheduled for March 18), alongside this poem:

> *In the scarlet robes of Oxford,*
> *Who's this personage we see?*
> *Gad, it's Churchill on a dais,*
> *To accept his L.L.D!*
>
> *O, the scarlet robe of old Oxford*
> *(Let it evermore be said),*
> *For a gentleman of England,*
> *Is the proper shade of red.*

Not for him the carmine, crimson,
Not for him cerise, or rose,
Such he scorned, and decent scarlet,
Is the color Winston chose.

Not for him the blooming redness,
Of the countenance of one,
Who's regretful of words spoken,
Or of deeds untimely done.

O, the scarlet of old Oxford,
Is a safer red, m'lud,
Than the flaming red of riot,
Ruby, Russian red of blood![21]

Yet American media reaction to the Fulton speech was not entirely hostile. The *New York Times* was one of the few newspapers to focus on Churchill's plea for an accord with the Soviet Union, reprinting the speech in its entirety under the header "Mr. Churchill's Address Calling for United Effort for World Peace." An editorial in the next section praised Churchill as a "towering leader" and affirmed his argument that "if the western democracies headed by Anglo-American fraternity pool their strength they can reach a good understanding with Russia on all points."

The *Pittsburgh Post-Gazette* sang Churchill's praises for his Fulton address, stating that "to an English-speaking world grown increasingly troubled over relations with Russia, Mr. Churchill's message is a welcome tonic. It reaffirms faith in our strength, and a determination to see that the fruits of victory are not lost through hesitancy and fear." Churchill also found support from the *Wall Street Journal*, which, though disregarding his call for Anglo-American military alliance, told its readers that the speech "had a hard core of indisputable fact."[22]

A measured editorial in *Life,* informed by veteran writer George Scadding's reporting from Fulton and the presidential train trip, described how Churchill had "called on the Western World to act while time remains" to prevent World War III. "Coming from the man who warned of World War II before the world was ready to listen, his words commanded sober thought," Scadding believed. William Allen White, influential editor of the *Emporia Gazette* (nicknamed "The Sage of Emporia"), told Churchill that should his speech "fail to pull the democratic world together to meet the crisis, I don't think that anything else can succeed." His sentiments were echoed by the industrialist J. H. Rand, who sent Churchill a new Remington noiseless typewriter from his Remington Rand plant in Elmira, New York. (This was the brand that Churchill had imported for the Cabinet War Rooms during World War II, because he loathed persistent background noise.) Rand's note declared the Fulton speech to be "an articulate, forthright statement of the kind which is needed if the present clouds of misunderstanding are to be cleared."[23]

There was also some support from Britain's dailies, particularly the conservative outlets. Though the Labour Party–supporting paper *The Daily Herald* declined to comment on Churchill's speech and *The Times* (London) offered several criticisms, *The Daily Telegraph* defended his argument, stating that "Mr. Churchill's purpose is not to divide the world into two opposing camps but to see whether frankness could not unite the two camps into which the world is already tending to divide itself." *The Daily Mail* went one step further, insisting that "Russia's disastrous course can and must be arrested. Who can doubt that the way to do it is the one proposed by Mr. Churchill?" Even the *Yorkshire Post*, printed in a traditional left-wing stronghold, was in favor of Churchill's proposals, with one writer believing they offered "the one true remedy that can rid the freedom-loving powers of their present great anxieties."[24]

Arriving at the Waldorf-Astoria Hotel in New York on March 15 to deliver another speech, Churchill faced a reception even colder than the chilly evening air. Picketers yelled "GI Joe is home to stay, Winnie, Winnie, go away!" and held up signs stating "Mr. Truman, Repudiate Churchill's Call for War Against Soviet Union," "No Americans Shall Die for Churchill's Empire," and "Blood, Sweat, and Tears for Churchill's World War III." These protesters were only kept from rushing the Briton by New York Police Department officers who had set up barriers and a human cordon to ensure Churchill's safe passage into the lobby. The NYPD arrested twenty demonstrators from a crowd of more than seven hundred who massed outside the Waldorf-Astoria that night, bundling the offenders roughly into the back of black vans and slamming the heavy double doors behind them. This inhospitable welcome inspired Churchill's performance at the podium later that evening, in which he defended "The Sinews of Peace," growling defiantly, "I do not wish to withdraw or modify a single word."[25]

Columbia University gave Churchill another opportunity to emphasize his position on Russia before returning to England. Arriving at the New York campus to receive an honorary degree on March 18, Churchill braved the catcalls of 250 picketers and then delivered a telling analogy: "Our Communist friends should study . . . the life and the soul of the white ant. That will show them not only a great deal about their past but will give a very fair indication of their future."[26]

Two days later, Churchill gave the final interview of his U.S. trip to his son, Randolph, who was on assignment for the United Press. Seated in his modest suite aboard *The Queen Mary,* the elder Churchill told the younger that the UNO should not meet Stalin's demand to postpone its hearing on the Red Army occupation in Iran. "It would be very dangerous to let matters go from bad to worse in Persia and on the frontiers of Turkey and Iraq," he said. "It is very easy to raise disorders in those countries." He then took a direct stab at Moscow: "With money, force, and inflammatory propaganda, lawful governments may be overthrown, a state of disorder created and a Quisling government installed."[27]

Churchill claimed that "all the Communists in the world would have seen England sunk forever beneath the waves by Hitler's Germany; it was only when Soviet Russia was attacked that they put themselves in line with the modern world." And, he insisted, Communism "means in fact the death of the soul of man." This was an even stronger condemnation of Soviet malfeasance than he had made at Westminster College, the Waldorf-Astoria, or Columbia University—a parting shot across the bows indeed. "Have you any message to give the United States on your departure?" Randolph asked. "The United States must realize its power and its virtue," his father replied. "It must pursue consistently the great themes and principles that have made it the land of the free. All the world is looking to the American democracy for resolute guidance. If I could sum it up in a phrase, I would say, 'Dread nought, America.'"[28]

CONCLUSION

The most important speech of my career.

—Winston Churchill's view of "The Sinews of Peace,"
expressed to Clark Clifford and Charles Ross
(March 5, 1946)

O N DECEMBER 4, 1946, Churchill wrote to New York Governor Thomas E. Dewey. Reflecting on the recent transgressions of the Soviet government, he declared, "If I made the Fulton speech today it would be criticized as consisting of platitudes." Later that week, he penned another letter in the same vein to Frank Clarke, his host in Florida, expounding: "Fulton still holds its own!"[1]

Indeed, Fulton would continue to hold its own for the rest of his life and career, and for the duration of the Cold War. In the short term, "The Sinews of Peace" solidified the thoughts and actions of the Attlee and Truman governments on Russia and transatlantic relations, directed the remainder of Churchill's political efforts, and created the most powerful visual image of the division between the democratic, capitalist West and the totalitarian,

Communist East. "The Sinews of Peace" also rhetorically paved the way for the Truman Doctrine and the massive injection of American aid to Europe encapsulated in the Marshall Plan, both conceived in 1947.[2]

Of course there were significant other economic and political factors in play—not least American trade interests in Europe—and other influential men of the age shared Churchill's views on Russia—most notably George Kennan, James F. Byrnes, and Ernest Bevin. But it was Churchill's message in Missouri that brought their collective opinions to a global audience and kick-started new policy initiatives. As Truman told Churchill in October 1947, the month after the formation of the Cominform (the agency that coordinated international Communist policy with guidance from Moscow), and with Soviet puppet rulers entrenched in Hungary and on the verge of claiming Czechoslovakia: "[Y]our Fulton . . . speech becomes more nearly a prophecy every day." Rarely lacking in self-confidence, Churchill shared similar sentiments with old friend Frank Clarke in March 1948, telling him that "Fulton has turned out to be a signpost that hundreds of millions have followed."[3]

Though the American and British governments were soon to diverge over how to deal with Communism in the Far East, they continued to heed Churchill's call for transatlantic solidarity in April 1949. That month, Truman, Attlee, and leaders of ten other nations signed the North Atlantic Treaty, which guaranteed that the signees would come to each other's aid in the event of attack by a hostile power—Russia being the likely perpetrator. Churchill reacted favorably to the agreement that his Fulton address inspired, declaring it to be "a very considerable advance in opinion as far as the United States are concerned."[4]

On February 14, 1950, Churchill shared his continued belief in personal diplomacy with an audience in Edinburgh, Scotland. There, he reasserted his hope for "another talk with Russia upon the highest level." He then explained to the crowd: "The idea appeals to me of a supreme effort to bridge the gulf between the two worlds, so that each can lead their life, if not in friendship, at least without the hatreds of the cold war. . . . It is not easy to see how things could be worsened by a parley at the summit." This was the first time the word *summit* had been used to describe a personal meeting between national leaders, and it soon became the standard term for such formal talks.[5]

After his unlikely return to 10 Downing Street in 1951, at age seventy-six, Churchill focused the three and a half years of his second premiership on achieving such a tri-nation meeting. However, despite his lofty hopes and the friendly rapport between them, Churchill's visit to Truman in January 1952 did not lead to a summit, and showed that Churchill had overestimated his personal sway with the president while underestimating Britain's fall from influence with the United States and Russia.[6]

Undeterred, Churchill doggedly pressed on. When Stalin died on March 5, 1953, fittingly the seventh anniversary of "The Sinews of Peace," Churchill believed that the Russians might be more amenable to a meeting and redoubled his efforts to organize it. His deputy Anthony Eden, members of the Tory Cabinet, and first-year President Dwight Eisenhower, who was skeptical at best about his old wartime colleague's plans, strongly discouraged this idea. Churchill also proposed going on a "lonely pilgrimage" to Moscow for peace talks, only to again be rebuffed by Eisenhower and his secretary of state, the proud, forceful, and principled John Foster Dulles.[7]

Despite his best efforts, Churchill failed to organize the era-defining postwar summit that he pushed so hard for before his death on January 24, 1965. He also did not live to see lasting peace between the powers divided by the iron curtain, his primary goal in his final years as politician, statesman, and world citizen.[8]

Yet he did see incremental progress. In February 1959, a Conservative prime minister—Harold Macmillan—followed through on Churchill's plan for a personal visit to Moscow. Though Macmillan would return to London without a definitive peace agreement, his visit was a symbolic step in lessening the tension between Whitehall and the Kremlin. And while Britain was not, as Churchill had argued it must be, present at the first summit between the Russian and American superpowers, such a historic meeting did take place when Eisenhower and Khrushchev finally came together at Camp David on September 25, 1959. Though Khrushchev was often critical of Churchill, he later conceded that "[i]t was actually Churchill's idea for the Western powers to open lines of communication with the new Soviet government after Stalin's death."[9]

"The Sinews of Peace" also had a profound impact on the next generation of world statesmen, across the political spectrum. Visiting John F. Kennedy when he was hospitalized as a teen, family friend Kay Halle found him engrossed in an abridgement of Churchill's multi-volume World War I commentary, *The World Crisis.* From that point on, Kennedy enthusiastically followed Churchill's literary career. Indeed, the title for Kennedy's undergraduate thesis-turned-book *Why England Slept* was a play on the title of Churchill's *While England Slept,* and the structure for Kennedy's 1955 Pulitzer Prize winner *Profiles in Courage* was inspired by Churchill's *Great Contemporaries.*

Kennedy also diligently studied Churchill's speech craft. During his 1960 presidential campaign, he used variations of Churchill's phrase *we arm to parley* more than a dozen times when talking about the relationship between America's military buildup and hopes for peace with Russia. Churchill had uttered this expression in 1949, though it had its roots in "The Sinews of Peace." At a Democratic fundraiser in Manhattan on September 14, 1960, Kennedy went further in reusing Churchill's Fulton rhetoric when he stated "A Democratic administration can never and will never negotiate with the Russians from a position of weakness."[10] Kennedy most notably put this philosophy into practice when navigating the fraught hours of the Cuban Missile Crisis in October-November 1962—forcing Russia to back down without triggering nuclear war.

On April 9, 1963, Kennedy made Churchill just the second foreign national (after the Marquis de Lafayette) to receive honorary American citizenship. At that ceremony, JFK stated that this "son of America" had "expressed with unsurpassed power and splendor the aspirations of peoples everywhere for dignity and freedom." This was as true of Churchill's quest for Cold War peace as it was of his wartime leadership. Kennedy also sought to memorialize Churchill's legacy in other ways. A month after conferring citizenship upon Churchill, JFK assumed the honorary chairmanship of a committee overseeing the creation of a monument on the Westminster College campus commemorating Churchill's visit there—a Christopher Wren–designed church shipped stone by stone from London. In the fall of that year, artist, businessman, and presidential adviser Leo Cherne made a bust in Churchill's likeness and Kennedy asked for a replica. Upon receiving it in September, the president placed Cherne's tribute in pride of place in the Oval Office, where it would sit for thirty-six years.[11]

When Richard Nixon assumed the presidency in 1969, he took up the mantle for Churchillian diplomacy. He later credited the Fulton address for his appraisal divide between what Churchill had called "the Soviet sphere" and the Western democracies: "It was Churchill's Iron Curtain speech . . . that profoundly affected my attitude to Communism in general and the Soviet Union in particular. I was jolted by these words." Nixon also remembered the impact of Churchill's visit to Washington in 1954 (when Nixon was Eisenhower's vice president). At the White House, Churchill again advocated "a policy of patience and vigilance," Nixon recalled. "He said we could not deal with the Communists on the basis of weakness—that it had to be a policy of strength."

Nixon's meetings with Soviet premier Leonid Brezhnev—particularly those in Moscow in 1972, at Camp David the following year, and in the Russian capital again in 1974—established a regular pattern of superpower diplomacy at the highest level, as Churchill had urged. Nixon later recalled his initial exchange with Brezhnev during his first trip to the Kremlin: "I said that I had studied the history of the relationships between Stalin and Roosevelt and Stalin and Churchill. I had found that during the war the differences between subordinates were usually overcome by agreement at the top level. 'That is the kind of relationship I should like to establish with the General Secretary,' I said.

'I would be only too happy, and am perfectly ready on my side,' he replied."[12]

Ten years later, Margaret Thatcher and Ronald Reagan advanced détente to achieve Churchill's primary goal in his dotage: the peaceful and permanent conclusion of the Cold War. Thatcher was as unequivocal about the necessity of Anglo-American unity as Churchill had been, declaring, "The Anglo-American relationship has done more for the defense and future of freedom than any other alliance in the world."

Speaking in Fulton to commemorate the fiftieth anniversary of Churchill's appearance, Thatcher explored the factors that ended the standoff between Russia and the West: "It happened in large part because of what Churchill said here fifty years ago. He spoke at a watershed: one set of international institutions had shown themselves to be wanting; another had yet to be born. And it was his speech, not the 'force' celebrated by Marx, which turned out to be the midwife of history."[13]

Ronald Reagan also appreciated the powerful legacy of March 5, 1946. He often quoted Churchill, and they shared a strong belief in personal diplomacy. During the early days of his relations with Gorbachev, Reagan mused that if the two men sat down one-on-one, "I really think we could see big changes in the Soviet Union."

In 1920, Churchill wrote that Bolshevism would fail because it was "fundamentally opposed to the needs and dictates of the human heart, and of human nature itself." Such thinking resonates in a speech Reagan made fifty-five years later, when he decried Communism as "a form of insanity—a temporary aberration which will one day disappear from the earth because it is contrary to human nature." Reagan also shared Churchill's belief that the founding principles of Western democracy were unshakeable, and would outlast Communism, which, as Reagan correctly predicted in 1982, was destined for "the ash-heap of history."

Furthermore, Reagan reiterated Churchill's Fulton advice for dealing with the Soviet Union militarily: "[T]here is nothing they admire so much as strength, and there is nothing for which they have less respect than for weakness, especially military weakness." In March 1978, Reagan made a near-identical sentiment, saying, "We want to avoid a war and that is better achieved by being so strong that a potential enemy is not tempted to go adventuring." He again paraphrased "The Sinews of Peace" in his "Evil Empire" address of 1983, declaring that "simple-minded appeasement or wishful thinking about our adversaries is folly." By acting on such policies and bolstering America's military (even when this included follies such as the ill-fated "Star Wars" missile defense project), Reagan helped end the Cold War without, as Churchill put it in Missouri, "the firing of a single shot" directly at Moscow.[14]

Transformative Soviet leader Mikhail Gorbachev also recognized the vital role Churchill's words had played in the latter years of the Cold War. On May 6, 1992, he delivered his own address at Fulton, fittingly using the same leather-topped podium that held Churchill's notes nearly half a century earlier. Gorbachev revealed that the Russian people had been exposed only to the iron curtain aspect of Churchill's speech and its supposed role in "the formal declaration of the Cold War." Due to media censorship, they had not been allowed to view the full text and thus were unable to appraise the more subtle elements of the address, as Gorbachev saw them: "Churchill's analysis of the postwar situation in the world, his thoughts about the possibility of preventing a third world war, the prospects for progress, and methods of reconstructing the postwar world."

Invoking Churchill's 1946 plea, Gorbachev called for all nations to pursue "the principles of democracy, equality of rights, balance of interests, common sense, freedom of choice, and willingness to cooperate." The former Russian premier noted, too, that when Churchill spoke in Fulton, he urged us to think "'super-strategically,' meaning to rise above the petty problems and particularities of current realities, focusing on the major trends and being guided by them."[15]

In an age in which our political philosophies are ever more reductionist and reactionary, and in which nuance is too often overlooked on the world stage, we would do well to embrace such an approach.

Today, there are many nontraditional assaults on the principles of freedom that Churchill lived by and enunciated in March 1946—terrorism, rogue states seeking to acquire nuclear weapons, and authoritarian leaders denying their citizens' most basic freedoms. Not to mention censorship of the Internet, with its "dangerous" ideas from the outside world, and restriction of social media tools that can expose nondemocratic regimes' abuses for all to see. These challenges are in some ways very different from those Churchill evaluated at Fulton. But perhaps the solutions to such problems and those of his era are not so different.[16]

Commitment to active diplomacy backed by restrained strength, determination to protect the tenets of democratic government and personal liberty at all costs (even as relentless opponents push us to compromise them), and a desire to avert global conflict still ring true today, in our own "anxious and baffling times."[17] Indeed, it is vital that we stand beside our allies in peace and in war, and proudly celebrate our shared heritage, language, and traditions together.

As recent uprisings in the Middle East and North Africa have shown, all people hunger for the right to elect their leaders, to freely speak their minds, and to practice personal beliefs in the comfort and safety of what Churchill called "cottage homes." To ensure that we are not guilty of a "mere frothing of words," we must encourage and support this pursuit of freedom, continuing the legacy of "The Sinews of Peace," which will continue to endure as Churchill's most influential speech and one of the defining statements of the twentieth century.[18] Perhaps if we look to it for guidance often, "the high-roads of the future," as Churchill put it, "will be clear, not only for us but for all, not only for our time, but for a century to come."[19]

AFTERWORD

A s CHURCHILL CONCLUDED HIS TRIP in the United States, he
stayed in close contact with the man whose invitation
brought him to Fulton, Franc "Bullet" McCluer. On March 9,
McCluer wrote that "The Sinews of Peace" was "an address of
enduring significance in the world" and closed his letter with
these words: "Some have described this as a great small college—
it is the greater because of your visit."[1]

Later that week, McCluer sent Churchill a Callaway County
ham and Ida Belle's cooking instructions, along with a copy of
Churchill's wartime speeches and programs from the March 5
address, which he asked the Briton to sign and return. In the accompanying note, McCluer predicted: "The Green Foundation
lecture of 1946 will be held in memory not only by the college
community but by the world."[2]

A few days later, McCluer opened a reply from Churchill, in
which the ex–prime minister wrote: "I think you know how highly
I valued the opportunity and the privilege you accorded me of
speaking at Westminster College. The ceremony and the warm
welcome I received . . . will ever be a living and happy memory

for me. Thank you so much for the kindness and consideration you and Mrs. McCluer and your friends showed me."[3]

This was just one of the hundreds of letters McCluer received after his big day. Dr. Howard A. Rusk, a graduate of the University of Missouri and a pioneer in rehabilitation medicine as well as a *New York Times* columnist, sent congratulations for "one of the most spiritual and dramatic things I have ever witnessed," and Richard Nacy, executive vice chairman of the Democratic National Committee, commended McCluer for his "stroke of genius" in bringing Churchill to Fulton.[4]

At the same time, McCluer continued his college duties, and his diligence paid off when the Westminster College registrar's office enrolled a record 552 students for the fall 1946 semester, with 70 percent of the new undergraduates receiving tuition assistance from the GI Bill.[5] Before the war a mere 10 percent of the student body had come from outside Missouri, but in this new, large class, a quarter were from other states—a result of Westminster's higher profile after Churchill's visit. Bullet could not have given his alma mater a better parting gift.

To the dismay of all at Westminster College, McCluer made the difficult decision to leave the school, agreeing in late summer 1947 to take the helm at Lindenwood, an all-female college just west of St. Louis. In his thirty-five years at Westminster, he steadied the school through the financial and social storms of the Great Depression and World War II and achieved his career-long goal of enhancing his students' minds through quality teaching, administration, and the establishment of the Green Lecture Series. Yet his lasting legacy would remain the composition of an ambitious, shot-in-the-dark letter that, with the backing of President Harry Truman, brought Winston Churchill to Westminster College on March 5, 1946. Arriving in St. Charles with Ida Belle in September 1947, Bullet made an immediate impact at the red-brick campus. "Dr. McCluer stressed the need for better housing for the faculty, a new chapel, dormitory and auditorium and a larger gymnasium," wrote Russell L. Dearmont, his longtime friend who was a trustee at Westminster and Lindenwood.[6] After nineteen years of service at Lindenwood, McCluer returned to Fulton with Ida Belle to give the Green Foundation Lecture at Westminster College, continuing the series that he created and that Churchill brought to international fame with "The Sinews of Peace" more than two decades before.

ACKNOWLEDGMENTS

> *Writing a book is an adventure. To begin with it is a toy,
> then an amusement. Then it becomes a mistress, and
> then it becomes a master, and then it becomes a tyrant
> and, in the last stage, just as you are about to be recon-
> ciled to your servitude, you kill the monster and fling him
> out to the public.*
>
> —Winston Churchill on book writing
> (November 2, 1949)[1]

A S I SIT DOWN TO WRITE these acknowledgments, I fear that
they may become like the proclamations of an overenthused
actor who is cut off unceremoniously by cheesy award-show music. Despite this concern, I hope you will stick with me as those
who deserve credit get it.

First, this book would not have come into being had not my
lovely wife, Nicole, been so patient. She has endured my absen-
teeism on research trips and, on too many nights to count,
played the role of "writer's widow" as I shuttered myself in my
office, surrounded by books, folders, paper, and cups of what
used to be coffee but soon morphed into something more potent

and penicillin-like. Thank you, Nicole, for putting up with me and this project, which must have seemed endless at times. I am also grateful for your passionate and detail-focused reading and rereading of the drafts, which means more than you can know.

I'd also like to commend my boys, Johnny and Harry, for their patience with Daddy. I made a rigorous effort to not cut short our precious time together during the writing process. While on the subject of family I must acknowledge Mum and Dad, who've been tremendous encouragers. Without my mother's inspirational writing and determination to push me in my own endeavors and my father's example of what true hard work is, I would never have attempted, let alone finished, this project. Thank you also to Barrie, Jacqui, and Debbie for displaying long suffering, as only siblings can, as I made a consistent case for winning the Worst Sibling of the Year award by neglecting the regular phone calls and e-mail contact you deserve during the writing process. Barrie, our spirited weekly discussions are special to me, and I wish we were not separated by an ocean. Lisa, Molly, Mike, and Ollie, you too have been wonderful.

On the Stephens side, Dr. Randall has been a fine editor and critic, and his exemplary writing has spurred me to up my game, while Janice, David, and Nicole (not my wife but, rather, her sister-in-law) have kept me positive at times when I was tired and in need of a pep talk.

The catalyst for this project was an idea presented to me by my friend Henry Worcester. He has been at my side throughout this three-year journey—on research jaunts to Fulton and the University of Missouri at Kansas City and as a first reviewer, sounding board, and sage counselor. The early support and later incisive and insightful editing from Rob Havers, director of the National Churchill Museum in Fulton, were also key to this book's genesis. Rob knows more about Churchill than I ever will, and I sincerely thank him for all his efforts. I would also like to acknowledge Daniel Hannan and Laragh Rose Widdess for giving their time to review the manuscript and for offering constructive criticism and encouragement. Staying on the subject of reviewers, thanks to Barney Forsythe at Westminster College, who is a worthy heir of Bullet McCluer as president of Westminster College and who kindly read the first chapters. Dr. Larry Arnn at Hillsdale College was also nice enough to do this, which came about because of Mike Harner's introduction.

At a critical juncture, my friend and former editor Yaniv Soha put me in touch with the fantastic Rob McQuilkin at Lippincott Massie McQuilkin—in my opinion, the best agent and literary agency a humble scribe could hope to partner with. Rob's diligent reworking of the proposal, keen attention to detail, and, ultimately, skilled representation transformed my initial concept into the words you're reading now. Christina Shideler at LMQ was also a big help.

And that brings me to the PublicAffairs team who connected with Rob and put their confidence in me to write a book that people would want to read. I'd like to thank Clara Platter, my incomparable editor, for her vision, commitment, and wisdom, which guided the ship through choppy waters. I also appreciate the investment that Susan Weinberg and Clive Priddle have made in my work. A hat tip to Tessa Shanks, Melissa Raymond, Jaime Leifer, and Robert Kimzey for their important contributions, to art director Pete Garceau and designer Linda Mark for their design expertise, and to the rest of the staff for all they do. And thanks to Lindsay Farmer for signing this project.

On the research front, Richmond McCluer, Jr., opened his family's archives to me, invited me into his home, and has become a dear friend. Sara Winingear, Kit Freudenberg, and especially Liz Murphy at the National Churchill Museum have freely given their time and expertise to the cause and have been fantastic hosts on many occasions. Philip Mohr was also most helpful when he was helping organize the museum's archives. If you've never been to this venue, I implore you to go. Not just a fine exhibit, it is also situated in the basement of the splendid Church of St. Mary the Virgin, Aldermanbury, a twelfth-century building from the middle of London that was redesigned by Sir Christopher Wren in 1677, bombed in the Blitz, and shipped stone by stone to Fulton in 1964. Later that year it was Harry Truman who, fittingly, turned the first shovel in a reconstruction that took five years.

Going back to those who helped with this book, the openness of O. T. Harris, Jack Marshall, Baxter Watson, Bob Craghead, Bill Johnson, Frieda Lubkeman, Bill Franklin, Thomas Potts, Harvey Clapp, and John Bell added color to the Fulton sections. Glenn Acree, who I also interviewed, sadly passed away before publication, but the hospitality that he and his lovely wife, Marlene, showed to Nicole and me was a testament to the life of this great man, and even more valuable than the information he shared about Fulton. Thank you, too, to Barbara Huddleston at the Callaway County Historical Society for helping me set up these interviews, and to Kristen Zeimet at the Callaway County Chamber of Commerce for providing several key details. David Strawhun was a gracious host who took me in during my second research trip to Fulton when there was (I'm not making this up!) no room at the inn.

I also value the generosity of Allen Packwood at the Churchill Archives Centre, who kindly welcomed me to Cambridge in May 2011. Allen, Katharine Thomson, and their colleagues at CAC have also been patient and responsive to many e-mail requests before and since, and have always come up trumps. Glenda Seifert at MidAmerica Nazarene University performed magic in obtaining obscure interlibrary loans for me that I thought were out of reach, and her colleague Lon Dagley was also most helpful. Cindy Peterson, Rocky Lamar, Mark Hamilton, and Roy Rotz at MNU have also been very supportive. At The State Historical Society of Missouri, Laura Jolley spent a lot of time trawling through the papers of McCluer and his associates, and then sent them up to UMKC, where the archives team was great to work with. I would also like to thank David Clark and Pauline Testerman at the Harry S. Truman Library.

I am lucky to have a lot of friends in my life who bear with my many flaws, compel me to be a better writer and a better man, and never let me settle for "good enough." Luke Crisell is a confidant, and an inspiration with everything he writes—thanks for setting the bar so high, sir. Brett Chalmers and Tom Seibold pushed me to make this book happen from day one. Though four thousand miles away, Jono Lloyd, Ben Spicer, Antony and Chloe Spencer, and Jon Manley have made this English expat feel among friends during late-night e-mail exchanges. The GMC members—Sascha Ohler and Mike and Jason Slattery—have also kept me going, as have Paul and Jenny Hunt, my fellow British expats. Another countryman, Jonathan Sandys, has also been a great encourager. In addition, I appreciate the impact of Justen Wack, Cory Maxwell, Mark Johnston, Taylor Johnson, Matt Korte, Brett Craven, Tim Elliott, Matt Feeney, Kevin Potts, Karen Palmer, Cary DeCamp, Eric Palmer, Jared Blankenship, Dusty Laun, David Wells, Jeremy Snyder, Cody Strate, and Margaret and Rollin Gilliland on my life.

As I've wandered this path, I have also been lucky enough to call several exceptional people mentors. Thank you to Daniel Vanderpool, Phil Towle, Tyler Blake, Jeannie Millhuff, Shanti Thomas, and Dean Nelson for all the hours you put into my life. And, without the passion for history and writing modeled by John Lucas, Tim Godfrey, Melanie Marshall, and Jo Hall, there would be no book.

And with that, let the music play, if it hasn't already. Finally, this work would have gone nowhere without the Lord's blessings.

Notes

A *note regarding the abbreviations herein:* For simplicity's sake, I have abbreviated several sources that appear often throughout this book, as follows:

CHUR The Churchill Papers, provided by the Churchill Archives Centre, Churchill College, Cambridge, England, accessed October 2010 and May 2011

CPPC Churchill Papers Press Clippings, provided by the Churchill Archives Centre, Churchill College, Cambridge, England, accessed May 2011

CTMDC Churchill, Truman, McCluer Day Collection, provided by the National Churchill Museum Archives, Fulton, Missouri, accessed summer 2009, summer 2010, and October 2010

MFP McCluer Family Papers, provided by Richmond McCluer, Jr., accessed from November 2009 until January 2011

ONSL The Papers of Nina, Lady Onslow (née Sturdee), provided by the Churchill Archives Centre, Churchill College, Cambridge, England, accessed October 2010 and May 2011

WHM   Western Historical Manuscripts, provided by the
Missouri State Historical Society and accessed at the
University of Missouri–Kansas City, October 2009

Introduction

1. Richard Langworth, *Churchill by Himself: The Definitive Book of Quotations* (New York: PublicAffairs, 2008), 381; Winston S. Churchill, *The World Crisis: The Aftermath, 1919–1929* (New York: Charles Scribners' Sons), 65.

2. Clementine Churchill to Winston Churchill, December 22, 1950, quoted in Martin Gilbert, *Winston S. Churchill: Never Despair* (Boston: Houghton Mifflin, 1971), 570.

3. Winston S. Churchill, "Constituency Meeting 10 July 1948," in Randolph Churchill, ed., *Europe Unite* (Boston: Houghton Mifflin, 1948), 374.

4. André Fontaine, *History of the Cold War: From the October Revolution to the Korean War, 1917–1950,* translated by D. D. Paige (New York: Pantheon, 1968), 39–41.

5. Martin Gilbert, "From Yalta to Bermuda and Beyond: In Search of Peace with the Soviet Union," in James W. Muller, ed., *Churchill as Peacemaker* (Cambridge: Cambridge University Press, 1997), 304; Winston S. Churchill, ed., *Never Give In: The Best of Winston Churchill's Speeches* (New York: Hyperion, 2003), 199.

6. Martin Gilbert, *Churchill: A Life* (New York: Henry Holt, 1991), 630, 695.

7. Winston S. Churchill and Martin Gilbert, *The Churchill War Papers, 1941: The Ever-Widening War* (New York: W. W. Norton, 2001), 832.

8. Fontaine, *History of the Cold War,* 235–236.

9. Winston Churchill to Franklin Roosevelt, March 8, 1945, quoted in Warren Kimball, ed., *Churchill and Roosevelt: The Complete Corres-*

pondence, Vol. 3 (Princeton: Princeton University Press, 1984), 547–551; Warren F. Kimball, *Forged in War: Roosevelt, Churchill, and the Second World War* (Lanham, Md.: Ivan R. Dee, 2002), 277; John Lukacs, *Churchill: Visionary, Statesman, Historian* (New Haven: Yale University Press, 2002), 46.

10. Winston Churchill to Harry Truman, May 12, 1945, quoted in G. W. Sand, ed., *Defending the West: The Truman-Churchill Correspondence, 1945–1960* (Santa Barbara: Praeger Publishers, 2004), 136.

Chapter 1   The Black Dog

1. David McCullough, *Truman* (New York: Simon and Schuster, 1992), 384.

2. Donald Rayfield, *Stalin and His Hangmen: The Tyrant and Those Who Killed for Him* (New York: Random House, 2005), 85–87.

3. Roy Jenkins, *Churchill: A Biography* (New York: Hill and Wang, 2001), 750.

4. Martin Gilbert, *Winston S. Churchill, Volume VIII: Never Despair* (Boston: Houghton Mifflin, 1971), 42–45.

5. Robert Lloyd George, *David & Winston: How the Friendship Between Lloyd George and Churchill Changed the Course of History* (New York: Woodstock, 2008), 166.

6. Martin Gilbert, *Churchill: A Life* (New York: Henry Holt, 1991), 625.

7. "Royal Setting for Big Three," *Life,* October 17, 1955, accessed June 2011.

8. McCullough, *Truman,* 503.

9. Winston S. Churchill, *The Second World War, Volume 6: Triumph and Tragedy* (Boston: Houghton Mifflin, 1953), 499.

10. Charles L. Mee, Jr., *Meeting at Potsdam* (New York: M. Evans & Co., 1975), 83–84.

11. Josephine and Ray Cowedery, *The New German Reichschancellery, in Berlin, 1938–1945* (Rogers, Minn.: Victory WW2 Publishing, 2003), 46, 47, 52, 84.

12. Mee, *Meeting at Potsdam,* 84.

13. "Royal Setting for Big Three"; Gilbert, *Never Despair,* 63.

14. "The Truman Memoirs," *Life,* October 17, 1955, accessed June 2011; Gilbert, *Never Despair,* 65.

15. Charles Wilson (Lord Moran), *Churchill: The Struggle for Survival, 1945 to 1960* (London: Constable, 1966), 292–293.

16. Winston S. Churchill, *Memoirs of the Second World War* (abridged) (Boston: Houghton Mifflin, 1959), 983; Churchill, *Triumph and Tragedy,* 654.

17. "The Truman Memoirs."

18. Churchill, *Triumph and Tragedy,* 635.

19. "The Truman Memoirs"; Churchill, *Triumph and Tragedy,* 636.

20. Jan Gross, "War as Revolution," *The Establishment of Communist Regimes in Eastern Europe, 1944–1949,* edited by Norman Naimark and Leonid Gibianiski (New York: Westview Press), 30–34.

21. Fraser J. Harbutt, *The Iron Curtain: Churchill, America, and the Origins of the Cold War* (Oxford: Oxford University Press, 1986), 113; "The Truman Memoirs"; Gross, "War as Revolution," 30–32.

22. "The Truman Memoirs."

23. "Churchill Reviews Famed Unit," *Evening Independent,* July 21, 1945, accessed June 2011; "Schloss Cecilienhof im Neuen Garten Potsdam," *Visit Berlin,* date not posted, available online at http://www .visitberlin.de/en/spot/schloss-cecilienhof-im-neuen-garten-potsdam, accessed May 2011.

24. Churchill, *Triumph and Tragedy,* 655–656.

25. André Fontaine, *History of the Cold War: From the October Revolution to the Korean War, 1917–1950,* translated by D. D. Paige (New York: Pantheon, 1968), 235, 254.

26. Churchill, *Triumph and Tragedy,* 655–656.

27. McCullough, *Truman,* 432.

28. Churchill, *Triumph and Tragedy,* 658–659.

29. Harbutt, *The Iron Curtain,* 108; "The Truman Memoirs"; Churchill, *Triumph and Tragedy,* 659–660.

30. Harbutt, *The Iron Curtain,* 113.

31. Churchill, *Triumph and Tragedy*, 668.

32. Winston S. Churchill, *Victory: War Speeches by Right Hon. Winston S. Churchill, O.M., C.H., M.P., 1945*, edited by Charles Eade (London: Cassell and Company, 1946), 244.

33. Peter Hennessy, *Never Again: Britain 1945–1951* (New York: Pantheon, 1993), 85; "Churchill Raps British Critics of His Campaign," *St. Petersburg Times*, June 29, 1945, accessed October 2009.

34. Jenkins, *Churchill*, 794; Wilson, *Churchill*, 304.

35. Churchill, *Triumph and Tragedy*, 662.

36. Archie Brown, *The Rise and Fall of Communism* (New York: Ecco, 2009), 164.

37. Gilbert, *Never Despair*, 95–98.

38. Churchill, *Triumph and Tragedy*, 665–670.

39. Gilbert, *Never Despair*, 105; Churchill, *Triumph and Tragedy*, 674.

40. Maureen Waller, *London 1945: Life in the Debris of War* (New York: St, Martin's Press, 2004), 320, 326.

41. Hennessy, *Never Again*, 94, 169; Norman Davies, *No Simple Victory: World War II in Europe, 1939–1945* (New York, Penguin, 2008), 276.

42. Gilbert, *Never Despair*, 105; Ben Hoyle, "War Diaries and Cigar Light Up Winston Churchill Auction," *The Times* (London), May 7, 2010, accessed May 2010.

43. Churchill, *Triumph and Tragedy*, 674–675.

44. William Manchester, *The Last Lion, Winston Spencer Churchill: Alone, 1932–1940* (New York: Delta Publishing, 1989), 8.

45. Gilbert, *Never Despair*, 106.

46. Churchill, *Triumph and Tragedy*, 675.

47. Jenkins, *Churchill*, 797.

48. Gilbert, *Never Despair*, 108.

49. Mary Soames, *Clementine Churchill: The Biography of a Marriage* (Boston: Mariner Books, 2003), 510.

50. Jenkins, *Churchill*, 824.

51. Wilson, *Churchill*, 5.

52. Churchill, *Triumph and Tragedy*, 573.

53. "Foreign News: Loyal Opposition," *Time,* August 27, 1945, accessed October 2009.

54. Rhodes James, *Churchill Speaks,* 873–874; G. W. Sand, ed., *Defending the West: The Truman-Churchill Correspondence, 1945–1960* (Santa Barbara: Praeger Publishers, 2004), 136.

55. "Churchill Decries Dictatorship Spread," *The Milwaukee Sentinel,* August 17, 1945, accessed June 2011.

56. Rhodes James, *Churchill Speaks,* 874; "Foreign News: Loyal Opposition," *Time,* August 27, 1945, accessed October 2010.

57. "Churchill Visits Mussolini's Grave," *St. Petersburg Times,* September 9, 1945, accessed June 2011; Barbara Leaming, *Churchill Defiant* (New York: Harper, 2010), 59.

58. Leaming, *Churchill Defiant,* 38.

59. Sarah Churchill, *A Thread in the Tapestry* (London: Dodd & Mead, 1967), 94.

60. Soames, *Clementine Churchill,* 518.

61. Sarah Churchill, *A Thread in the Tapestry,* 94.

62. Wilson, *Churchill,* 324.

63. "Churchill on Riviera," *New York Times,* September 23, 1945, accessed June 2011.

64. Mary Soames, ed., *Winston and Clementine: The Personal Letters of the Churchills* (Boston: Houghton Mifflin Harcourt, 1999), 541.

65. Winston S. Churchill, *The Gathering Storm* (Boston: Houghton Mifflin, 1948), 7–9.

Chapter 2   Determination of Another Kind

1. Author interview with Richmond McCluer, Jr., Winona, Minnesota, November 2009.

2. Margaret M. Pinet, "Dr. Franc L. McCluer, Westminster College President Is the Man of the Hour," *Jefferson City News and Tribune,* February 24, 1946, MFP, accessed November 2009; author interview with O. T. Harris, March 5, 2011.

3. Pinet, "Dr. Franc L. McCluer."

4. Author interview with Richmond McCluer, Jr.

5. Charles F. Lamkin, *A Great Small College* (St. Louis: Horace Barks Press, 1946), 414, 419, 432–433.

6. William E. Parrish, *Westminster College: An Informal History, 1851–1969* (Fulton, Mo.: Westminster College Press, 1971), 82; Pinet, "Dr. Franc L. McCluer."

7. "Letter from Augustus Hockaday to Chief Signal Officer on December 8, 1917, MFP, accessed November 2009; J. R. Baker to Whom It May Concern, December 10, 1917, MFP, accessed November 2009; certificate of service from Missouri Fourth Minute Men, undated, MFP, accessed November 2009.

8. Author interview with Richmond McCluer, Jr.

9. Russell Dearmont, *Russell L. Dearmont Papers, 1929–1965*, date not listed, Box C2665, Folder 4847, WHM, accessed October 2009.

10. Lamkin, *A Great Small College*, 489.

11. Franc Lewis McCluer, *Living Conditions Among Wage-Earning Families in Forty-One Blocks in Chicago* (Chicago: University of Chicago, 1928), 1.

12. Parrish, *Westminster College*, 171–173.

13. Lamkin, *A Great Small College*, 514–515; Parrish, *Westminster College*, 173.

14. Charles F. Lamkin, "Westminster College: The Second Century," date unknown, CTMDC, accessed October 2009.

15. Parrish, *Westminster College*, 175.

16. "Inauguration of Franc Lewis McCluer as President of Westminster College," October 28, 1933, MFP, accessed November 2009.

17. Lamkin, *A Great Small College*, 527–528; Dearmont to C. L. Miller, Dean of The James Milikin University, Decatur, Illinois, November 21, 1944, *Russell L. Dearmont Papers, 1929–1965*, Box C2665, Folder 4847, WHM, accessed October 2009.

18. Parrish, *Westminster College*, 176; Ellen Schrecker, "The Bad Old Days: How Higher Education Fared During the Great Depression," *Chronicle of Higher Education*, date unknown, accessed December 2009.

19. Russell Dearmont, untitled document, *Russell L. Dearmont Papers, 1929–1965,* date not listed, Box C2665, Folder 4830, WHM, accessed October 2009.

20. Parrish, *Westminster College,* 184.

21. Russell Dearmont, "McCluer's Report to the Board of Trustees," November 10, 1942, *Russell L. Dearmont Papers, 1929–1965,* Box C2665, Folder 4821, WHM, accessed October 2009; Russell Dearmont, Minutes of Franc McCluer's speech to Delta Tau Delta fraternity, date unknown, *Russell L. Dearmont Papers, 1929–1965,* Box C2665, Folder 4813, WHM, accessed October 2009.

22. "Education: Undergraduate Sideshow," *Time,* May 13, 1940, available online at http://www.time.com/time/magazine/article/0,9171 ,884038,00.html, accessed June 2009.

23. Lamkin, *A Great Small College,* 555.

24. Russell Dearmont to C. L. Miller, November 21, 1944, Russell L. Dearmont Papers, 1929–1965, Box C2665, Folder 4821, WHM, accessed October 2009.

25. Dr. Edgar Dewitt Jones, "Stars Fall on Fulton, Mo.," *Detroit News,* March 2, 1946, MFP, accessed November 2009.

26. Parrish, *Westminster College,* 186.

27. Clarence Cannon, *Clarence Cannon Papers, 1896–1964,* date unknown, Box C2342, Folder 3090, WHM, accessed October 2009.

28. Ron Calzone, "Notes on the Constitutional Convention of 1943–1944," 2007, accessed September 2009; author interview with Richmond McCluer, Jr.

29. Franc McCluer to Russell Dearmont, November 25, 1943, *Russell L. Dearmont Papers, 1929–1965,* Box C2665, Folder 4821, WHM, accessed October 2009.

30. Franc McCluer, notes written May 19, 1944, *Franc McCluer Papers, 1943–1945,* Box C0022, Folder 4, WHM, accessed October 2009; McCluer, undated notes, "Section Two: School Funds," Committee on Finance, Box C0022, Folder 5, accessed October 2009; McCluer, undated notes, "Section 10: Public Libraries," Committee on Finance, Box

C0022, WHM, accessed October 2009; McCluer, January 18, 1944, Committee on Public Health, Box C0022, WHM, accessed October 2009; J. A. Thompson to Franc McCluer, April 27, 1944, Committee on Education, Box C0022, WHM, accessed October 2009.

31. Franc L. McCluer, address delivered at Westminster College, April 15, 1968, MFP, accessed November 2009.

32. Chester A. Bradley, "The Old College 'Try' Draws Churchill to Fulton, Missouri," *Kansas City Star,* January 20, 1946, reprinted in the *Fulton Daily Sun-Gazette* on February 1, 1946, accessed November 2009.

33. Richmond McCluer, Sr., to Catherine Eileen McCluer, October 1, 1949, MFP, accessed November 2009.

34. Author interview with Richmond McCluer, Jr.

35. Franc McCluer, 1945 report to the Board of Trustees, MFP, accessed November 2009.

36. Ida Belle McCluer, "Churchill Day," April 1946, MFP, accessed November 2009; "Churchill Memorial Ground Breaking Slated," *New York Herald Tribune,* date unknown, accessed November 2009; "Fulton's Big, Little College Has Its Biggest Day," *Fulton Sun-Gazette,* March 5, 1946, accessed October 2010.

37. Franc McCluer to Estill I. Green, September 10, 1945, CT-MDC, Box 2, Invitations & Misc. Correspondence Folder, accessed July 2009.

38. Bradley, "The Old College 'Try' Draws Churchill to Fulton, Missouri"; Harry H. Vaughan interview with Charles T. Morrissey for the William Jewell College Oral History Project, January 16, 1963, The Harry S. Truman Library and Museum, accessed March 2009; Gary Partney, "Bringing Churchill to Fulton," *Fulton Sun-Gazette,* 1986 (full date unknown), Callaway County Library Churchill Day Collection, accessed March 5, 2011.

39. Author interview with O. T. Harris, March 5, 2011; Bradley, "The Old College 'Try' Draws Churchill to Fulton, Missouri."

40. Ida Belle McCluer, "Churchill Day."

41. Winston Churchill to Harry Truman, November 29, 1946, Churchill Archive Centre, CHUR 2/230 A, accessed October 2010; Winston Churchill to Frank Clarke, November 22, 1946, CTMDC, Winston Churchill to Frank Clarke Folder, accessed August 2011.

42. "Education: Bull's Eye," *Time*, February 11, 1946, available online at http://www.time.com/time/magazine/article/0,9171,854176,00 .html, accessed June 19, 2009.

43. "The Administration: The Deep Freeze Set," *Time*, August 22, 1949, available online at http://www.time.com/time/magazine/article /0,9171,800578,00.html, accessed May 2010.

44. Partney, "Bringing Churchill to Fulton."

45. Harry H. Vaughan interview with Charles T. Morrissey.

Chapter 3   A Date Is Set

1. Franc McCluer to Winston Churchill, October 3, 1946, MFP, with postscript from Harry Truman, accessed November 2009.

2. Fraser J. Harbutt, *The Iron Curtain: Churchill, America, and the Origins of the Cold War* (Oxford: Oxford University Press, 1986), 160.

3. Winston Churchill to Harry Truman, November 8, 1945, Churchill Archive Centre, CHUR 2/230 A, accessed October 2010.

4. Ibid.

5. Harry Vaughan interview with Charles T. Morrissey, Alexandria, Virginia, January 16, 1963, Harry S. Truman Library, available online at http://www.trumanlibrary.org/oralhist/vaughan3.htm, accessed October 2010; Franc McCluer to Harry Vaughan, November 30, 1945, CTMDC, Box 2, Invitations & Misc. Correspondence Folder, accessed October 2010.

6. "Fulton's Big, Little College Has Its Biggest Day," *Fulton Sun-Gazette*, March 5, 1946, MFA, accessed October 2010; Chester A. Bradley, "The Old College 'Try' Draws Churchill to Fulton, Missouri," *Kansas City Star*, January 20, 1946, reprinted in the *Fulton Daily Sun-Gazette* on February 1, 1946, MFP, accessed November 2009.

7. Author interview with Baxter Watson, March 6, 2011.

8. Franc McCluer to Westminster College alumni, December 10, 1945, Allen P. Green Papers, WHM, accessed October 2009; press release to Missouri newspapers from Westminster College, January 17, 1946, CTMDC, Box 2, Publicity Folder, accessed October 2010.

9. Allen P. Green to Franc McCluer, December 13, 1945, Allen P. Green Papers, WHM, accessed October 2009.

10. "A. P. Green Biography," The State Historical Society of Missouri, date unknown, available online at http://shs.umsystem.edu /famousmissourians/entrepreneurs/green/index.html#portrait, accessed March 2011.

11. Franc McCluer to Harry Truman, December 13, 1945, CTMDC, Box 2, Invitations & Misc. Correspondence, accessed July 2009; Harry Vaughan to Franc McCluer, December 10, 1945, CTMDC, Churchill, Truman, McCluer Day Collection, Box 2, Invitations and Misc. Correspondence Folder, accessed July 2009.

12. Franc McCluer to Phil Donnelly, December 19, 1945, Phil M. Donnelly Papers, WHM, accessed October 2009.

13. Franc McCluer to Estill I. Green, December 6, 1945, CTMDC, Box 2, Invitations & Misc. Correspondence Folder, accessed July 2009.

14. William E. Parrish, *Westminster College: An Informal History, 1851–1969* (Fulton, Mo.: Westminster College Press, 2000), 199; Tom Van Sant to Phil Donnelly, December 20, 1945, Phil M. Donnelly Papers, WHM, accessed October 2009.

15. Parrish, *Westminster College,* 199.

16. Franc McCluer to Harry Vaughan, December 19, 1945, CTMDC, Box 2, Invitations & Misc. Correspondence Folder, accessed October 2010.

17. Ida Belle McCluer, "Churchill Day," April 1946, MFP, accessed November 2009.

18. Margaret Maunder, "Fulton, Mo., Prepares for Churchill Visit," *St. Louis Globe-Democrat,* January 27, 1946, MFP, accessed November 2009.

19. *Kansas City Times,* article title and date unknown, MFP, accessed November 2009.

20. Author interview with Jack Marshall, March 5, 2011.

21. Truman L. Ingle to Franc McCluer, January 31, 1946, CTMDC, Box 2, Folder 24, accessed October 2010.

22. Telegram from Allen P. Green to W. B. Coullie, February 25, 1946, Allen P. Green Papers, WHM, accessed October 2009.

23. Larry Hall, "Callaway County Anxiously Awaits Churchill-Truman Trip," *The News and Courier,* January 27, 1946, accessed January 2011; Bradley, "The Old College 'Try' Draws Churchill to Fulton, Missouri."

24. Larry Hall, "Missouri County in Dither over Churchill, Truman Visit," *Newark Sunday Call,* January 27, 1946, accessed January 2011.

25. Maunder, "Fulton, Mo., Prepares for Churchill Visit"; author interview with Bill Franklin, February 28, 2011.

26. Fulton Historical Society and Callaway County of Commerce records, conveyed by Barbara Huddleston and Kristen Zeimet via e-mails to author, January 3 to January 12, 2011.

27. Author interviews with Bill Franklin, February 28 and March 4, 2011, and with Glenn Acree, February 2 and March 5, 2011; "1945 Films," *Films 101,* http://www.films101.com/y1945r.htm, accessed January 2011; author interview with Glenn Acree, March 5, 2011.

28. Walter R. Ruch, "Wilson Denies Plan for Capital Talks on GM Strike Today," *New York Times,* November 28, 1945, accessed January 2011; John Patrick Diggins, *The Proud Decades: America in War and in Peace, 1941–1960* (New York: W. W. Norton, 1988), 98–103; James T. Patterson, *Grand Expectations: The United States, 1945–1974* (Oxford: Oxford University Press, 1996), 10; author interviews with Bill Franklin, February 28, 2011, and O. T. Harris, March 5, 2011.

29. Author interview with Bill Franklin, February 28, 2011; Gary Donaldson, *Abundance and Anxiety: America, 1945–1960* (Westport, Conn.: Praeger Publishers, 1997), 8.

30. Author interview with Glenn Acree, February 2, 2011, *Milwaukee Journal,* January 25, 1946, accessed February 2011; "In Defense of Fulton," *St. Joseph News-Press,* January 11, 1946, accessed February 2011.

31. "Music: Sincere Sounds," December 23, 1946, *Time,* accessed February 2011; author interview with Jack Marshall, February 25, 2011.

32. "Danny Gage on Westminster's Faculty 65 Years," *Fulton Sun-Gazette,* March 5, 1946, MFP, accessed November 2009.

33. Ibid.

34. Ibid.

35. Parrish, *Westminster College,* 195.

36. Franc McCluer to Allen P. Green, December 21, 1945, Allen P. Green Papers, WHM, accessed October 2009.

37. Allen P. Green to Franc McCluer, January 28, 1946, Allen P. Green Papers, WHM, accessed October 2009.

38. Franc McCluer to Westminster military alumni, January 3, 1946, CTMDC, Box 2, Invitations & Misc. Correspondence Folder, accessed October 2010; Franc McCluer to Westminster college alumni, January 3, 1946, Box 1, Folder 2, CTMDC, accessed July 2009.

39. Franc McCluer to Allen P. Green, February 4, 1946, Allen P. Green Papers, accessed October 2009.

40. Author interview with Jack Marshall, February 25, 2011.

41. "President McCluer Named to Study Child Welfare in State," *Westminster College Bulletin,* October 1945, *Russell L. Dearmont Papers, 1929–1965,* Box C2665, Folder 4821, WHM, accessed October 2009.

42. E-mail from Jack Marshall to author, March 2, 2011; author interview with Jack Marshall, February 25, 2011.

Chapter 4   Finding a Kettle Drum

1. Frank A. Mayer, *The Opposition Years: Winston S. Churchill and the Conservative Party, 1945–1951* (New York: Peter Lang, 1992), 63.

2. Roy Jenkins, *Churchill: A Biography* (New York: Hill and Wang, 2001), 807.

3. Martin Gilbert, *Winston S. Churchill, Volume VIII: Never Despair* (Boston: Houghton Mifflin, 1971), 159.

4. Randolph S. Churchill, "*Winston S. Churchill, Volume I: Youth 1874–1900* (Boston: Houghton Mifflin, 1966), 108, 118, 121, 162, 171.

5. "Mackenzie King Wins," *Time*, April 8, 1940, available online at http://www.time.com/time/magazine/article/0,9171,763787,s00.html, accessed March 2011.

6. Diaries of William Lyon Mackenzie King, entry dated October 26, 1945, Library and Archives of Canada, Ottawa, available online at http://www.collectionscanada.gc.ca/databases/king/001059-119 .02-e.php?&page_id_nbr=27886&interval=20&&PHPSESSID =glus4rhtvhta03p2ohuefc2oa4, accessed January 2011.

7. Gilbert, *Never Despair,* 161–162.

8. Diaries of William Lyon Mackenzie King, entry dated October 26, 1945.

9. Ibid.

10. Donald Rayfield, *Stalin and His Hangmen: The Tyrant and Those Who Killed for Him* (New York: Random House, 2005), 86.

11. "Basic Principles Still There," *Tuscaloosa News,* October 27, 1946, accessed February 2011; "Hint Sino-Soviet Pact Periled, Russia Linked with Chinese Reds," *Youngstown Vindicator,* October 27, 1945, accessed February 2011; Walter Lippmann, "Soviet Position Undergoing Drastic Change," *Pittsburgh Post-Gazette,* October 27, 1945, accessed February 2011.

12. Dean Acheson, *Present at the Creation: My Years in the State Department* (New York: W. W. Norton, 1987), 500.

13. Bela Zhelitski, "Postwar Hungary, 1944–1946," in Norman Naimark and Leonid Gibianiski, eds., *The Establishment of Communist Regimes in Eastern Europe, 1944–1949* (New York: Westview Press, 1998), 74–76.

14. André Fontaine, *History of the Cold War: From the October Revolution to the Korean War, 1917–1950,* translated by D. D. Paige (New York: Pantheon, 1968), 280–285; Jan Gross, "War as Revolution," in Norman Naimark and Leonid Gibianiski, eds., *The Establishment of Communist Regimes in Eastern Europe, 1944–1949* (New York: Westview Press, 1998), 32.

15. Gross, "War as Revolution,"32.

16. John Micgiel, "Bandits and Reactionaries: The Suppression of the Opposition in Poland, 1944–1946," in Norman Naimark and Leonid Gibianiski, eds., *The Establishment of Communist Regimes in Eastern Europe, 1944–1949* (New York: Westview Press, 1998), 97.

17. "Churchill's Son Is Guest When Moscow Celebrates," *Toronto Daily Star,* November 7, 1945, accessed February 2011; David Reynolds, *From World War to Cold War: Churchill, Roosevelt and the International History of the 1940s* (Oxford: Oxford University Press, 2006), 260.

18. Klaus Larres, *Churchill's Cold War: The Politics of Personal Diplomacy* (New Haven: Yale University Press, 2002), 96.

19. "Churchill's Son Is Guest When Moscow Celebrates."

20. "Molotov Declares Soviet Union Seeks Accord," *Los Angeles Times,* November 7, 1945, accessed March 2011.

21. "Foreign Policy (President Truman's Declaration)," *Hansard,* November 7, 1945, available online at http://hansard.millbanksystems .com/commons/1945/nov/07/foreign-policy-president-trumans, accessed March 2011.

22. "Gallacher Accuses Churchill," *New York Times* via the Associated Press, November 8, 1945, accessed March 2011.

23. "Foreign Policy (President Truman's Declaration)."

24. "Belgians Acclaim Mr. Churchill," *The Glasgow Herald,* November 16, 1945, accessed December 2010; Barbara Leaming, *Churchill Defiant: Fighting On, 1945–1955* (New York: Harper, 2010), 48.

25. "Churchill Gets Great Welcome in Brussels," *Milwaukee Journal* via the Associated Press, November 15, 1946, accessed December 2010; John Ramsden, *Man of the Century: Winston Churchill and His Legend Since 1945* (New York: Columbia University Press, 2003), 287.

26. Winston S. Churchill, "Brussels University," *Sinews of Peace* (Boston: Houghton Mifflin, 1949), 37–43.

27. Churchill, "Brussels University," 44.

28. Larres, *Churchill's Cold War,* 55.

29. Ibid., 55, 61, 140–141.

30. Reynolds, *From World War to Cold War,* 278.

31. "Charge Russia Won't Allow Teheran to Fight Rebels," *Toronto Daily Star,* November 29, 1945, accessed February 2011.

32. Reynolds, *From World War to Cold War,* 275.

33. Jenkins, *Churchill,* 806; Harbutt, *The Iron Curtain,* 137.

34. Leaming, *Churchill Defiant,* 48.

35. "Government Policy (Motion of Censure)," *Hansard,* November 27, 1945, available online at http://hansard.millbanksystems.com /commons/1945/dec/06/government-policy-motion-of-censure #S5CV0416P0_19451206_HOC_287, accessed February 2011.

36. Leaming, *Churchill Defiant,* 49.

37. Martin Gilbert, *Churchill and America* (New York: Free Press, 2005), 363.

38. Winston Churchill to Harry Truman, November 29, 1946, CHUR 2/230 A, accessed October 2010.

39. Jenkins, *Churchill,* 80.

40. William Manchester, *The Last Lion, Winston Spencer Churchill: Alone 1932–1940* (Boston: Little, Brown, 1988), 6.

41. Richard Langworth, *Churchill by Himself: The Definitive Collection of Quotations* (New York: PublicAffairs, 2008), 13.

42. Manchester, *The Last Lion: Alone,* 261, 262, 365, 385.

43. Ibid., 14.

44. Langworth, *Churchill by Himself,* 13–14.

45. Kathleen Hill to Albert Canning, December 10, 1945, CHUR 2/230, accessed October 2010; Nina "Jo" Sturdee to her parents, March 10, 1946, ONSL, accessed October 2010.

46. Gilbert, *Never Despair,* 174–175.

Chapter 5   Preparation in Earnest

1. Ida Belle McCluer, "Churchill Day," April 1946, MFP, accessed November 2009.

2. Margaret Pinet, "Dr. Franc L. McCluer, Westminster College President, Is the Man of the Hour," *Jefferson City News and Tribune,*

February 24, 1946, accessed March 2009; Chester A. Bradley, "The Old College 'Try' Draws Churchill to Fulton, Missouri," *Kansas City Star,* January 20, 1946, reprinted in the *Fulton Daily Sun-Gazette* on February 1, 1946, accessed November 2009; *Westminster College Bulletin,* October 1945, WHM, accessed November 2009.

3. Allen P. Green to Franc McCluer, January 2, 1946, Allen P. Green Papers, WHM, accessed October 2009.

4. Franc McCluer to Allen P. Green, January 2, 1946, Allen P. Green Papers, WHM, accessed October 2009.

5. "Postwar American Television," Early Television Foundation, available online at http://earlytelevision.org/postwar_american.html, accessed January 2011.

6. Helen Sioussat to Franc McCluer, December 27, 1945, CTMDC, Box 1, Folder 6, accessed July 2009; Franc McCluer to Helen Sioussat, December 28, 1945, CTMDC, Box 1, Folder 6, accessed July 2009; "Postwar American Television"; Franc McCluer to Winston Churchill, January 15, 1946, CTMDC, Box 2, Invitations & Misc. Correspondence Folder, accessed October 2010.

7. Franc McCluer to Winston Churchill, January 26, 1946, CTMDC, Box 2, Invitations & Misc. Correspondence Folder, accessed October 2010.

8. Winston Churchill to Franc McCluer, January 30, 1946, CHUR 2/230 B, accessed October 2010.

9. Winston Churchill to France McCluer via Western Union, February 5, 1946, CTMDC, Box 1, Folder 9, accessed October 2010.

10. Franc McCluer to Winston Churchill, February 9, 1946, CHUR 2/230 B, accessed October 2010.

11. "Newspaper Men in Fulton for C-T Day," undated, CTMDC, Box 2, Invitations & Misc. Correspondence Folder, accessed July 2009.

12. A. C. Huber to William Newton, February 15, 1946, CTMDC, Box 2, Folder 4, accessed October 2010.

13. "Newspaper Men in Fulton for C-T Day."

14. Jack Bennett to Governor Phil Donnelly, March 1, 1946, Phil M. Donnelly Papers, WHM, accessed October 2009; Gene W. Dennis

to Joe Humphreys, February 13, 1946, CTMDC, Box 2, Folder 4, accessed July 2009; Thomas Velotta to Joe Humphreys, CTMDC, February 13, 1946, Box 1, Folder 8, accessed July 2009.

15. Terry Savage to A. C. Huber, February 14, 1946, CTMDC Box 1, Folder 9, accessed July 2009; A. C. Huber to the manager of the Daniel Boone Hotel in Columbia, Missouri, February 22, 1946, CT-MDC, Box 1, Folder 9, accessed July 2009.

16. Winston Churchill to Franc McCluer, February 14, 1946, CHUR 2/230 B, accessed October 2010.

17. Larry Hall, "Rural Missouri County in a Dither over Churchill, Truman Visit, March 5," *Newark Sunday Call*, January 27, 1946, MFP, accessed January 2011; "Missouri Town Awaits Big Guns," *Telegraph Herald* (Dubuque, Iowa), March 4, 1946, accessed February 2001; e-mail from O. T. Harris to author, March 30, 2011.

18. Franc McCluer to Neal Wood, December 19, 1945, CTMDC, Box 2, Invitations & Misc. Correspondence Folder, accessed October 2010.

19. Joe Humphreys to Lewis Shumate, February 27, 1946, CT-MDC, Box 1, Folder 6, accessed July 2009.

20. Joe Humphreys to John W. Tinnen, February 20, 1946, CT-MDC, Box 1, Folder 5, accessed July 2009.

21. "Margaret Maunder, "Fulton, Mo., Prepares for Churchill Visit," *St. Louis Globe-Democrat*, January 27, 1946, MFP, accessed November 2009; Dorothy Carter to Franc McCluer, January 8, 1946, CTMDC, Box 2, Housing and Feeding, accessed October 2010; Anna S. Hoffmeyer to Franc McCluer, January 7, 1946, CTMDC, Box 2, Housing and Feeding, accessed October 2010; Bradley, "The Old College 'Try' Draws Churchill."

22. Franc McCluer, quoted in Westminster College press release, January 17, 1946, CTMDC, accessed October 2010; John Raeburn Green to Franc McCluer, February 15, 1946, CTMDC, Box 2, Invitations & Misc. Correspondence Folder, accessed October 2010.

23. Edward W. Sowers to Franc McCluer, February 9, 1946, CTMDC, Box 1, Folder 9, accessed October 2010; Clarence Cannon to Franc McCluer, undated letter, Clarence Cannon Papers, WHM,

accessed October 2009; Franc McCluer to Phil Donnelly, January 31, 1946, Phil M. Donnelly Papers, WHM, accessed October 2009.

24. Pinet, "Dr. Franc L. McCluer, Westminster College President, Is the Man of the Hour."

25. Harold Grams to Franc McCluer, February 13, 1946, CTMDC, Box 1, Folder 7, accessed October 2010; author interview with Bill Franklin, February 28, 2011.

26. Colonel L. P. Bonfoey to Allen P. Green, February 25, 1946, Allen P. Green Papers, WHM, accessed October 2009.

27. Allen P. Green to Franc McCluer, February 26, 1946, Allen P. Green Papers, WHM, accessed October 2009.

28. A.C. Huber to Phil Donnelly, February 26, 1946, Phil M. Donnelly Papers, WHM, accessed October 2009.

29. Author interview with Martha Bolton, née Payne, February 10, 2011.

30. Ida Belle McCluer, "Churchill Day"; "Fulton in Holiday Mood for Eminent Visitors," *The Southeast Missourian*, March 4, 1946, accessed March 2011.

31. "History," Fulton Country Club, available online at http://www.fultonccgolf.com/aboutus.html, accessed March 2011.

32. E-mail from O. T. Harris to author, March 30, 2011.

33. Ida Belle McCluer, "Churchill Day."

34. William E. Parrish, *Westminster College: An Informal History, 1851–1969* (Fulton, Mo.: Westminster College Press, 1971), 204.

35. "Fulton in Holiday Mood for Eminent Visitors"; "Arrangements for Churchill Visit," memo from Huber and Humphreys to Franc McCluer, February 6, 1946, CTMDC, Box 2, Folder 24, accessed October 2010.

Chapter 6   A Message to a Baffled World

1. Martin Gilbert, *Churchill: A Life* (New York: Henry Holt, 1991), 862.

2. "Scientist Says Russia Has New Atomic Bomb," *Ottawa Citizen*, January 8, 1946, accessed February 2011.

3. "Senior Officers," January 10, 1946, CHUR 2/229, accessed October 2010; "An Odyssey of the Sea," *Montreal Gazette,* June 23, 1945, accessed March 2011; "N.Y. Greets Churchill, Canadians; War Leader Will Stay at Tory Helm," *Montreal Gazette,* January 14, 1946, accessed December 2010; "RMS Queen Elizabeth," quoted in N.R.P. Bonsor, *North Atlantic Seaway,* 5 vols. (Newton Abbot, Devon, England: David & Charles, 1975–1980), available online at http://www.ocean-liners.com /ships/queenelizabeth.asp, accessed February 2011.

4. Ralph Allen, "Churchill Gives Warning," *Toronto Globe and Mail,* quoted in the *Windsor Daily Star,* January 14, 1946, accessed December 2010.

5. "N.Y. Greets Churchill, Canadians; War Leader Will Stay at Tory Helm," *Montreal Gazette,* January 14, 1946, accessed January 2011; Barbara Leaming, *Churchill Defiant* (New York: Harper, 2010), 59.

6. Roy Jenkins, *Churchill: A Biography* (New York: Hill and Wang, 2001), 809.

7. "The Baruch Program," *Time,* February 28, 1944, available online at http://www.time.com/time/magazine/article/0,9171,796478,00.html, accessed March 2011.

8. Martin Walker, *The Cold War: A History* (New York: Macmillan, 1995), 23; Bertrand D. Hulen, "British State Case at Financial Talks; Keynes Indicates U.S. Help Is Vital to United Kingdom During Reconversion Period," *New York Times,* September 14, 1945, accessed March 2011.

9. John Ramsden, "Mr. Churchill Goes to Fulton," in James W. Muller, ed., *Churchill's "Iron Curtain" Speech Fifty Years Later* (Columbia, Mo.: University of Missouri Press, 1999), 25; Hulen, "British State Case at Financial Talks"; Leaming, *Churchill Defiant,* 28–29.

10. Fraser J. Harbutt, *The Iron Curtain: Churchill, America, and the Origins of the Cold War* (Oxford: Oxford University Press, 1986), 184–185; Klaus Larres, *Churchill's Cold War: The Politics of Personal Diplomacy* (New Haven: Yale University Press, 2002), 97.

11. General Passenger Manager of Cunard White Star to Mr. P. Solly-Hull, March 9, 1946, CHUR 2/229, accessed October 2010.

12. "Churchill in New York," *Milwaukee Sentinel* via the Associated Press, January 14, 1946, accessed January 2011.

13. Winston Churchill to Harry Truman, November 8, 1945, CHUR 2/230 A, accessed October 2010.

14. "Churchill to Rest on Visit Here," *Miami News,* January 15, 1946, accessed January 2011; "Churchill Relaxes Without Tie on Miami Beach," *Windsor Daily Star,* January 17, 1946, accessed January 2011.

15. "Winston Churchill," *Miami News,* January 16, 1946, accessed January 2011.

16. Martin Gilbert, *Churchill and America* (New York: Free Press, 2005), 365.

17. Walter Locke, "Churchill in Miami," *Miami Daily News,* January 17, 1946, accessed January 2011.

18. Ibid.

19. Gilbert, *Never Despair,* 184.

20. Jo Sturdee to her parents, March 8, 1946. ONSL, Box 2, accessed May 2011; "Jungle Island (formerly Parrot Jungle)," *Roadside America,* http://www.roadsideamerica.com/story/11308, accessed June 2011; "Churchill Takes Ease in Miami," *Saskatoon Star-Phoenix* via the Associated Press, January 18, 1946, accessed June 2011.

21. Claude Pepper to Winston Churchill, January 17, 1946, CHUR 2/229, accessed May 2011.

22. Mary Soames, *Clementine Churchill: The Biography of a Marriage* (Boston: Houghton Mifflin Harcourt, 2003), 441.

23. Leaming, *Churchill Defiant,* 61–62; William S. White, "Ferguson Fails in Churchill Bid," *New York Times,* January 19, 1946, accessed February 2011.

24. Soames, *Clementine Churchill,* 441.

25. "Arnold Luncheon Guest of Churchill," *Palm Beach Post,* January 19, 1946, accessed January 2011; "Churchill Takes Role of Artist," *Baltimore Sun,* January 20, 1946, accessed January 2011; Walter Locke, "Churchill in Miami," *Miami News,* January 16, 1946, accessed January 2011.

26. Gilbert, *Never Despair,* 184–185.

27. Gilbert, *Never Despair*, 188; "British War Secret Bared," *Tuscaloosa News* via the United Press, January 25, 1946, accessed February 2011; "Churchill Feared Japs Might Overrun Large Parts of India," *The Indian Express*, January 26, 1946, accessed February 2011.

28. Jo Sturdee to Clementine Churchill, undated, CHUR 2/229, accessed October 2010.

29. James F. Byrnes, *All in One Lifetime* (New York: Harper, 1958), 349; David McCullough, *Truman* (New York: Simon and Schuster, 1992), 370.

30. André Fontaine, *History of the Cold War: From the October Revolution to the Korean War, 1917–1950*, translated by D. D. Paige (New York: Pantheon, 1968), 280; Winston Churchill to Harry Truman, January 29, 1946, CHUR 2/230/350, accessed October 2010; David Reynolds, *From World War to Cold War: Churchill, Roosevelt and the International History of the 1940s* (Oxford: Oxford University Press, 2006), 262.

31. "Track History: Hialeah Park Is Eternal," *Hialeah Park Racing*, available online at http://www.hialeahparkracing.com/index.php?option =com_content&view=category&layout=blog&id=55&Itemid=62, accessed June 2011; "Churchill Picks Two Winners," *Calgary Herald*, January 31, 1946, accessed June 2011.

32. "AP Release on Mr. Churchill's Arrival," Associated Press, February 1, 1946, CHUR 2/231, accessed October 2010.

33. Ben Ross, "48 Hours in: Havana," *The Independent*, February 6, 2010, available online at http://www.independent.co.uk/travel/48-hours -in/48-hours-in-havana-1890524.html, accessed January 2011.

34. "Churchill Sees Continued Unity," *Pittsburgh Press*, January 2, 1946, accessed January 2011.

35. "AP Release on Mr. Churchill's Arrival"; G. W. Sand, ed., *Defending the West: The Truman-Churchill Correspondence, 1945–1960* (Santa Barbara: Praeger Publishers, 2004), 157.

36. Gilbert, *Never Despair*, 191.

37. R. Henry Norweb to Harry Truman, February 7, 1946; Sand, *Defending the West*, 157–158.

38. Harbutt, *The Iron Curtain,* 161–163.

39. McCullough, *Truman,* 463; Felix Belair, Jr., "Truman Upholds Yalta on Balkans," *New York Times,* January 9, 1946, accessed February 2011.

40. P. J. Philip, "More Canadians Rounded Up as King Implicates Russians," *New York Times,* February 16, 1946, accessed February 2011; "Soviets Score Atomic Gain," *Baltimore Sun,* February 1, 1946, accessed February 2011.

41. Archie Brown, *The Rise and Fall of Communism* (New York: HarperCollins, 2009), 160, 175; Tony Judt, *Postwar: A History of Europe Since 1945* (New York: Penguin, 2005), 131–132; C. L. Sulzberger, "Hoxha Shows Dictator Hand to Offset Soviet[s] in North," *Montreal Gazette,* March 7, 1946, accessed February 2011.

42. "Churchill Mobbed in Washington," *Glasgow Herald,* February 11, 1946, accessed February 2011.

43. "Churchill Plans to See Truman," *St. Petersburg Times,* February 10, 1946, accessed February 2011.

44. Ramsden, "Mr. Churchill Goes to Fulton."

45. The Diaries of William D. Leahy, 1897–1956, February 10, 1946, Iowa State University, accessed at MidAmerica Nazarene University, November 2010.

46. "Abroad, Mr. Bevin and Mr. Vishinsky Fight It Out," *New York Times,* February 2, 1946, accessed February 1946; "U.S. Says 'Atom Spies' Are Under Control," *Christian Science Monitor,* February 19, 1946, accessed February 2011.

47. "The Man Behind the Legend," *Time,* July 2, 1965, available online at http://www.time.com/time/magazine/article/0,9171,833836,00.html, accessed February 2011.

48. Jordan A. Schwarz, *The Speculator: Bernard Baruch in Washington, 1917–1965* (Chapel Hill: University of North Carolina Press, 1981), 489.

49. McCullough, *Truman,* 563.

50. "Boom & Bust?," *Time,* December 10, 1945, http://www.time.com/time/magazine/article/0,9171,852615,00.html, accessed February 2011;

"The Congress: What Can We Do?," *Time,* January 28, 1946, available online at http://www.time.com/time/magazine/article/0,9171,855290,00 .html, accessed February 2011; McCullough, *Truman,* 564.

51. Winston Churchill to Clement Attlee, February 17, 1946, quoted in Gilbert, *Never Despair,* 192.

52. Byrnes, *All in One Lifetime,* 349.

53. Gilbert, *Never Despair,* 193, Leaming, *Churchill Defiant,* 76; Larres, *Churchill's Cold War,* 109.

54. "Churchill Wants to Return," *Glasgow Herald,* February 27, 1946, accessed February 2011; *Miami Herald,* story title unknown, Joe Humphreys to Helen Sioussat, February 27, 1946, National Churchill Museum Archives, CTMDC, Box 1, Folder 6, accessed October 2010.

55. This term was a misnomer owing to the utter absence of democracy in Russia.

56. Judt, *Postwar,* 108; Bernard A. Weisberger, *Cold War, Cold Peace: The United States and Russia Since 1945* (New York: American Heritage, 1984), 47–49.

57. Charles E. Bohlen, *Witness to History, 1929–1969* (New York: W. W. Norton, 1973), 240.

58. W. Averell Harriman and Elie Abel, *Special Envoy to Churchill and Stalin, 1941–1946* (New York: Random House, 1975), 294.

59. George Kennan, quoted in Harriman and Abel, *Special Envoy to Churchill and Stalin,* 548.

60. Harbutt, *The Iron Curtain,*153; Harriman and Abel, *Special Envoy,* 548–549; McCullough, *Truman,* 548–549.

61. "Churchill Begins Portrait Sittings Roosevelt Requested," Associated Press, February 14, 1946, accessed February 2011; Gilbert, *Never Despair,* 185.

62. Jo Sturdee to Charles Campbell, February 2, 1946, CHUR 2/158, accessed October 2010.

63. Harbutt, *The Iron Curtain,* 162.

64. Larres, *Churchill's Cold War,* 45, 117.

65. "Frank Policy with Russia Urged by Sen. Vandenberg," *St.*

Petersburg Times via the Associated Press, February 28, 1946, accessed March 2011.

66. "Byrnes Warns Force from U.S. Behind Peace," *Montreal Gazette,* March 1, 1946, accessed March 2011.

67. Byrnes, *All in One Lifetime,* 349; David Lawrence, "Today in Washington," *Schenectady Gazette,* March 1, 1946, accessed March 2011.

68. McCullough, *Truman,* 486.

69. Diaries of William Lyon Mackenzie King, February 28, 1946, Library and Archives of Canada, available online at http://www.collections canada.gc.ca/databases/king/001059-119.02-e.php?&page_id_nbr=28213 &interval=20&&PHPSESSID=qm2h9mqe2njl9mque8at5knv12, accessed March 2011.

70. Byrnes, *All in One Lifetime,* 334–339; "U.S. Protests to Russia," *San José News* via the Associated Press, March 2, 1946, accessed April 2011.

71. "Churchill Will Get a Missouri Feast," *Chicago Tribune,* March 2, 1946, accessed March 2011.

Chapter 7   The New Missouri Gang

1. "Truman and Churchill Fulton-Bound," *Spartansburg Herald,* March 4, 1946, accessed January 2011; "Truman, Churchill Leave Today for Briton's Address at Fulton, Mo.," *New York Times,* March 4, 1946, accessed January 2011; Sir Winston Churchill, *His Father's Son: The Life of Randolph Churchill* (London: Trafalgar, 1997), 279.

2. "The Ambassador's Residence," website for British Embassy in Washington, available online at http://ukinusa.fco.gov.uk, accessed December 2010.

3. Fraser J. Harbutt, *The Iron Curtain: Churchill, America, and the Origins of the Cold War* (Oxford: Oxford University Press, 1986), 180.

4. John Chamberlain, "The Earl of Halifax," *Life,* March 19, 1945.

5. "Ambassador's Residence: The Dining Room," website for British Embassy in Washington, http://ukinusa.fco.gov.uk/en/about -us/our-embassy/location-access/residence/residencediningroom,

accessed March 2011; "Ambassador's Residence: The Staircase & Bed-
rooms," website for British Embassy in Washington, http://ukinusa
.fco.gov.uk/en/about-us/our-embassy/location-access/residence
/residencebedrooms, accessed December 2010; James F. Byrnes, *All in
One Lifetime* (New York: Harper, 1958), 349.

6. Byrnes, *All in One Lifetime,* 349.

7. The Diaries of William D. Leahy, 1897–1956, March 3, 1946,
Iowa State University, accessed at MidAmerica Nazarene University,
November 2010.

8. Truman, Churchill Are Missouri-Bound," *Schenectady Gazette*
via the Associated Press, March 1, 1946, accessed January 2011.

9. "Truman Tries Hand as Train Engineer," *Lewiston Daily Sun* via
the Associated Press, March 4, 1946, accessed January 2011; "Churchill
on Way to Join President," March 2, 1946, *New York Times,* accessed
December 2010; Patrick Wright, *Iron Curtain: From Stage to Cold War*
(Oxford: Oxford University Press, 2007), 30; "Fulton Gets Its Big Day,"
Kansas City Times, March 4, 1946, MFP, accessed November 2009.

10. "Mighty Warm for March," *Time,* March 25, 1946, accessed December 2010.

11. David McCullough, "Fighting Chance," in Jack Beatty, ed., *Pols:
Great Writers on American Politicians from Bryan to Reagan* (New
York: PublicAffairs, 2004), 201.

12. Major General Harry Vaughan interview with Charles T. Morrissey, Alexandria, Virginia, January 16, 1963, Harry S. Truman Library
and Museum, available online at http://www.trumanlibrary.org/oralhist
/vaughan3.htm, accessed October 2010.

13. Clark Clifford, *Counsel to the President* (New York: Random
House, 1991), 101.

14. Bruce Barrington to Franc McCluer, February 22, 1946, Na-
tional Churchill Museum Archives, CTMDC, Box 1, Folder 8, accessed
October 2009; Richard Everett, "Fulton Welcome Prepared, Awaits
Churchill and Truman," *St. Louis Star-Times,* March 4, 1946, accessed
January 2011; Margaret Maunder, "Fulton, Mo. Prepares for Churchill

Visit," *St. Louis Globe-Democrat*, January 26, 1946, accessed January 2011.

15. "Fulton Awaits Notables," *St. Louis Star-Times*, March 4, 1946, accessed February 2011.

16. "Glow in Fulton," unknown newspaper, March 4, 1946, MFP, accessed January 2011; Everett, "Fulton Welcome Prepared."

17. *Fulton Sun-Gazette*, March 4, 1946, Churchill Day Collection, Callaway County Library, accessed March 5, 2011.

18. Clementine Paddleford, "Churchill Enjoys Home-Cooked Missouri Meal," *New York Herald Tribune*, March 6, 1946, MFP, accessed November 2009.

19. Margaret Hamilton, "Hostess of Truman and Churchill Puts Final Dainty Touch to Home," *Kansas City Star,* March 4, 1946, accessed February 2011.

20. "Churchill-Truman Parade at Noon Today," *Fulton Sun-Gazette,* March 5, 1946, MFP, accessed November 2009; "Glow in Fulton"; "World Spotlight Turns on Westminster College," *Westminster College Bulletin,* April 1946, CTMDC, Box 2, Publicity Folder, accessed October 2010; H. R. Schuessler to Mr. Woodson, January 8, 1946, CTMDC, Box 2, Folder 14, accessed October 2010.

21. "Arrangements for Churchill Visit," memo from Huber and Humphreys to Franc McCluer, February 6, 1946, CTMDC, Box 2, Folder 24, accessed October 2010; "Fulton Gets Its Big Day."

22. "World Spotlight Turns on Westminster College"; Charles F. Lamkin, *A Great Small College* (St. Louis: Horace Barks Press, 1946), 502.

23. Joe B. Humphreys to Gene W. Dennis, February 15, 1946, CTMDC, Box 2, Folder 24, accessed October 2010.

24. Jo Sturdee to her parents, March 8, 1946, Churchill Archives Centre, ONSL, Box 2, accessed October 2010.

25. Untitled document with diagram of sleeping arrangements for the journey from Washington, D.C., to Jefferson City, CAC, CHUR 2/230 B, accessed October 2010; Ernest B. Vaccaro, "Truman Leaves

for Missouri," *Tuscaloosa News,* March 4, 1946, accessed February 2011.

26. David Brinkley, *A Memoir* (New York: Alfred A. Knopf, 1995), 71.

27. "National Affairs: Fun and Troubles," *Time,* March 18, 1946, available online at http://www.time.com/time/magazine/article/0,9171 ,934437,00.html, accessed March 2011.

28. "Churchill Speaks," *Life,* March 18, 1946, accessed May 2011; "Truman Runs Train, Churchill Recites," *Daytona Beach Morning Journal* via the Associated Press, March 5, 1946, accessed February 2011; Harold B. Hinton, "Truman, Churchill Travel to West," *New York Times,* March 4, 1946, accessed February 2011.

29. "Truman Runs Train, Churchill Recites."

30. "Churchill Speaks."

31. "National Affairs: Fun and Troubles"; Brinkley, *A Memoir,* 71.

32. Clifford, *Counsel to the President,* 102–104.

33. Matthew Algeo, *Harry Truman's Excellent Adventure: The True Story of a Great American Road Trip* (Chicago: Chicago Review Press, 2009), 10; "Churchill's Political Offices, 1906–1955," The Churchill Centre, available online at http://www.winstonchurchill.org/learn /reference/churchills-political-offices, accessed April 2011.

34. Clifford, *Counsel to the President,* 102–104.

35. "Truman Decides Child Must Be Republican," *Fulton-Sun Gazette* via the Associated Press, March 5, 1946, MFP, accessed November 2009.

36. "Pressing Harsh Terms on Iran," *Calgary Herald,* March 5, 1946, accessed May 2011.

Chapter 8   "C-T Day"

1. Ida Belle McCluer, "Churchill Day," April 1946, MFP, accessed November 2009; "World Spotlight Turns on Westminster College," *Westminster College Bulletin,* April 1946, CTMDC, Box 2, Publicity Folder, accessed July 2009.

2. "Churchill Gets Cigars, Truman a Country Ham," *Fulton Sun-Gazette,* March 6, 1946, accessed January 2011; Sarah Churchill, *A Thread in the Tapestry* (New York: Dodd, Mead and Company, 1966), 38.

3. "Representatives from Student Groups on Campus Who Are Designated to Meet President Truman and Mr. Churchill," undated, CTMDC, Box 2, Invitations & Misc. Correspondence Folder, accessed October 2010.

4. James F. King, "Excited in State Capital," *Kansas City Times,* March 5, 1946, accessed February 2011; "Governor Gives Churchill Hard-to-Get Cuban Cigars," *St. Louis Globe-Dispatch,* March 5, 1946, accessed February 2011.

5. Franc McCluer to Phil Donnelly, February 28, 1946, CTMDC, Box 2, Invitations & Misc. Correspondence Folder, accessed October 2010; A. C. Huber to Phil Donnelly, February 26, 1946, Phil M. Donnelly Papers, WHM, accessed October 2009.

6. "Churchill's Fulton Speech Termed 'Most Important,'" *Minneapolis Star-Tribune,* March 5, 1946, accessed February 2011; "Churchill Gets Cigars, Truman a Country Ham"; "Churchill Visit Proves a Tonic for Doc Simpson," *Jefferson City Post-Tribune,* March 5, 1946, accessed February 2011.

7. Franc McCluer to Phil Donnelly, February 28, 1946, accessed October 2009; Jo Sturdee, letter to her parents, March 8, 1946, Churchill Archives Centre, ONSL, Box 2, accessed October 2010.

8. "Fulton's Big Day," unknown newspaper, March 6, 1946, MFP, accessed November 2009; "William E. Parrish, *Westminster College: An Informal History, 1851–1969* (Fulton, Mo.: Westminster College Press, 2000), 205; "Fulton Awaits Notables," *St. Louis Star-Times,* March 4, 1946, accessed January 2011; author interview with Bob Craghead, March 5, 2011.

9. Donald Grant, "Fulton Expects 30,000 Visitors to Greet Truman and Churchill," *St. Louis Globe-Dispatch,* March 5, 1946, accessed January 2011.

10. Author interview with Frieda Lubkeman, née Franklin, February 12, 2011.

11. Author interview with Glenn Acree, February 2, 2011; "Churchill's Fulton Speech Termed 'Most Important.'"

12. Author interview with Martha Bolton, February 10, 2011; Matthew Algeo, *Harry Truman's Excellent Adventure: The True Story of a Great American Road Trip* (Chicago: Chicago Review Press, 2009), 16; e-mail from Marlene Acree to author, February 2, 2011.

13. Author interview with Bill Johnson, February 7, 2011.

14. "Churchill-Truman Visit Thrills Fulton," *The Missouri Record,* January 16, 1946, accessed February 2011; Margaret Pinet, "Carnival Spirit Takes Fulton as Winnie Arrives," *Jefferson City Post-Tribune,* March 5, 1946, WHM, accessed October 2009; Parrish, *Westminster College,* 206; Gary Partney, "Bringing Churchill to Fulton," *Fulton Sun-Gazette,* 1986 (full date unknown), Churchill Day Collection, Callaway County Library, accessed March 2011.

15. Ibid.; A. C. Huber to P. F. Drury of the AAA Automobile Club of Missouri, February 22, 1946, CTMDC, Box 2, Passes Folder, accessed October 2010.

16. "Missouri Awaits Churchill Visit," *St. Petersburg Times* via the Associated Press, March 3, 1946, accessed February 2011; "25,000 Line the Streets for Parade," *St. Louis Post-Dispatch,* March 6, 1946, accessed January 2011; "Fulton," *Minneapolis Star-Tribune,* March 3, 1946, accessed January 2011.

17. Author interview with Glenn Acree, February 2, 1946; author interview with Bill Johnson.

18. Author interview with Thomas Potts, March 23, 2011.

19. "World Spotlight Turns on Westminster."

20. Ida Belle McCluer, "Churchill Day."

21. Margaret Hamilton, "Hostess of Truman and Churchill Puts Final Dainty Touch to Home," *Kansas City Star,* March 4, 1946, accessed January 2011; Mary Kimbrough, "Too Many Hot Dogs," *St. Louis Star-Times,* March 6, 1946, accessed February 2011; Ida Belle McCluer, "Churchill Day."

22. Clementine Paddleford, "Churchill Enjoys Home-Cooked Missouri Meal," *New York Herald Tribune,* March 6, 1946, MFP, accessed October 2009; "A Confederate Stronghold Puts on a Show for Churchill," *Chicago Sun,* March 5, 1946, accessed February 2011.

23. Ida Belle McCluer, "Churchill Day."

24. "Churchill-Truman Parade at Noon Today," *Fulton Sun-Gazette,* March 5, 1946, MFP, accessed November 2009; "London Paper Mentions Us," *The Record,* quoting "Day by Day" in *The Daily Telegraph,* March 5, 1946, Missouri School for the Deaf, accessed January 2011; "Our Pupils Present Gold Card to Mr. Churchill," *The Record,* Missouri School for the Deaf, undated, accessed March 2011; Paddleford, "Churchill Enjoys Home-Cooked Missouri Meal"; Rich Gleba, "Pasley Recalls Meeting Churchill," March 6, 1996, Churchill Day Collection, Callaway County Library, accessed March 2011; Jo Sturdee, letter to her parents.

25. "Truman-Churchill Day," CTMDC, Box 2, Folder 24, accessed October 2010; "In Pursuit of a Ticket," March 8, 1981, *Kingdom Daily News,* Callaway County Library, Churchill Day Collection, accessed March 2011.

26. Larry Hall, "Wild Excitement Precedes Churchill Visit," Associated Press, January 27, 1945, accessed February 2011; *Milwaukee Journal* (article title unknown), March 4, 1946, accessed April 2011; Margaret Hamilton, "Churchill Joins Truman in a Political Hand-Shaking Spree," *Kansas City Times,* March 5, 1946.

27. Ida Belle McCluer, "Churchill Day"; H. R. Schuessler to Mr. Woodson, January 8, 1946, CTMDC, Box 2, Folder 14, accessed October 2010.

28. Harry H. Vaughan, "General Vaughan," speech in summer 1969 at Westminster College, *Westminster College Magazine,* Churchill Day Collection, Callaway County Library, accessed March 2011.

29. Jo Sturdee, letter to her parents; "Shoot If You Must," *Time,* March 18, 1946, available online at http://www.time.com/time/magazine /article/0,9171,934435,00.html, accessed November 2009.

30. Ida Belle McCluer, "Churchill Day."

31. Jon Hetzel, "Churchill's Visit Through the Eyes of . . . ," *Fulton's Finest Hour* supplement to *The Fulton Sun,* March 1, 2006, Callaway County Library, Churchill Day Collection, accessed March 5, 2011; "200 with Tickets Fail to Get into Gym," *Fulton Sun-Gazette,* March 6, 1946, Callaway County Library, Churchill Day Collection, accessed March 2011.

32. Lisa Yorkgitis, "Looking Back," *Jefferson City News Tribune,* March 3, 1996, Churchill Day Collection, Callaway County Library, accessed March 2011; Kimbrough, "Too Many Hot Dogs"; "Churchill-Truman Parade at Noon Today"; author interview with Bob Craghead; e-mail from Bob Craghead to author, March 29, 2011; Partney, "Bringing Churchill to Fulton."

33. "World Spotlight Turns on Westminster College," *Westminster College Bulletin,* Franc McCluer to Professor R. F. Wood, Central Missouri State Teachers College, February 18, 1946, CTMDC, Box 2, Folder 16, accessed October 2010.

34. "Churchill Warns Against Russian Aims," *St. Louis Globe-Dispatch,* March 6, 1946, accessed October 2010; author interview with Baxter Watson, March 11, 2011; "The John Findley Green Lecture" program, March 5, 1946, CTMDC, Box 2, Folder 23, accessed July 2009; Clark Clifford, *Counsel to the President* (New York: Random House, 1991), 104.

35. "William B. Lampe Invocation," March 5, 1946, CTMDC, Box 2, Publicity Folder, accessed October 2010; "Churchill Urges U.S.-British Coalition," unknown author and newspaper, MFA, accessed October 2009; Jo Sturdee, letter to her parents.

Chapter 10   A Firebrand

1. "Message for Presentation of Gold Watch to Churchill," March 6, 1946, CTMDC, Box 2, Folder 26, accessed October 2010; "Benton Picture for Churchill, Who Refused Fee," *St. Louis Post-Dispatch,* March 6, 1946, MFA, accessed March 2011.

2. Margaret Hamilton, "Churchill Joins Truman in a Political Hand-

Shaking Spree," *Kansas City Times*, March 5, 1946, accessed March 2011.

3. "Churchill Warns Against Russian Aims," *St. Louis Globe-Dispatch*, March 6, 1946, accessed March 2011.

4. Anthony J. Leviero, "Churchill Will Take Spotlight; May Slant Speech at the Kremlin," *New York Times*, March 3, 1946, accessed April 2011.

5. Clark Clifford, *Counsel to the President* (New York: Random House, 1991), 106.

6. The Diary of Charles Ross, entry dated March 7, 1946, Charles G. Ross Papers, Harry S. Truman Library and Museum, accessed December 2010; "Charles G. Ross Papers," Harry S. Truman Library and Museum, available online at http://www.trumanlibrary.org/hstpaper /ross.htm, accessed December 2010.

7. Harry Truman to Winston Churchill, March 12, 1946, CHUR 2/158, accessed May 2011.

8. Felix Belair, Jr., "President Hopeful; Doubts Moscow Will Go 'Down One-Way Street,'" *New York Times*, March 8, 1946, accessed April 2011; Archie Brown, *The Rise and Fall of Communism* (New York: HarperCollins, 2009), 178.

9. Fraser J. Harbutt, *The Iron Curtain: Churchill, America, and the Origins of the Cold War* (Oxford: Oxford University Press, 1986), 180–181.

10. Bernard A. Weisberger, *Cold War, Cold Peace: The United States and Russia Since 1945* (New York: American Heritage, 1984), 57. (An exception to the administration's unified stance was Secretary of Commerce Henry A. Wallace, whose soft line on Russia infuriated his hawkish colleagues.)

11. Martin Gilbert, *Winston S. Churchill, Volume VIII: Never Despair* (Boston: Houghton Mifflin, 1971), 207; Pamela Harriman, "The True Meaning of the Iron Curtain Speech," in *Finest Hour*, "The Journal of Winston Churchill," volume 58, Spring 1988, accessed May 2011.

12. The Diaries of William D. Leahy, 1897–1956, entry dated

March 5, 1946, Iowa State University, accessed at MidAmerica Nazarene University, November 2010.

13. Winston Churchill to Clement Attlee and Ernest Bevin, March 7, 1946, CHUR 2/4, accessed May 2011.

14. "Russian Broadcasts Denounce Churchill as War Monger," *Pittsburgh Post-Gazette* via the United Press, March 11, 1946, accessed March 2011; David Reynolds, *From World War to Cold War: Churchill, Roosevelt and the International History of the 1940s* (Oxford: Oxford University Press, 2006), 262.

15. "Stalin Takes the Stump," *Time*, March 25, 1946, available online at http://www.time.com/time/magazine/article/0,9171,888130,00 .html, accessed December 2010; Bill Jones, *The Russia Complex: The British Labour Party and the Soviet Union* (Manchester, England: Manchester University Press 1978), 115.

16. "Business of the House," *Hansard,* March 14, 1946, available online at http://hansard.millbanksystems.com/commons/1946/mar/14 /business-of-the-house#S5CV0420P0_19460314_HOC_315, accessed June 1946.

17. The Diaries of William D. Leahy, 1897–1956, entry dated March 5, 1946.

18. "Proposal Viewed as 'Body Blow' to United Nations, Affront to Reds," *St. Louis Post-Dispatch,* March 6, 1946, accessed February 2011; "Churchill in Fulton," *St. Louis Globe-Democrat,* March 6, 1946, accessed November 2010.

19. Reynolds, *From World War to Cold War,* 260.

20. Robert L. Beisner, *Dean Acheson: A Life in the Cold War* (New York: Oxford University Press, 2009), 38; "Churchill Urges Armed Alliance," *Chicago Sun,* March 6, 1946, accessed May 2011; Martin Gilbert, *Churchill and America* (New York: Free Press, 2005), 373.

21. "The Redness of Winston," *Chicago Tribune,* March 6, 1946, accessed April 2011.

22. "Post-Gazette Holds Interest of Churchill," *Pittsburgh Post-Gazette,* March 7, 1946, accessed March 2011; "Mr. Churchill's Warning," *Pittsburgh Post-Gazette,* March 6, 1946, accessed March 2011;

"Mr. Churchill's Address Calling for United Effort for World Peace," *New York Times,* March 6, 1946, accessed April 2010; "Mr. Churchill's Message," *New York Times,* March 6, 1946, accessed April 2011; "Mr. Truman's Balloon," *Time,* quoting the *Wall Street Journal,* March 18, 1946, available online at http://www.time.com/time/magazine/article /0,9171,934436,00.html, accessed December 2010.

23. George Scadding, "Churchill Speaks," *Life,* March 18, 1946, accessed December 2010; William Allen White, quoted in John Ramsden, "Mr. Churchill Goes to Fulton," in James W. Muller, ed., *Churchill's "Iron Curtain" Speech Fifty Years Later* (Columbia, Mo.: University of Missouri Press, 1999), 25–26; J. H. Rand to Winston Churchill, March 15, 1946, CHUR 2/229, accessed May 2011; "Remington 'Noiseless' Typewriter," Churchill War Rooms, available online at http://www .iwm.org.uk/collections/item/object/30005886, accessed May 2011.

24. "Churchill Talk Causes Surprise in the Commons: Bevin Likely to Be Asked If He Knew About It," *St. Louis Star-Times* via the Associated Press, March 6, 1946, accessed April 2011; summary of press reaction to "The Sinews of Peace," March 6, 1946, CPPC, June 1945 to May 1946 Folder, accessed May 2011.

25. Winston Churchill, "Speech at the Waldorf-Astoria Hotel," March 15, 1946, in Churchill, *Sinews of Peace* (Boston: Houghton Mifflin, 1949), 115.

26. "Consider the Termite," *Time,* April 1, 1946, available online at http://www.time.com/time/magazine/article/0,9171,792727,00.html, accessed June 2011.

27. Gilbert, *Churchill and America,* 320; Jack Bisco, "Churchill Warns Against UNO Delay on Iran," *The Herald-Journal* via the United Press, March 21, 1946, accessed June 2011.

28. Bisco, "Churchill Warns Against UNO Delay on Iran."

Conclusion

1. Winston Churchill to Thomas E. Dewey, quoted in Clark Clifford, *Counsel to the President* (New York: Random House, 1991), 108.

2. Larry P. Arnn, "True Politics and Strategy," in James W. Muller, ed., *Churchill's "Iron Curtain" Speech Fifty Years Later* (Columbia, Mo.: University of Missouri Press, 1999), 130; Daniel J. Mahoney, "Moral Principle and Realistic Judgment," in Muller, *Churchill's "Iron Curtain" Speech Fifty Years Later*, 70.

3. Harry Truman to Winston Churchill, October 14, 1947, quoted in G. W. Sand, ed., *Defending the West: The Truman-Churchill Correspondence, 1945–1960* (Westport, Conn.: Praeger Publishers, 2004); Bela Zhelitski, "Postwar Hungary, 1944–1946," in Norman Naimark and Leonid Gibianiski, eds., *The Establishment of Communist Regimes in Eastern Europe, 1944–1949* (New York: Westview Press), 77–79; Igor Lukes, "The Czech Road to Communism," in Naimark and Gibianiski, *The Establishment of Communist Regimes in Eastern Europe, 1944–1949*, 247–248; Winston Churchill to Frank Clarke, March 28, 1948, CTMDC, Winston Churchill and Frank Clarke Correspondence Folder, accessed August 2011.

4. "Churchill and the Great Republic," Library of Congress, available online at http://www.loc.gov/exhibits/churchill/wc-coldwar.html, accessed May 2011.

5. Martin Gilbert, *Churchill and America* (New York: Free Press, 2005), 889; "Great Britain," in David Reynolds, ed., *The Origins of the Cold War in Europe: International Perspectives* (New Haven: Yale University Press, 1998), 77.

6. Klaus Larres, *Churchill's Cold War: The Politics of Personal Diplomacy* (New Haven: Yale University Press, 2002), 156; Barbara Leaming, *Churchill Defiant* (New York: Harper, 2010), 154–158.

7. Robert Rhodes James, "The Largest Human Being of Our Time," in James W. Muller, ed., *Churchill as Peacemaker* (Cambridge: Cambridge University Press, 1997), 22; Manfred Weidhorn, "A Contrarian's Approach to Peace," in Muller, *Churchill as Peacemaker*, 47; Larres, *Churchill's Cold War*, 302; Richard H. Immerman, ed., *John Foster Dulles and the Diplomacy of the Cold War* (Princeton: Princeton University Press, 1992), 2–6.

8. Spencer Warren, "A Philosophy of International Politics," in Muller, *Churchill's "Iron Curtain" Speech Fifty Years Later*, 121.

9. John W. Young, *Winston Churchill's Last Campaign* (Oxford: Clarendon Press, 1996), 321.

10. Shelley Sommer, *John F. Kennedy: His Life and Legacy* (New York: HarperCollins, 2004), 17; Thurston Clarke, *Ask Not: The Inauguration of John F. Kennedy and the Speech That Changed America* (New York: Macmillan, 2005), 81, 226.

11. Douglas B. Cornell, "But His Acceptance Honors Us Far More," *Eugene Register-Guard* via the Associated Press, April 10, 1963, accessed May 2011; "Kennedy in Fulton Memorial Group," *Kansas City Times*, May 25, 1963, accessed June 2011; Andrew F. Smith, *Rescuing the World: The Life and Times of Leo Cherne* (Albany: SUNY Press, 2002), 141.

12. Richard M. Nixon, *The Memoirs of Richard Nixon* (New York: Grosset and Dunlap, 1978), 45, 158, 610; Winston Churchill, *Sinews of Peace* (Boston: Houghton Mifflin, 1949), 100.

13. Patrick J. C. Powers, "Rhetorical Statesmanship," in Muller, *Churchill's "Iron Curtain" Speech Fifty Years Later*, 144; Martin Fletcher and Michael Binyon, "Special Relationship Struggles to Bridge the Generation Gap—Anglo-American," *The Times* (London), December 22, 1993; Margaret Thatcher, "New Threats for Old," Speech at Westminster College, Fulton, Missouri, March 9, 1996, available online at http://www.churchillmemorial.org, accessed December 2010.

14. Stephen F. Hayward, *Greatness: Reagan, Churchill, and the Making of Extraordinary Leaders* (New York: Three Rivers Press, 2006), 139–140; Spencer Warren, "Reagan and Churchill," The Claremont Institute, October 6, 2004, available online at http://www.claremont.org/publications/pubid.368/pub_detail.asp, accessed December 2010; Churchill, *Sinews of Peace*, 103–104.

15. Mikhail Gorbachev, "The River of Time and the Imperative of Action," May 6, 1992, http://www.churchillmemorial.org/lecture/green/Pages/TheRiverofTimeandtheImperative.aspx.

16. Arnn, "True Politics and Strategy," 137.

17. Mahoney, "Moral Principle and Realistic Judgment," 71; Churchill, *Sinews of Peace*, 93.

18. Churchill, *Sinews of Peace*, 95.

19. Ibid., 104–105.

Afterword

1. Franc McCluer to Winston Churchill, March 9, 1946, CTMDC, Box 2, Invitations & Misc. Correspondence Folder, accessed October 2010.

2. Franc McCluer to Winston Churchill, March 15, 1946 (first of two letters that day), CHUR 2/230 B, accessed May 2011; "For Mr. Churchill," Ida Belle McCluer to Winston Churchill, March 15, 1946, CTMDC, Box 2, Invitations & Misc. Correspondence Folder, accessed October 2010; Franc McCluer to Winston Churchill, March 15, 1946 (second letter that day), CHUR 2/230 B, accessed May 2011.

3. Winston Churchill to Franc McCluer, March 16, 1946, CHUR 2/230 B, accessed May 2011.

4. Dr. Howard A. Rusk to Franc McCluer, Richard Nacy to Franc McCluer, all dated March 1946, CTMDC, Box 2, Invitations & Misc. Correspondence Folder, accessed October 2010.

5. William E. Parrish, *Westminster College: An Informal History, 1851–1969* (Fulton, Mo.: Westminster College Press, 2000), 213.

6. Minutes of the Lindenwood Finance Committee, October 8, 1947, Russell L. Dearmont Papers 1929–1965, Lindenwood College, Folder 2754, WHM, accessed October 2009.

Acknowledgments

1. Richard Langworth, ed., *Churchill by Himself: The Definitive Collection of Quotations* (New York: PublicAffairs, 2008), 49.

INDEX

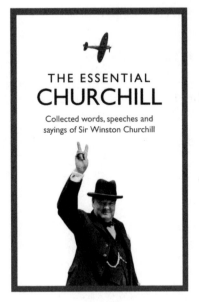